COP

A TRUE STORY

MICHAEL L. MIDDLETON

CONTEMPORARY
BOOKS
CHICAGO

Library of Congress Cataloging-in-Publication Data

Middleton, Michael L.
Cop : a true story / Michael L. Middleton.
p. cm.
ISBN 0-8092-3736-9 (cloth)
1. Middleton, Michael L. 2. Police—California—Los Angeles—Biography. 3. Los Angeles (Calif.). Police Dept. I. Title.
HV7911.M5A3 1994
363.2′092—dc20
[B] 93-44373
CIP

Published by Contemporary Books, Inc.
Two Prudential Plaza, Chicago, Illinois 60601-6790
Manufactured in the United States of America
International Standard Book Number: 0-8092-3736-9
10 9 8 7 6 5 4 3 2 1

This book is dedicated to Martha, my wife of more than twenty-five years. Throughout its writing she was a tireless editor as well as a benevolent critic. Without her love, support, and encouragement, it may be simply stated that I could never have amounted to anything.

WHILE THIS BOOK IS THE STORY of my years as a police officer, in reality it is the story of the men and women who risk their lives to protect and serve. It is an account of the good in them as well as the evil. Some of their names were changed. Some of the places were altered. The stories are true, and the men and women who lived them are real.

CONTENTS

Introduction 1

Chapter One

DEATHS

Some You Can't Remember, Others You Can't Forget 8

Chapter Two

HEROISM

Heroes Are Like That 36

Chapter Three

SIEGE MENTALITY

". . . And Remember, It's Us Against Them." 67

Chapter Four

DRUGS

". . . Coon Can! Come On, Open the Door!" 106

Chapter Five

GANGS

Competition for the Streets 141

Chapter Six
DEADLY FORCE
When Death Is Close Enough to Touch 178

Chapter Seven
THE CRIMES
"All Units! Any Unit Available to Handle. . . ." 216

Chapter Eight
IN RETROSPECT 263

INTRODUCTION

"ALL UNITS. THE AIR UNIT ADVISES one suspect has just discarded his shotgun and is now running between the apartments. The other two suspects are no longer visible and may have entered the last building to your left at the end of the walkway. All units be advised. South Pasadena PD states shots have been fired by the suspects."

"3-L-50, roger."

"Sarge, they've got to be right up in there at the end. It looks like an entryway to the apartments. That's gotta be where they are."

"OK. Dave, Bill, let's go down in here. The rest of you guys cover us, and don't move until we check the stairwell."

"Sarge, he's comin' out at the end of the building! That's gotta be the guy that dumped the shotgun."

"All right, let's go! Guys, watch that entry to the left."

"OK, asshole, freeze! Down! Down! Out flat! Keep your hands out where we can see 'em! Touch that fuckin' gun and you're dead! Cover me, I'm goin' to cuff him. Call two more guys up here to take this asshole."

"Sarge, we've got him. The K-9 unit's comin' over."

"OK, I'm going with the dog. You guys stay out front, and we're goin' up to see if those guys made entry into any other apartments."

"Mike, you want Liberty to check the hallway?"

"Yeah, Norm. Are you all set?"

"Yeah, Mike. Liberty smells somethin'. They have to have gone up in here; she smells it. I don't think there's any way out. I've been in these apartments before. If they're up there, and they didn't go into any unit, they're trapped. Watch it, Mike. They could have a good shot at us as we go up the stairs."

"Right, Norm. You're gonna let Liberty go?"

"Yeah."

"I'll cover the stairwell, and when you get to the top of each flight, I'll follow."

"OK, Mike. She's got one! Out, girl, out! Liberty, out! I've got one here, Mike! Get your fuckin' hands out where I can see 'em! Watch him, Mike, he's got a piece."

"Toss me your cuffs. I used mine on the other guy. Roll over, facedown! Put one hand behind your back. This is L-50. Dave, Bill, come up to the second floor. We have one in custody, and there's still one outstanding. OK, shithead, where's your partner?"

"He's up there, man. Don't shoot 'im."

"Has he got a gun?"

"Yeah, man, but he won' use it."

"This is the Los Angeles Police Department. We know you are up there. Drop your weapon and walk out where we can see you. If you don't come out, my dog is coming up."

"All right! All right! I'm comin' out! I don' have a gun!"

"Norm, I can see him. All right, keep your hands out where we can see them! Lace your fingers together! Turn around. Face the other way. Don't move! Keep your hands right there! Dave, let me have your cuffs."

"I'll cuff him, Sarge."

"OK. Go ahead, Dave. Bill, don't go down with that guy yet. Let's take this guy first."

"Keep facing away from me. Don't move. I'll tell you what to do. Don't you fuckin' move! Put your right hand down behind your back. Now bring your other hand down. He's cuffed, Sarge. He didn't have a piece on him."

"All right, where's your fuckin' gun, asshole? We know you had one."

"I left it up there. I never shot at that guy. It was the other guys, I swear! You can look at my gun. I'd never shoot at no police. I swear! I done a lot of stupid things, but I never done that, no sir!"

"Norm, Dave, let me check up there and make sure there's nothing else, and then we'll go down. There's no one up here. I've got his gun. OK, let's go. Great fuckin' work, guys! Great job! 3-L-50 to Control One. Show code four at our location. Suspects in custody."

Control One was the designation for police communications downtown, and we had just advised them that no further assistance was needed (code four). I drove back to Southwest Station, sat for about thirty seconds looking around my police car, took my ROVER (a radio system that can be removed from the police car for use as a hand-held radio in the field) out of its holder, and turned off the engine. This was my last radio call, the final chapter in my police career. Those twenty-one years had gone by so fast.

That's how it ended, but not how it began.

It was not my lifelong ambition to be a police officer. The fact is, I didn't really have any goals during that summer of 1966. I was twenty-one years old and adrift.

Immediately after high school I joined the navy and ended up being assigned to an aircraft carrier, the USS *Independence*. The ship was deployed to

Vietnam, and as a member of the catapult crew I helped launch bomb-laden planes. My Vietnam experience left me pretty disillusioned; I came to believe we were throwing lives away to accomplish nothing.

My discharge was scheduled for the middle of February, which would have caused me to miss the start of the spring college term. The navy had a program to help veterans start college on time, so I applied for a release thirty days early, and it was granted. With my "early out" I was off to Pasadena City College and there fell in with a pretty liberal crowd, which began to challenge my conservative thinking on social issues. This began a process that would put me in direct opposition to some of my police peers over the years.

In addition to attending school, I was working more than forty hours a week at a veterinary hospital. Being a full-time student and a full-time employee was very difficult, but I completed the spring semester at Pasadena City College, and was looking forward to summer. The coming months would be a time of change for me. I wasn't sure which direction my life was going in.

Following World War II, the LAPD had grown dramatically to meet the needs of the city. These officers were now eligible for retirement, so there was quite a recruitment drive. In spite of the replenishment effort, Los Angeles had the smallest police force per capita of all large cities in the world. A friend of mine had taken the examination for the police department and failed. After a few friendly verbal jabs a bet was made, and I was off to take the test, too.

The general-knowledge exam hadn't seemed hard at all, and I passed, making me eligible to go on to the physical agility test. Next came a complete medical examination. Having come this far, I was starting to become interested in the police department as a long-term career opportunity.

The department psychologist conducted a variety of psychological tests and an interview. Following that examination came several days with a police background investigator assigned to me. The testing began in June 1966; I didn't start at the academy until that October.

The whole process made me realize that growing up in poor surroundings had helped me understand poverty. (It was a view from the outside, looking into a window at all the nice things you didn't have.) My father was killed in World War II before I was born, and my mother became the sole breadwinner. My family's fortunes definitely took a turn for the worse.

We were forced out of a comfortable home in the Highland Park area of the city. The only housing we could now afford was a sixteen-foot trailer in a rundown neighborhood. My mother, sister, grandmother, grandfather, and I shared these cramped living quarters for almost three years before we moved to an even rougher area along Whittier Boulevard. Even though we lived in an old house divided in two, it did have a yard. On more than one occasion my grandmother would chase off Latino gang members from in front of our home. They developed a great respect for her cast-iron skillet and her way with the English language as she chased them down the street. She had more spunk than anyone I ever knew.

One day, as we went grocery shopping, my grandmother gave me some advice that I never forgot. "Michael, if you hold your head high, no one will know we're poor. Don't let it bother you and don't let them know."

Sometimes my sister and I would go a few blocks down Whittier Boulevard to stare in the windows of the stores. Being the elder at twelve, she would hold my hand as we walked along that busy street. Donna would also protect me, and with the absolute trust of a six-year-old I knew we would be all right. It was a tough neighborhood, but Donna was tougher.

The experience of those formative years in the slums helped make me a better police officer. Perhaps it was an unconscious desire to help people that was formed while I was growing up in the poor section of East Los Angeles. I had not only seen the other side of the coin; I had lived it. Poverty was the enemy, and I knew the nature of the beast better than most. A few years later my family moved out of the central city area to a better place, but as it turned out, I would return to those mean streets of Los Angeles where I had started.

A lot went on in my old neighborhood, but nothing I ever saw in my childhood would prepare me for the wild ride I would take in a black-and-white police car wearing the LAPD uniform for more than twenty years. There would be powerful moments, poignant moments, moments that remain as fresh as when they happened.

Images like the little boy whose father slit his throat with a bread knife and threw him on the floor like yesterday's garbage.

Images like the young police officer I saw for the last time lying in the gutter at Figueroa and College, covered with his own blood, killed in the line of duty.

Narcotics that take everything you have and then your life. White boys in their Beemers reduced to mindless cokeheads looking to score in the ghetto.

Racism within the police department that I would become a part of. Sexism directed at female officers. The search for some way to find a shred of sanity expressed in black humor.

Police officers are not made upon graduation from the academy. It's one day, one call at a time. All of those images you're exposed to, that you react to, coupled with your own life experience, help shape you.

These stories are grouped into categories, spanning my time on the Los Angeles Police Department, and are my personal experiences. There are happy moments, moments of terror, moments of sorrow—significant moments in my police career.

So hang on. We have calls to handle.

Chapter One

DEATHS
Some You Can't Remember, Others You Can't Forget

FROM THE MOMENT YOU PUT ON that blue uniform, pin the badge to your shirt, get in the police car, and head out into the street, you know a lot is going to happen. You don't know when, you don't know what, you don't know how often, but things are going to happen, and you'll be there. It can't be avoided. It's this sense of anticipation, an undercurrent of excitement that gives uniformed patrol its thrill. You will see death, you will see dying, and you'll see plenty of both.

We were told this in the police academy, and they didn't lie. Some guys know exactly how many homicide scenes they've been at. That's what they're called—scenes. It's all so impersonal. It's not the deprivation of life, the end of dreams, the end of hope, or the beginning of despair for the survivors; it's just called "the scene." I'm not sure how many homicide scenes I've been at, but it had to be more than five hundred. Some of them you can't remember, and others you can't forget.

The first one is easy to recall.

Upon graduation from the academy I was in undercover narcotics, where I worked in high schools for a little more than three months. Afterwards I was given a choice of divisions. The captain of personnel walked me into the position control officer and said, "Give Officer Middleton any division he wants."

I had already heard about Newton Division in the academy, where it was always referred to as "Shootin' Newton." It was a tough area, and to me it had a romantic image, somewhat like the wild and woolly Old West. The Newton area is a run-down section just south of downtown Los Angeles. It was the northernmost division of the city affected by the Watts riots of 1965, and I wanted to go there. Having grown up in another poor area of the city, I felt comfortable in such surroundings and wasn't intimidated by a rough division. I couldn't wait. My initial assignment was on the busy P.M. watch, which started at 3:00 in the afternoon and finished at 11:45 at night.

It was an incredible thrill driving out of the station and onto Newton Street. I really had made it. I'll never forget the first time I drove down Central Avenue. The Watts riots had occurred eighteen months before. The smoke had cleared, but the wounds were still fresh. Nearly all of the burned-out shells had been leveled, sometimes leaving behind a block-long string of foundations waiting for buildings that would never come.

I don't remember the name of my partner that first tour, but I remember that night, and I remember his words.

"Kid, while you were in Vietnam, we had our own 'Nam right here. See that building? That's Gold's Furniture Store. We're only three blocks from the station. That's how close the riots came. It's been rebuilt, but that son of a bitch was burned to the ground. I'll tell you what—a few people were inside when it went up, or at least that's what the guys say that saw it torched and looted. I missed this one. I was at the

White Front Store on Alameda when this baby went. It was just one fire after another those nights.

"I never fired a shot during the riots, but a lot of guys did. I could've, but it just didn't seem worth it. Officially thirty-four people were killed, but one guy told me he had to call the coroner's office about a homicide and heard that they had more than thirty-four John Does already. There's no way only thirty-four people went, and everyone knew it. I always thought the numbers were deliberately kept down so there wouldn't be more trouble. I'm tellin' you, Mike, you wouldn't believe how much shooting was going on. You just went from one [officer needs] help call to another.

"It might look like everything's over, but the riots are gonna come again. Wait and see. Next time even more people will die because there's more guns out there now. When it happens, we'll never stop it. Shit, we couldn't stop it the last time."

The first night was uneventful. The next brought reality. My partner for the evening was a six-year veteran. He was the basic hard-bitten cop stereotype. My first contact with him came in roll call, where I had taken a seat in the back row. My thinking was to keep a low profile and blend in quietly. Unknown to me, the back row was reserved for senior officers, referred to as the "old-timers." He had been off the previous night, and we had never met. However, when he walked into the roll call room, he knew who his partner was right away.

"I'm your partner, and I don't know what the fuck you're doing in the back row, but get your ass up front, sit down, and keep your fucking mouth shut, because you're here to learn." He pointed at the soft drink I was holding. "Why do you have that? You haven't got enough fucking time on the job to drink anything in the roll call room."

He scooped up my soda and dropped it in the

nearby trash can. The roll call room was full of police officers, many of whom were enjoying a good chuckle at my expense. I was mortified and wished that it was possible to crawl under something as I moved to my new spot in the front row. A probationary police officer like me was the lowest form of life in Newton Division during the spring of 1967. Strike one.

After roll call we headed for his favorite spot, Orthopaedic Hospital, and the small coffee room just off the emergency room exit. It was ideal. You could have a cup of coffee and still hear your radio. I was about to receive my second strike for the evening from my ever-so-charming partner.

Just after we arrived and had gotten our coffee, an old Buick rattled down the ramp to the entrance of the emergency room. A black man in his late twenties jumped out of the car and ran inside.

"She's havin' it! She's havin' it! Help!" It then became apparent that there was a woman inside the car, leaning against the passenger door, slouched down so much she was barely visible.

Arriving at the same moment was a Los Angeles Police motorcycle officer with his red lights on. The father-to-be came back out with a team of doctors and nurses right behind him.

"It's the baby! The baby's comin'!"

My initial reaction was How neat! He gave them an escort. But wait. We had been taught at the academy that escorts were a violation of department policy.

The man was frantic as the motor officer calmly walked up to him and said, "Give me your license and registration."

"Officer, I know I went through the light, but she's havin' a baby, and I was afraid."

The motor officer was unmoved. "Your license, sir."

The man fumbled in his wallet and fished out

what appeared to be his driver's license. He handed it to the officer, who had already started to write the traffic ticket, or "greenie" as they were known. Meanwhile the doctors and nurses seemed to have everything under control, or, what was probably more correct, the impending baby had the doctors and nurses under control.

The new father ran back and forth between the officer and his wife, answering the officer's questions as he did so. The motor officer was quite nonchalant about the whole situation and seemed very much at ease, his left boot resting on the Buick's bumper while he wrote the ticket.

"What do you think of that, Mike?" Things were improving. He had called me by my first name. I didn't think I could miss with this answer.

"Well, it doesn't seem very fair to give him a ticket with his wife having a baby. I think I'd probably just warn him."

He went nuts. "What makes you think you have the right to criticize a brother officer in his line of duty? You don't know a fucking thing, so keep your mouth shut until you do!" Strike two.

Shortly afterward, we left the hospital and were on patrol. He maintained a fairly regular stream of talk, but it was as though I wasn't there. He had stories about the Watts riots, too, but from a very different perspective.

"Yeah, we busted some caps [fired some shots] on those fuckin' niggers. The best one was when Gold's burned. It was fuckin' beautiful. Those niggers were taking everything in sight. I mean they were cleaning the fucking place out! To show you how stupid one asshole was, he firebombed the place before they finished looting it. A whole bunch of us were outside watching when the fire started. Shit, we must've been outnumbered ten to one. What could we do? You would've thought that with the building burning, they'd split. Not Newton niggers. They had to steal the last fucking chair. One of the guys started busting caps on 'em, and then all of us started shooting. It was so bitchin'! Every time they'd try to run out of the store, we fire off a volley of shots, and they'd run back in. Then the roof caved in, and nobody else tried to run out, so my partner and I split. Fuck those assholes."

"How many people do you think were inside?"

"I wasn't countin'; maybe a dozen, but they never found evidence of any dead bodies in that place when they cleared the rubble." My partner was quite pleased with his story, laughing and shaking his head when he finished.

I didn't say one word in response. Not because I was shocked or horrified—I couldn't think of anything to say. Everyone in Newton who'd been there had a riot story. No matter what they said, it was clear to me that it had been a terrifying experience. The locker room war story bravado might conceal those fearful memories, but I was certain that everyone involved was either very frightened or too stupid to be scared. There was no doubt in my mind where my partner belonged.

"13-Adam-43. Shots fired. 5500 block Staunton Avenue."

"Roger," I responded.

In the cool darkness of the spring night we pulled off Fifty-Fifth Street and onto Staunton Avenue. There was a large commotion in the street about halfway down the block. Just before we got to the crowd, a man ran into the street, waving broadly at us with both arms. My partner brought the car to an immediate stop, and the man halted, placing his hands over his head.

"Officers, I'm the one you're here for. I did it. I shot him."

My God, he was surrendering. In a flash my

partner had his door open and was putting handcuffs on the suspect.

"Go over there and see what you can do," my partner yelled without stopping his work with the suspect.

I ran toward a four-unit green stucco apartment house the man had run out of. It had two units on the top, two on the bottom, like hundreds of others in Newton. Even though the building was fairly new, it already looked past its prime.

"Officer, he's in there! Hurry! He's been shot! I think it's bad!" a woman screamed as I ran toward an open door with about a dozen or so people clustered around it. Inside the apartment a middle-aged black man was lying on his back on the floor. Somehow he'd missed the threadbare sofa when he collapsed, but he did tag a low lamp table, breaking it. Parts of the table were underneath him, and other pieces were scattered about the bare linoleum floors.

"Save him, save him, officer! He been shot real bad. Save him!"

"What happened, lady?"

"My husband came home, and my friend, well, my boyfriend, he shot him. I ain't even been seein' him lately. It was over and everything, but he shot him anyways. I thought he was just goin' to talk to him."

About every five seconds it looked to me that the victim was trying to breathe, but something was stopping him. The only light in the room was from my flashlight, so I was aware of but couldn't really see the other people inside. The victim was my primary concern anyway. A couple of times when the man appeared to breathe the people would chant, "Save him! Save him!"

His eyes were open in a glassy stare. He looked dead to me, or what I thought someone would look like if he was dead, since I had never seen anyone dying up close like this. Rookies are taught artificial resuscitation at the academy, and all I could remember was the instructor bellowing out, "I don't care if he's a Skid Row bum; you will get down on your hands and knees and give mouth-to-mouth resuscitation." It was long before AIDS became a threat.

There wasn't any room for interpretation in that instructor's words, but this guy was filthy. I finally settled on a compromise. Kneeling next to the victim, I placed my hands over his mouth. That way I could employ my own sanitized version of mouth-to-mouth resuscitation. I vigorously exhaled, and his chest began to expand. The onlookers responded in unison. "Look, he's breathin'! He's breathin'!"

As the air went out of the man's chest, the same pattern developed. What I didn't know is that the victim had taken three rounds in the back, and one of those bullets went right through his heart. His breathing was actually agonal respiration, or death throes, involving involuntary muscle reactions that give the appearance of attempts to breathe.

One more try, one more breath, and maybe he'll be all right, I thought, bending down to repeat the resuscitation process. As the man's lungs expanded for a second time, unknown to me, my partner entered the room.

"What the fuck are you doing? Someone's tryin' to make a good nigger out of him. Don't fuck it up!"

At that point my partner kicked me square in the ass, causing me to lose my balance and land on top of the man, who was in fact dead. Strike three.

I was handling my first homicide.

The dead man's wife would have to be questioned later at the police station, so I was instructed to take her out to the police car and get some basic information on her and her husband. Any questioning regarding the crime would be done at the station by homicide detectives. All I had to obtain were the couple's complete names, addresses, dates of birth, and whether or not any other witnesses were present at the time of the shooting. My partner took care of clearing the other people from the room to make sure the scene was preserved for the investigation.

After I situated her in the backseat, I sat down in front on the passenger side. Each time I turned around to ask her a question, she responded with a query about her husband. At first I was noncommittal, trying to avoid the subject because I'd never given a death notification. Finally I decided to give her a truthful answer.

"Ma'am, I'm very sorry, but your husband has passed away."

What a mistake. I thought she had figured it out, but apparently not. She went wild in the backseat of the police car, kicking the seat, stomping the floor, banging her hands on the window, and punching the headliner of the car, wailing and screaming the whole time. It was the "Newton Death Dance," a phrase coined by the division's officers to describe the reactions of relatives and friends to the death of loved ones. Any other Newton officer would have known exactly what her reaction to the news would be. All I could think was, how could that much activity go on in the backseat of a car?

Asking any other questions was definitely out, and I immediately realized that a serious tactical error had just been made. It was a lesson well learned, because I never again notified a husband or wife of a spouse's passing before I had asked all the necessary questions.

"What the fuck's going on?" My partner returned and sat down in the driver's seat. "What's her problem?"

"She didn't know her husband was dead, and I told her."

"What the fuck did you do that for?"

"Well . . . she wanted to know, so I told her."

"Fuck her!" He started the car, and we set off for Newton Station.

How could it be possible? Strike four.

AT MY FIRST HOMICIDE the murder victim was already dead when we arrived. It's one thing to see a person who has already been killed and quite another to watch the culmination of the crime unfold before you. In about two weeks I would have the opportunity to witness this most horrible event—the exact moment when an assault with a deadly weapon changes to murder.

Hooper Avenue winds south from Washington Boulevard through a run-down section of the city. The residents knew all about the streets, and I knew nothing. We had received a radio call involving an "ambulance stabbing" on Hooper. My partner was a streetwise veteran who had joined the department at the close of World War II. He had worked Newton precinct for years and knew it like the back of his hand. It was about four in the afternoon, and we had just left roll call. The station was only a few blocks away from the crime scene, so we were right on top of the location. This was my first stabbing call.

People usually gather at a crime scene, which makes it easy to find when you're approaching a call. It doesn't really matter if the action is inside the location or outside on the street; people are milling about. There's excitement in the air, and that's the way it was this particular afternoon.

We pulled our black-and-white next to the curb on the wrong side of the street so we could be as close as possible to the scene. My partner coolly got out of the car and walked slowly up the sidewalk toward a white clapboard duplex. Like most of the neighborhood, it had been built in the 1920s and was long past its prime. As he waded through the group of about twenty people, mostly kids, it was as though the waters parted for him. I was right behind him, and the crowd quickly closed back around us.

"Hey, what happened? What's goin' on here?" my partner asked a man crouched next to the victim. This particular casualty appeared to be about twenty years old, only a little younger than me.

"Hey, man, I don't know. We was just comin' out of the store over there, and some fool come up and was arguin' with him. The next thing I know is that mo-tha-fucker stabbed him and run up the street. Man, we wasn't doin' nothin'."

"Get back. Let me look at him." My partner knelt down to look at the wound, a ten-ring [bull's-eye] shot. It looked as if the knife had entered the chest just under the sternum, and while I didn't think about it then, it must have gone straight into his heart.

"Hey, kid," my partner said to me, "you better make sure the ambulance is coming, because I think this fuckin' guy is going to be history directly. The rest of you, get back!" he shouted at the crowd.

I sprinted to the police car, an awkward, gangly novice who was trying unsuccessfully, like most rookies, to hold on to my hat while I ran. The RTO (radio telephone operator) confirmed that the ambulance was indeed en route. By now the crowd had moved back, and my partner was asking if anyone had seen anything. Of course no one had. You really couldn't blame them, because, as I was to learn, they had to protect themselves since we sure as hell couldn't. We couldn't be there every minute. Just about the time one of them came forward and told us what had happened, we took the statement, and left to go back to the station to write the report, another unit would get a call for the same thing. No, they didn't see a thing. It wasn't worth it.

I guess I was expecting my partner to perform a

miracle. It didn't seem right that we just stood there and watched this man die on that sidewalk. At first it looked to me like he would be OK. After all, no blood was coming out. Shows you how stupid I was. He seemed awfully scared; I guess I was too. I don't know why, because I wasn't dying. Then, slowly but surely, he seemed to become more distant and stopped breathing.

In the movies death is often shown with sudden jerking motions put in to make sure the audience doesn't miss the fact that this character is dying. It wasn't like that at all on Hooper Avenue that warm spring afternoon in 1967. He just stopped moving; his eyes closed about halfway, as though he was simply staring into the sky. You knew then he wasn't there anymore. At that time in my life it was one of the most profound things I had ever seen. It was the first time I'd ever watched anyone actually die, but it wouldn't be the last. Over the years I would be at somewhere between five and six hundred homicide scenes, and perhaps a hundred of those victims would still be clinging to life when I arrived.

THERE ARE TIMES WHEN YOU THINK you can change the course of things. You really believe it. Maybe you've just had something happen, and through your efforts it worked out right. Then comes a reminder you're not in control, and ultimately all of your training, all of the equipment at your disposal, all of your hopes are simply not going to be enough.

"Ambulance cutting. See the woman." Larry and I were the field sergeants for the shift, working separate cars and available to help the officers under our supervision. The call was in a shoddy neighborhood off Hooper Avenue. We had just left the station and were on our way to have coffee when the call came out. No other patrol units were clear, so it was assigned to us. I was right behind Larry, and we pulled up to the scene at the same time.

A Latin woman in her late thirties ran out into the street as we approached to make sure we knew where the call was. She told me in Spanish her son had been attacked and was cut very badly. Other witnesses who had seen the attack said that the young man had been robbed while coming back from the grocery store about a hundred yards away. Some gang-bangers (gang members) had stopped him and demanded money, but when he told them he had none, one of them swung at him with a knife, catching the victim on the left side of his neck. After he was slashed, the teenager tried to run back toward his house, but he didn't make it. He was lying on the driveway between two houses. Several women had gathered around him, covering him with blankets and putting a pillow under his head. He was only sixteen years old.

While I spoke with the woman, the other sergeant went over to the young man to see what he could do. Larry knelt down by him, inspecting the wound with the aid of his flashlight. It was about 11:45 at night and very dark between those houses. The teenager's neck was opened up more than an inch on the left side and had been covered by a towel one of the women brought out. There was no question in my mind that this kid was in danger of bleeding to death in the next few minutes. When Larry took the towel away, you could see a lot of bleeding, but fortunately the main blood vessels, the jugular and carotid, were still intact. If they had been nicked during the initial attack, the boy would already be dead, and if they had been partially severed and opened up further, the amount of blood would have been much greater.

We were both on our hands and knees now. Larry was holding the towel, which was folded to form a compress, and I was talking to the boy, telling him not to move because an ambulance was coming. He looked absolutely terrified but remained motionless. He was doing just what we told him to do. His mother was standing behind us, bent over, looking at her son, telling us over and over in Spanish, "Help him, help him. Oh, God, help him. He's my boy. Oh please, help him . . . You're going to be all right. The officers are going to help you."

One mistake, and this kid was gone. I couldn't have been happier to see the red lights from the ambulance reflecting off the buildings and down the driveway.

"What you got?"

Larry looked up at the paramedic, never turning loose of the makeshift compress. "He's cut very deeply. Looks like a knife wound . . ."

"The witnesses said that a couple of gangbangers sliced him with a knife across the neck, like this." I gestured.

Larry broke in. "The carotid and jugular are still OK, I think, but I'm afraid if we move him they might go."

"OK, we're going to put him on a gurney and hold him real still as we lift him. In fact, let's backboard him to hold his neck while we do it." One of the paramedics retrieved a long plywood board normally used for back and cervical injuries. In this case it was going to be used to stabilize the neck in an attempt to prevent tearing of the blood vessels.

The boy was on his back, so we rolled him over to his left side, sliding the board underneath him while Larry held the towel tightly against the wound. Then we placed him on the ambulance gurney—so far, so good. One of the paramedics put a foam block on either side of the boy's head and began wrapping an elastic bandage around the gurney to prevent his head from moving from side to side.

Larry noticed something was wrong. Without

warning, blood started to go everywhere. Larry moved the towel away to look, and blood poured and spurted from the wound. It was like a garden hose that had been turned on full force. The gurney began to fill with blood around the left side of the boy's immobile head, running around his shoulder and arm.

"OK, come on, guys. Let's get him up and in. We've got to hurry. Get him in." As the gurney was jerked into position, the towel moved again, and blood shot everywhere. Larry quickly clamped the compress back on, but life continued to pour out of the boy's body. As we slid the gurney into the ambulance, the boy's face began to change. A check of his pulse by one of the paramedics revealed it was very weak and fading. Then his eyes became dilated in a fixed stare. The doors of the ambulance slammed shut, and they were off to the hospital. By now other officers had arrived at the scene, and one jumped into the back of the ambulance to assist in whatever way he could.

With the victim en route to the hospital, we directed the officers to begin the preliminary investigation at the scene. I telephoned the station and told them we had a possible 187 (the Los Angeles Police Department frequently uses Penal Code section numbers as part of radio transmissions; e.g., 187 is the section number for murder) and it looked very bad for the victim. Larry's hands were covered with the boy's blood, so he rinsed them off with a garden hose attached to the side of the house and returned to the station. I drove back a few minutes later, meeting him there. On the way the officer we had sent to the hospital advised me by radio that the boy didn't make it and was pronounced dead on arrival.

At the station Larry and I sat in the coffee room and finally had that cup of coffee. I don't think we spoke during that fifteen- or twenty-minute period. As we finished and walked out, Larry said to me,

"God, Mike, I tried so hard . . ."

"I know you did, Larry. I know you did."

OCCASIONALLY DEATH IS VIEWED from a very different perspective. You're glad someone has died. You don't care how. You don't care why. The person is dead, and the world is better for it. You hope deaths like these will even the score in some small way for previous injustices, but they really don't settle anything.

"All Newton units. See the woman. Ambulance shooting. Be advised we have numerous calls to this location reporting shots fired, and we also have an unknown trouble call at the location."

"All Newton units" is just what responded. Every car not already on another call rolled to the shooting location. The address was on one of those east-west streets lined with palm trees planted in the 1920s and 1930s as part of a development scheme to lure potential buyers to southern California's "tropical" setting. On the surface not a bad-looking neighborhood. Most of the houses were well taken care of; a few had apartment houses built behind the primary dwelling.

It was easy to tell where the problem was as I rolled up to the call. People were gathered on the sidewalk and in the driveway that led to the two-story, two-unit apartment house in the rear. The call was upstairs. It was about 2:30 in the morning, and I remember there was no moon as it was very dark walking back to the call. The crowd was buzzing about what had happened inside; faceless voices muttering in the night.

"I can't believe he's gone."

"I can't believe he did it."

As I reached the stairwell, a woman ran downstairs, crying hysterically as she passed me. A young man in his twenties followed her a few seconds later.

He stopped in the doorway, looking at me with contempt. "You motha-fuckers ain't goin' to do nothin'! I don' know what you motha-fuckers is even here for!"

"Fuck you, dude. Get out of my way." I pushed him to one side and walked up the stairs, where the door to the apartment at the top was partially open. Already inside the room were two officers, another sergeant, a woman, and two other men in their mid-twenties. The real subject of the call, however, was on the floor.

One of the officers was attempting to soothe the woman and find out what exactly had happened. "Ma'am, I know you're upset, but please try to calm down and tell me what happened."

"We was havin' a party, and he comes out with the gun and starts puttin' bullets in it."

"How many did he put in, ma'am?"

"I don't know. Three, four . . . I don't know, an' I told him, 'Leroy, put the gauge [shotgun] away. Don't be pointin' it 'round. You goin' hurt somebody.' They told him, too—same thing. Well, he jacks [loads] one in it.

" 'It ain't nothin'. I'm just havin' some fun.'

" 'Don't be playin'. Put the motha-fucker away.'

" 'OK. Shit, man, I'm just playin'.'

"And he takes the bullets out. You know, like this." She moved her hands in a manner that showed the shotgun rounds being taken out of the magazine. She was becoming more excited and started to cry again.

"Just relax and tell me what happened next."

"Well, he held the gauge up to his head and said, 'Look, it ain't l—' and he pulled the trigger, and it went off."

It seems Leroy had forgotten to remove the round he had placed in the pump shotgun's chamber. The blast from the twelve-gauge shotgun literally blew Leroy's brains out. His brains were all over the ceiling and two walls. But the most amazing thing was Leroy's left eye. It had taken flight and stuck on the wall. It was like an anatomy class exhibit—still reasonably intact, with nerve endings hanging down.

It was hard to top the gruesome specter of Leroy, but my attention was drawn to what looked like a family album lying on the coffee table. I flipped it open, hoping to see a picture of Leroy intact. This wasn't a family album, yet maybe it was. It was a "211 book," kept by people who commit armed robberies for a living. When the criminals returned from a caper, they would record the robbery for posterity by taking a picture of the money they'd stolen along with the guns used in the holdup. The picture composition was usually one of two choices. They'd either lay the money and guns out on the rug, or they might stand facing the camera, fanning the money, holding a gun in the other hand. There's no way to tell what robbery this money came from, so you couldn't use these books as evidence for a specific crime.

Leroy's book contained at least twenty photographs depicting various people holding money and guns, as well as displays of money and guns on the rug, but there were some particularly significant factors that made his different. You could tell they were taken at separate times because the same people in each picture had different clothes on. Featured prominently in the "family album" were Leroy, Leroy's girlfriend, and—you guessed it—the trusty old "gauge."

As I looked over at the girlfriend, my sympathy was ebbing rapidly. To me Leroy's death was just another form of urban renewal—one less piece of trash to prey on the community. Holding the 211 book up, I said to her, "Nice family album. Looks like business has been good. I've got just one question. Do you think Leroy has committed his last robbery?"

The bereaved girlfriend let out a scream. "You

motha-fucker! You ain't got no respect for the dead!"

"In this case, lady, you're right."

I looked at the officers and said, "If you guys don't need me, I've got to go." And I left.

ONE OF THE SIGNIFICANT ELEMENTS of police work is that you see situations that are so unfair. The most startling example of this is when someone dies as a result of the capricious actions of another person. You feel incredible anger and enormous frustration because there is nothing you can do to set things right. You witness moments when families are ripped apart, when loved ones die senselessly. By virtue of your position as a police officer you are expected to be a detached and unbiased observer and take the appropriate actions under the law. Sometimes it's just not possible.

Just before seven one morning my partner and I got an "ambulance traffic—possible K/injuries" call. Whenever the dispatcher said this, it was never "possible K"; it was always a fatal traffic accident. We arrived at the crash scene, Ninety-Second and Main in Seventy-Seventh Division. The fire department was already there and had the fire almost out in a vehicle that was wrapped around a telephone pole.

The fire captain walked over to us as we crossed the street and said, "You've got a double, guys. Looks like a couple of women. They got hit by two cars; looks like those guys were racing." The other vehicles, still sitting in the intersection, were also pretty smashed up.

"Where are the suspects?"

"The traffic officer has them over there."

We were in luck. A T-unit [traffic car] had bought the call, and we just had to assist. I walked over to the car wrapped around the pole and saw two bodies inside. It had been broadsided by both of the speeding vehicles. Witnesses said the two kids were drag-racing as they went south on Main Street and never even slowed down for the car they hit. After impact this vehicle was propelled sideways with such force it ended up wrapped around a large telephone pole. The front and rear bumpers were almost touching each other.

The car made contact with the pole at the driver's door, collapsing the front seat. The collision had shoved both women together, making them appear to be hugging each other. They were horribly burned. Their skin looked like burned newspaper with huge cracks filled with oozing blood. Their hands were burned off, and they appeared to have clenched each other, perhaps in absolute terror as the fire engulfed their car and burned them to death.

There wasn't any smell of death in the air to separate this horrible scene from so many other vehicle fires, but I can picture those women today just as I did more than twenty years ago, clutching each other in the front seat of their car, their belongings strewn about the intersection for all to see.

A man separated himself from the crowd and approached me. "Excuse me, Officer. I'd like to talk with you a moment. I believe the driver of that car is my wife's mother. She's a nurse. I recognize her license plate. Once a week she and another nurse go into work early to volunteer in the children's ward. We live just down on Ninety-Second Street. I know it's her. My wife's here . . . I don't think she knows."

I turned around, and there was a very pretty, well-dressed young woman. She was wearing pink and holding a piece of paper burned around the edges. She was walking toward me, only a few feet away now, with her arms stretched out, tears streaming down her cheeks. She looked me in the eyes and choked, "That's my mom."

She put her arms around me, as I did to her,

while she quietly sobbed over and over, "That's my mom." She couldn't see my face, and I was glad. Cops are supposed to be tough, but this touched me personally. Tears filled my eyes, and I said what seemed painfully inadequate at the time, "It's OK. You're going to be all right."

It must have been some sight to see, the two of us standing in the middle of the intersection, tearfully embracing. So much for tough, inner-city police. For me this was something different. Until that moment I had never personally felt the anguish of the people I came into contact with. I had seen many deaths before that morning, but I was able to shut out the pain and remain detached. As a psychologist who worked for the police department would tell me many years later, I had violated all the rules of detachment when I put my arms around her. In that brief moment, in that intersection, we shared a moment of sorrow.

THE DEATH OF ANY INNOCENT person is horrible, but when it happens to a child, the atrocity of the crime is compounded significantly. If you haven't learned the lesson of detachment, and you touch again, you will pay. . . .

South Park in Newton Division was a neighborhood that had come back from the 1965 Watts riots. The burned-out carcasses of buildings were gone, and a whole new generation lived there, but make no mistake—this was a poor neighborhood, with the same kind of poverty that helped spark the violence in '65. Just north of Fifty-Second Street between Avalon and San Pedro were businesses and a few apartment houses that all looked like they came from the same set of plans. I'd worked other divisions, been promoted, and now was back in Newton as a sergeant. One of my units had a call.

The call seemed simple enough, a family dispute

with a cutting. Our problem this morning was in unit three on the ground floor of a two-story apartment house with four units on top, four units on the bottom. It was fall and still dark out at 5:30 A.M., but the sun was starting to lighten the sky to the east. It's the only time of day you can fool yourself into thinking that the air really is clean in L.A.

I pulled up in front behind the ambulance and another police unit already on the scene. There wasn't any activity in the ambulance, so I figured it couldn't be much of a call, probably a minor family dispute with a small wound. The apartment door was partially open, and I walked into unit three. A couple of women were sitting in the front room, not saying much. Two paramedics and my officers were standing next to a closed door.

"Sarge, you're not goin' to fuckin' believe it. This guy stabbed both of his kids and split. The door's locked, and we're tryin' to figure out how to open it."

"I accidentally pulled the door shut, and it locked from the inside," a slightly embarrassed fire fighter volunteered.

"Where are the kids?" I asked.

"They're inside, Sarge."

"Well, kick the fucking door open! What are you waiting for?"

Bang! The door was opened with a single well-placed kick from one of my officers. I knew as we stood in the hallway waiting for the door to open that a horrible sight would be unveiled.

There were two beds in the room with clothes strewn about from the partially opened dresser drawers. A sliding closet door, also slightly open, revealed a mess typical of two young children sharing the same room. Nothing in its place, clothes thrown around, punctuated with a toy here and there, but no pictures on the walls, no pennants, no bright posters of cartoon characters—none of that. As I looked into that room, my worst fears were not realized; they were vastly exceeded.

A little girl was lying on her back in her flannel nightgown, resting in a pool of her own blood. Her throat had been slit, causing her to bleed to death while choking on her own blood. Her face looked so peaceful, belying her violent death. She appeared to be only sleeping, but she was dead. On the floor her two-year-old brother was moving. He was trying to get away and hide beneath the bed. His throat too had been slit, and he was sliding in his own blood. The sticky, sweet smell of it permeated the air the way it always does in close spaces where humans bleed to death.

I reached down, picked him up, and cradled him, as you might hold any small baby, but it was as if his neck was hinged. His head flopped backward, revealing a gash halfway through his throat, making his windpipe clearly visible. I immediately snapped his head forward to close the wound. It was frightening because blood wasn't going everywhere the way it should have. He wasn't breathing, not even trying. The paramedics quickly came over. I tightened my arms around him, holding him close to me. He didn't cry. He couldn't. He was moving ever so slightly, the kind of movement that gives you hope.

"Sarge, he's finished. He's dead." No mistaking the air of finality in the paramedic's voice. In one of the few times I ever lost my temper, I screamed in his face, "He's not fucking dead till I say he's fucking dead—got it?"

"OK, Sarge, we'll try, we'll try." He seemed shocked by the tone of my voice, but he and his partner started to work on the child again. I opened his neck, and the paramedics carefully threaded an oxygen tube down that small windpipe. No need to go through this little one's mouth because a direct path had been established by the bread knife lying on the floor next to us. Together the three of us ran to the ambulance.

Finally I relinquished the little boy to one of the paramedics, who held him just as tenderly. By now a crowd of neighbors had gathered in the cool dawn. I guess they were like us. They had hope in their eyes. No one spoke—only silence. The kind of silence that means you're afraid to speak because you'll jinx it. The doors to the ambulance slammed shut, and the race north to Metropolitan Hospital began.

It wasn't going to turn out right. The little boy didn't make it. In my heart I already knew that as I returned to unit three. The paramedics were right, and I was wrong.

We still had a crime to investigate, a suspect to catch, evidence to secure, notifications to make, witnesses to interview. Inside that room of death I stood by myself in the company of only the little murdered girl lying in her bed. I looked at her, and I couldn't stop my sobs. I cried, for the only time in my twenty-one-year police career. It just wasn't fair the way things were turning out. Those kids didn't have a chance. It wasn't right, and it wasn't going to be right. Not that morning, maybe not ever.

A family dispute had started it, probably over something very simple. I don't really know. The husband was a PCP dealer, and the wife told us later that in her anger she had flushed a bottle of the drug down the toilet. To punish her, the husband had brought each of their children out and, in front of their mother, run a ten-inch bread knife across each of their throats. They must have looked up at him, trusting their father implicitly, and he returned their trust with death. He took the little girl back to her bed to die, but the little boy he threw down on the bedroom floor like trash that had no further use, just as he did with the bread knife; then he ran.

On the table was a family album filled with photographs. I asked the wife to remove all the photos of her husband. Taking the pictures outside, I asked the neighbors to help us find the man who had murdered his children. There was no hint of the usual attitude of "move on down the sidewalk, get back, there's nothin' goin' on here" this time. We needed their help, and help us they would. We wanted this guy, and we wanted him real bad. The neighbors did, too.

Every person standing there took a picture and fanned out through the area. By now two additional police units were there, and we checked the immediate vicinity of the apartment house. It seemed like only a few minutes before a young man came running back, so out of breath he couldn't talk. He pointed down the street, and I asked, "Is he over there?" He nodded. Officers and neighbors together began running down the street, following the youthful messenger.

We turned the corner, and two houses down on the left the boy stopped. Out stepped the suspect. He was easy to identify. Having seen several photographs of him, I knew he was the killer. My gun was drawn.

"Keep your hands out where we can see them. Come here slowly, down the steps. Come on, keep your hands up."

"You can kill me, motha-fucker, 'cause I ain't goin'."

I reholstered my weapon and told the officers to cover me as I went up the steps after him. Reaching him, I grabbed the murderer and extended my left leg as he went past me. He tripped and fell face first down the steps and onto the sidewalk. He tried to get to his feet to flee, and the fight was on. I seized him from behind and applied a chokehold harder than I have ever done. The absolute rage I felt blinded me. At that moment I really think I could have beaten him to death. It felt good having my arm around his neck, bringing him to his knees.

"Sarge, let go of him. Let go of him!" yelled a detective who had responded to the scene from headquarters. I thought it meant I'd choked the father to death, so I let go, but the detective wanted his turn. He stepped up and booted the man in the face harder than I have ever seen anyone kick. The detective had just wanted to vent his own anger before I was finished. Then he shouted, "Get that motherfucker, Sarge!" I resumed the chokehold until the man was unconscious. It was with great satisfaction that I rolled him over onto his stomach to slap handcuffs on him.

He regained consciousness almost immediately, so we stood him up and began walking him down the street toward the police cars. An elderly man who had watched the excitement unfold said to the person next to him, "See, I tol' you. Just stay back. They knows how to kick ass."

Later at the hospital the detective approached me. "Hey, Sarge, do you think we'll get in trouble for whipping that guy?"

"Fuck no, not the way he was fighting, and that's the way I'm writing it up in my log." I had wanted to retaliate for the little children who couldn't fight for themselves. Too bad he wasn't seriously injured.

I don't know if that was police brutality, and I don't really care. I never felt a second of remorse for choking that guy or for the kick delivered by the detective. I don't care what others think about what we did. They didn't hold that little boy. If he had given up initially, there would have been no fight, no matter how much I wanted it. It's hard to describe just how good it felt to choke him out cold, to even the score for those children in some small way.

The suspect was tried for two counts of first-degree murder with special circumstances. Special circumstance cases may lead to the death penalty or life imprisonment without possibility of parole. After the preliminary hearing we lost special circumstances. The wife didn't turn out to be nearly as good a witness as the case needed. She changed her tune and began to support her husband's actions, saying it was her fault because she had angered him. Maybe it was because all evidence pointed to the fact that she sold dust (PCP) along with her husband, and she valued the family business more than her children's lives.

On one of her visits to her husband prior to the preliminary hearing, her conversation was recorded. A detective handling the case relayed part of that exchange to me. She and her husband were calmly discussing the murder of the two children when she said to him, "It ain't no thing. We can makes more babies."

For some months following the murders I had a recurring dream. Each time, we'd be in the apartment house, and all the dialogue would be the same. We'd kick the door just as we had that morning, only this time my twin daughters, who were about the same age as the murdered boy, would be lying dead in the room.

Coincidentally, around this time there was an experimental program whereby the police department employed "station house shrinks." These psychologists would work with police officers and citizens in the station or on the street. The doctor assigned to Newton Street was Ryan Gray. He really understood police work and the pressures placed on police officers. As a sergeant you were charged with escorting Dr. Gray when he worked your shift. One night I decided it was time to talk.

"Dr. Gray, I've got a question for you. Not as a sergeant, but as Mike Middleton, patient." I then told him about my dreams.

"How do you feel about it?"

"I don't want to have them anymore. I'm tired of it, and I don't understand why now, after almost twenty years on the job, something like this is affecting me."

"You've seen a lot, Mike, but you violated the rules this time. You touched, and when you touch, the shield you use to protect yourself comes down."

He then advised me on how I should attack this situation. He told me to welcome remembrances of that terrible morning. "What's worse," he asked, "thinking about what happened or what actually happened? If what actually happened is worse, then thinking about it is going to help. The mind can cleanse itself, but you've got to help."

He was right. That day, before I went to sleep, I thought about everything that had happened in minute detail. I let the memories wash over me without rejecting them. Finally, I fell asleep, really asleep. I never had those dreams again, but I'll always remember what caused them.

DEATH IS AN INTEGRAL PART of violent, inner-city police work. Loss of lives or saving lives is the most important thing that happens. Regardless of which way it goes, there's always a reminder that it could be you that's dying or you whose life others are frantically racing to save. Death is a dirty part of the police business, and you hope it won't rub off on you. You become inured to its real impact and significance. By the end of your career, death doesn't mean much anymore, except you're glad it wasn't you.

Chapter Two

HEROISM

Heroes Are Like That

DURING MY YEARS ON THE Los Angeles Police Department I knew a lot of them. They literally came in all shapes and sizes. Sometimes they were brand-new to police work; other times they were veterans. A strange breed. It's not a class taught at the police academy, and you can't acquire a "how to" book on it. All had reasons for their actions but probably couldn't explain them very well. Most of the time they were rather shy, and maybe even a bit embarrassed about what happened to them. They called themselves police officers, but to everyone else they were heroes.

Sometimes they get "the Medal" for what they do, but not usually. "The Medal," as it's called by officers within the department, is the Medal of Valor, a silver and blue medallion that simply states

LOS ANGELES POLICE DEPARTMENT
FOR VALOR

Mayor George Cryer awarded the first Medal of Valor ever given to a Los Angeles police officer in 1925 to Sergeant Frank Harper, who had been involved in a shoot-out with a gang of robbers and ultimately captured several of them. Since that time about four hundred officers have been honored. Sometimes it's given posthumously to families of officers whose call to heroism cost them their lives.

Officers are expected to perform heroic acts day after day. "You will protect the citizens and the community through your own service." What follows are some stories of everyday officers who were selected.

NEWTON P.M. WATCH HAD ALREADY left roll call at about 3:45 one Saturday afternoon in October 1982. I was working the mid-P.M. watch, which started at 5:00 in the evening, and had just finished roll call for my officers. Roll call for Los Angeles police officers lasts about three-fourths of an hour and normally includes the calling off of assignments for each radio car, the reading of important information regarding wanted suspects, and a training period that could include such things as changes in department policies or updates on legal issues confronting officers. It's the only opportunity for all the officers working any one watch to sit down in the same room at the same time. This particular day I cut roll call short and was done in fifteen minutes. On Saturdays we usually ran short of personnel, and I wanted the officers to be out on the streets as soon as possible.

I had just checked out the keys for my sergeant's car when the relative silence of the watch commander's office was broken by the radio.

"13-A-43 requesting assistance. We have a major structure fire on San Pedro, just south of Jefferson." Immediately I was out of the station and en route to the call.

The two officers working 13-A-43 were Raymond Castro and Joseph Doherty. Castro was a police officer III, and the training officer for his probationary partner, Doherty. I had known Ray Castro for a few years. We had worked Central Division together before I made sergeant. He was not a shy person, but I suppose the best way to describe him was quietly outgoing. Joseph Doherty was a new officer, and I don't think I had ever spoken to him before that day. Probationary officers usually don't have too much to say to sergeants unless they're asked a specific question, as well I remembered from my own early days on the department. I knew he worked with Ray, but whenever Ray and I talked to each other or joked about something, Joseph was always very quiet. He struck me as rather shy.

About twenty people stood across from Avalon Boulevard, watching the free, action-packed show. Parked against the curb was a police car with its doors open, but the two officers were nowhere in sight. Their last transmission had indicated people were trapped upstairs in the burning building. It appeared that the apartments were on the second floor, over the top of several small storefront businesses. On one end of the apartment building was a small, inset patio with a wooden railing. An extension ladder was leaning next to the patio's railing, which gave access to the second floor.

I parked my car behind the abandoned police vehicle and retrieved my ROVER from its holder as I climbed out. "13-L-50 to 13-A-43, come in." I stood on the sidewalk and waited about fifteen seconds before repeating my transmission in an effort to find my missing officers. "43, come in."

An elderly man came down the sidewalk toward me. He apparently could tell that I was trying to locate the officers. "Man, they're up in there." He pointed to the apartment house. "They've already brought a bunch of people out, and—"

"Which way'd they go? Where're they at?"

"Last time I seen 'em, they went up that ladder.

At first they couldn't get up there, so we got 'em a ladder. I don't know how they can do it, 'cause it's bad, real bad."

"Did they both go up there?"

"Yeah, man, one after the other. They're somethin' else."

The second-floor balcony where they had climbed with the help of that ladder was now completely engulfed in flames. I looked back down the sidewalk and saw the entrance to the apartments. Smoke was rolling out of every window, and flames were coming through the roof of the building.

"13-A-43, come in! 43, come in!" Now I was worried about the safety of those officers.

Still no response. I ran to the entrance and started up the stairs when I encountered a wall of thick gray smoke. You couldn't see anything. It was as though the lights had been turned off. I retreated down the stairs to breathable air. A fire fighter also walked down the stairs right after me and back out onto the sidewalk. He had on breathing apparatus and a mask that completely covered his face. He unsnapped it, swinging it to one side.

"Don't go in there, Sarge; it's bad. You couldn't make it without an air pack."

"Have you seen my officers? Two of them are inside somewhere."

"We just got here, and I didn't see them. If they don't have something to help them breathe . . . I don't know. Maybe they came out the far end." He pointed down to the corner. "There's a stairway down there."

"Thanks," and I began to run down the sidewalk to the corner where most of the fire trucks from Engine Company 14 were parked. It was a maze of equipment as fire fighters pulled hoses into the building. At that moment a blue uniform appeared around the corner of one of the fire vehicles. It was Ray Castro, walking with another man. Ray's arm was around the man's waist, keeping him upright, while the victim had his arm around Ray's neck.

One of the fire fighters took the man from Ray and led him to the back of the fire truck to sit down. Approaching Ray, I asked, "Where's Joe?"

He looked at me, and his eyes rolled straight back in his head. Ray started to fall forward, like a tree that has just been chopped down. Another fire fighter and I grabbed him but were only partially successful in breaking his fall. Ray hit the street face first. Castro was out cold.

A paramedic unit had already arrived at the scene, treating several people for smoke inhalation. I picked Ray up and carried him to the ambulance. His arms were hanging loose, and his head flopped back and forth as I made my way. The fire fighter walked with me, supporting Ray's legs. It seemed strange to me at the time, but the onlookers were clapping and cheering as this was going on. Their accolades had nothing to do with me or the fire fighter but were a tribute to Officer Castro, who unfortunately was unable to appreciate it.

"Hey, Sarge, your other guy's over here. He's pretty well out of it, too." Another fire fighter was walking by, pointing back over his shoulder toward the stairway leading to the second floor. Officer Joseph Doherty was on his hands and knees, coughing convulsively. Compared to Castro, Doherty looked great.

The still unconscious Ray was now in the ambulance, being given oxygen by the paramedics. Doherty got up and barely made it to the ambulance under his own power. He sat on the bumper, elbows resting on his knees, head hanging down while one of the fire fighters gave him oxygen as well. His coughing had subsided. I was standing with Joe, crouched down with my hand on his shoulder, patting him, just letting him know I was there. He raised his head up and pushed the oxygen away for a brief moment. The words he spoke gave me for the first time a sense of what had gone on inside that building.

"Sarge, we tried to get them all. I think we did. We went back as much as we could. I think we got them all."

"Come on, Officer, just breathe the oxygen. It's going to help you." The paramedic was trying to take care of his responsibilities.

"Just relax, Joe. I'll talk to you guys in a bit."

"Sarge, he's going to be fine. He just needs to breathe this for a little bit more," the paramedic told me as he repositioned the oxygen mask on Doherty's face.

Looking inside the ambulance, I had more good news. Castro was moving his head slowly from side to side. Climbing in, I patted him on the leg. "Come on, Ray, just relax."

"I don't think he can hear you. He's still out." The paramedic was right about that; in fact Castro would remain unconscious for almost twenty minutes.

The blaze was now pretty well knocked down, and the fire department personnel were performing the last rites of their operation. Smoke was being sucked from the building with fans, and a careful inspection was being made to ensure there were no "hot spots" to flame up again. I spoke to the fire captain to find out the status of the people who had been in the building.

"Captain, do you know anything about some residents my guys helped get out?"

"You mean rescued." The fire captain was emphatic. "If they hadn't gone in there, we'd have bodies in those rooms now. I don't know how they did it without any breathing equipment. From what I understand, they didn't go in just once. They went in over and over. They're the ones who can tell you more." He gestured toward a group of people sitting on the curb. "They're the ones the officers brought out. You got me how they did it."

"Was anyone left inside?" I asked.

"No, that's just it. They got them all. I think it was a total of eight people or something like that."

The survivors, all middle-aged men or older, were huddled together, the full impact of what almost happened to them beginning to sink in. Their heads were down as they talked quietly to each other.

"Can any of you folks tell me about the fire and what happened?" I asked the question of no one in particular, but it seemed as though they answered me all at once. Their dazed expressions evaporated as they excitedly began to relate their own stories of rescue.

"They came to my door and kicked it in! They helped me out. I was choking, but they pulled me until we were outside."

"When they came up, they were bangin' on all the doors and yellin', 'Fire, fire! Everyone get out!' I was takin' a nap, and didn't know anythin' was goin' on. The hall was full of smoke, and I was afraid to go out, but that guy over there," the survivor pointed toward Doherty, "said it was OK to come on. He sort of helped me into the hall . . . no, I guess he pulled me into the hall, 'cause I was afraid to leave. Look at my room. The flames were comin' out of it! I'd be dead, because I don't think I would've left. I was too scared."

"You know when they got to me, they were pullin' the guy who lives at the end of the hall behind them. I think he's in the ambulance now. I guess the fire started in his room, but he was knocked out, and they was on the floor pullin' him. I mean crawlin'! Then they helped me out, too, and we all crawled down the hall together. You know what they did next? They went back in! I could barely breathe, but they didn't even stop. They just went in."

A man in his late sixties was seated on the curb and offered his version of the rescue. "Yeah, well when they got to our room, you know I lives with my friend"—he pointed to an elderly gentleman also seated on the curb—"I knew there was a fire, and I knew I was dead. I was in bed because I can't walk by myself. I called for help, but I guess with all the noise nobody could hear me except for the shorter guy—you know, the officer that passed out. He came to my door, and it was closed. I was afraid to open it because the fire was comin'. He banged on it, and I yelled back, 'We're in here!' Bang! He kicked it right in. You know, he was like a knight when he stood in that doorway. Just like a knight who came to rescue *me*! He walked right out of that smoke and into my room and says to me, 'I knew it. I knew there had to be more people. I had a feeling. I knew it. I couldn't stop. I knew there was someone left.'

"He helped me out of the bed—I told him I can walk if someone helps me, but I can't walk alone—so when we got to the door, he told me to get down near the floor because the air wasn't as bad there. I was worried 'bout my friend, but I could see he was with the other officer. The fire was comin' down the hall, and you could feel how hot it was. We got down, and that officer helped me along with him till we got to the stairs. Then he held me as we walked down and outside to the firemen. Sarge, you don't understand. I was gonna *die*, and he saved my life. He came to that door, and he saved me."

It went on like this, with everyone relating his personal story of rescue. I just wished I could have seen Ray Castro standing in that doorway "like a knight." It must have been something. Onlookers were now coming forward to tell their own stories of the rescues. One man who lived across the street had come out when the fire started.

"Sarge, I'm gonna tell you one thing. Those guys were everywhere! They'd go in and come out with somebody. They'd go back in and come out with somebody else. That big fat dude over there, they was draggin' him. I don't know who got that ladder for 'em, but they couldn't get upstairs because of the way the fire was, so I think the guy on the corner got it for 'em, and up they went. You know, there was flames comin' out of that apartment. They busted the glass and went right inside. God, it was amazin'!"

"Excuse me, Sergeant. I'm Margaret Davis, director of the Avalon Carver Community Center, and I stopped to see if I could be of assistance." A well-dressed woman who seemed very out of place in this motley crowd began to recount her own observations.

"The officers went into the building several times and always came out with people. Flames were shooting out of some of the windows while they were inside. I couldn't believe they weren't even coughing when they came out. Maybe they didn't have time to think about themselves. When they went up the ladder, that room was on fire, and they still went in! They just disappeared into the smoke and flames. You're going to do something, aren't you, Sergeant? I've never seen such courage. They were so brave they should be recognized, and I will be happy to give you my name as a witness. And I'll tell you something else. There were a bunch of men just standing around, like they're doin' now. None of them helped your officers. No sir. None of *them* came forward."

By now Officers Castro and Doherty had both pretty well recovered from the smoke inhalation. If you'd seen them forty-five minutes earlier, you would have sworn they needed to be hospitalized, but they bounced right back and appeared to be fine. Their faces and hands were blackened from the soot and smoke, while their uniforms, although outwardly maintaining a clean pressed appearance, were filthy. The fire scene was now secure, and I drove them to Metropolitan Hospital for examination while I assigned another officer to drive their car back to the station. Ray and Joe both protested this action; they wanted to go back on patrol.

Later, after the doctors had checked Ray and Joe over and released them, I interviewed them at Newton Station and heard their side of the story. They honestly didn't consider their actions remarkable. I reminded them that the building was on fire, they had rescued eight people, and the fire captain had told me he couldn't believe they had survived without some sort of breathing apparatus inside the building, let alone while they were in the process of rescuing all those people. Officer Castro said, "Well, I don't know, Sarge, but we were really afraid that there were kids trapped in those apartments. You know how the streets are filled with kids around there. What else could we do?"

"Did you ever think about waiting for the fire units? After all, they have the right equipment to go into the building."

"Yeah, but Sarge, they weren't there, and we were."

"Did you think that you might be unduly risking your own lives?"

"No. I don't know about Joe, but I never thought about that. I guess there wasn't time. It is kind of scary now."

"Well, Joe, what about you?"

He looked at me, shrugged his shoulders, and turned his gaze to the floor. He took a few seconds before he replied in a very soft tone, "It's like Ray said. There wasn't time."

I really think that they believed they might be in trouble for their actions. I was like the fire captain; I was amazed they had been able to do everything attributed to them, but they had. Reluctantly they told me essentially the same story I had been given by the various witnesses.

After listening to them, I knew two things for sure: they had entered that building to save the lives of people they didn't even know, and they had been successful, eight times. I went back and spoke with the fire captain, who told me that in his opinion, had the officers not entered the building and persistently gone door to door until they had rescued all of the people inside, there would have been bodies instead of survivors arranged along the curb. His only criticism of the incident was that the officers went into the inferno without proper equipment, putting their own lives at substantial risk. He was right on all counts.

I wrote a commendation for Officers Raymond Castro and Joseph Doherty, and they were awarded the Medal of Valor for their deeds. My wife and I attended that ceremony and sat at the table with the officers and their families. Ray Castro's mother said to me, "Sergeant, I worry so much about Raymond. I don't know if you're aware of this, but he did almost the same thing when he was a police officer in San Jose. Oh, they gave him a nice medal then, too, but he just doesn't think when these kinds of things happen. I just wish he'd be more careful. But they really were very brave, weren't they?"

Yes, they really were.

MOST EXAMPLES OF POLICE HEROISM occur after a response to a radio call or as a result of officers on routine patrol driving up to a situation like the apartment house fire. Other times trouble just finds the officer. On the rarest of occasions the situations change, and some of the names remain the same.

Earthquakes are a fact of life in southern California, but tornadoes are another thing entirely. It was front-page news in 1939 when a tornado struck. A tornado would be front-page news again when one touched down forty-four years later.

The weather report that March morning indicated only that another rainstorm, with the possibility of thunderstorms, would pass through the L.A. Basin. It was accurate. Heavy rain was falling, but there was no inkling of the havoc that would occur when the storm turned violent. A police officer on his way to court that morning at about 8:30 reported something was happening around Vernon and Broadway, but he wasn't sure just what. He thought it might have been an explosion, but with the wind he said it might be a tornado. About the same time the switchboards lit up at police communications with citizens calling to find out what was going on.

For several blocks on Broadway it was a disaster scene. Twenty-foot-tall cast-iron lampposts were gone—just disappeared. Cars had been picked up and thrown into second-story windows. Billboards were bent over, their huge steel girders twisted to a ninety-degree angle. Even a stop sign, while still standing, had all of the lettering removed, leaving just shiny aluminum behind. Telephone poles had snapped at their bases, been picked up and dropped in alleys half a block away. What caused this havoc would have been crystal-clear to someone from the Midwest, but to Angelenos this was a foreign occurrence.

The weather bureau confirmed that a tornado had traveled in a northerly direction through the downtown area and touched down in the vicinity of Vernon and Broadway. Thankfully, there had been no loss of life.

Like any major police department, Los Angeles's has a system to deal with major disasters. When events such as a tornado occur, a command post is established and large numbers of personnel are assigned to the area. In this type of event police officers come from every division in the city to deal with the situation and assist in the handling of radio calls, crime investigations, and routine patrol. This time the command post was set up at the corner of Fifty-First and Broadway. All officers assigned to Newton Division were placed on a schedule of twelve hours on, twelve hours off and no days off for anyone. My shift started at 7:00 P.M. and would last through the night until seven the next morning. At the time I was a sergeant and arrived at the command post about ten minutes before my shift started.

There is a church on the northeast corner of Fifty-First and Broadway where all personnel were to report and ultimately receive their work assignments. I went inside, hoping I would draw field duty, and discovered instead that I was going to be working inside the command post trailer, cryptically called the CP, located directly opposite the church.

A Bell Jet Ranger police helicopter was sitting in the middle of the intersection I had to cross to reach the CP. Helicopters are normally deployed to assist when a disaster occurs since they are able to quickly give an overview of the scene and effectively patrol a large area for looters. The helicopter had set down in the street earlier in the afternoon.

Its crew had been taking a break inside the church and was now back in the helicopter preparing to check out a citizen's report of a possible burglar on the roof of a building at Jefferson and Hill. This was in the immediate area affected by the tornado, and therefore the command post would be responsible for sending officers to check it out.

As the helicopter blades began to rotate, I turned to Carl Drake, another sergeant from Newton, and said, "I'm going to get inside the CP, because this thing's going to blow shit all over us. Talk to you later." I walked across the street and went into the command post trailer, where I was met by Officer Raymond Castro.

"Hey, Mike, looks like we'll be working together tonight."

"That's cool. What're we doing?"

"The deployment schedule for tomorrow's shift." This meant Ray and I would have to contact all the divisions in the city and get the number and names of officers who would be assigned to tomorrow's 7:00-to-7:00 shift. Although other divisions weren't placed on this twelve-on, twelve-off schedule, personnel would have to be contributed to the disaster scene.

Several of the additional units assigned to the disaster scene were from the Metropolitan Division. Their unit designation always started with *R*.

"R-39 to CP-13. Code four here at Jefferson and Hill. Only a plumber." The Metro unit, by advising of a code four, had let the command post know that the helicopter wasn't needed to inspect the roof at Jefferson and Hill.

"CP-13 to R-39, roger."

The air unit personnel decided to take off anyway and do some patrol. With its engine running at top speed, the Jet Ranger started to lift off the ground. The helicopter didn't take off perpendicular to the street but instead began to sweep in a southerly direction down Broadway as it gained altitude. It seemed caught by some invisible force that abruptly stopped the upward movement. Eyewitnesses immediately knew something was wrong.

Inside the command post we could hear little but the noise of the helicopter's engines as the unit took off. Suddenly the sound changed. It's easy to identify the normal sound a helicopter's blades make when they are biting into the air, lifting it skyward. Abruptly, it stopped.

Carl Drake was still standing on the corner and said that the helicopter seemed to be suspended in midair. Its forward motion was halted only twenty-five feet up. The helicopter had struck an unseen wire and began to fall toward the street, its motor still whining as the pilot attempted to gain control of the craft.

Inside the CP someone screamed, "It's the helicopter! Look out, it's coming in!"

For an instant in that trailer no one moved. Everyone, I'm sure, was thinking the same thing: is it going to land here? It was a split second of absolute terror.

The helicopter crashed into the street with a tremendous roar. Ray Castro and I were the first ones out the door and saw the helicopter sitting in the street, its blades whirling as the ship gyrated back and forth with a rocking motion. The tail section broke on impact, destabilizing the aircraft. Both of the nearly full fuel tanks had burst, and fluid was pouring onto the street.

"CP-13 to Control One. Be advised we are abandoning the CP." The RTO grabbed a ROVER radio and ran from the command post trailer, followed by several other staff persons. CP communications were now being run by a hand-held radio in the parking lot at Fifty-First and Broadway as the deadly drama unfolded. This was the first broadcast that indicated something was seriously wrong at the command post. It was 7:06 P.M.

Ray Castro began running toward the helicopter, holding his radio in his right hand. As he ran, he broadcast, "Fifty-one and Broadway. Helicopter down. We need fire units."

Many of us at the scene were Vietnam veterans and expected the ship to disintegrate upon impact. We had seen helicopters go in before and fully expected a massive explosion followed by a barrage of shrapnel going everywhere. I was about fifty feet from the craft and took cover behind a telephone pole.

There was no other shelter available, but I thought that even with this limited protection I might be able to survive the initial explosion.

Officers Victor Comparetto, Ron Vega, and Noah Walls were all blocking traffic immediately south of the helicopter's takeoff position. When the helicopter crashed, they dropped to the street, hoping to survive the anticipated blast.

Sergeant Jacob DeLeon and Officer Clinton Dona were positioned north of the intersection, blocking traffic in much the same manner as the other officers. They also sought the almost nonexistent protection offered by lying flat in the street.

Just before takeoff Carl Drake walked north on Broadway across Fifty-First Street to tell a motorist parked in the area to move for his own protection because the helicopter was ready to take off. The motorist had driven away only moments before, which undoubtedly saved his life. The helicopter would have crashed directly on top of his car, and the results would have been catastrophic for us all. Drake stood motionless as the helicopter went into the street, making no move to seek protection for himself.

The unthinkable never happened. The helicopter did not explode upon impact, and within seconds of the crash an incredible scenario of bravery started to unfold.

Raymond Castro was the first to act. As he ran toward the downed craft, the door on the left side opened. Thomas Brooks, the copilot, or observer, attempted to free himself from the seat. His legs were trapped under it, and he fell backward out the open door. The gyrating action of the copter, coupled with his legs being pinned, caused a whipping action of his body. The back of his head struck the pavement with such force that he was immediately knocked out. Brooks looked like a rag doll being tossed about as the helicopter tilted wildly from side to side.

Ron Vega and Noah Walls were on their feet and ran headlong toward the wreckage. They ducked low to avoid the deadly swath of the whirling blades and arrived at the open door immediately after Castro.

Officer Clinton Dona ran toward the airship and, as he got even with the tail section, started to crawl because of the low swing of the helicopter's blades. As he moved past the ruptured fuel tanks, he was drenched in jet fuel. It looked as though he were inching through a stream as the fuel splashed up his hands and over his legs.

Carl Drake, realizing that enough people were helping the unconscious observer, went to the right door to help free the pilot, Sergeant Ronnie Hansen. Drake opened the door and helped the aviator out of the craft. Hansen seemed dazed and disoriented to Drake, who grabbed hold of him and pulled him along as they ran under the still-spinning blades to safety. Carl timed their escape when the helicopter was tipping away from them so the blades wouldn't be as low.

Also manning the helicopter was Reserve Police Officer Stuart Tiara, an electronics specialist not normally assigned to Air Support Division. Reserve officers volunteer their time to assist in the policing operations all over the city. On this particular day he was riding with the air unit and acting as an observer in addition to Officer Brooks. Immediately after Officer Brooks was knocked out, Officer Tiara exited the rear of the helicopter. He was uninjured in the crash and began to run toward safety. He looked behind him and stopped when he saw his partner, Officer Brooks, still trapped and returned to join in the rescue effort.

Officer Vega began yelling at the others, "Keep your heads down! Watch the blades!" The five officers worked feverishly to free the trapped Brooks. Officer Tiara moved around the other officers to gain a position that would afford him a better opportunity to free his partner. Without warning there was a sound like the crack of a baseball bat, and a rotor blade struck Officer Tiara in the forehead. The majority of his helmet flew directly toward me.

Ray Castro and Noah Walls broke away from their rescue effort with Brooks and grabbed hold of Stuart Tiara's shirt. They never spoke a word to each other, but both knew they had to pull him away from the helicopter immediately. Later both officers told me they felt if they could get him away from the copter they could start emergency first aid and save his life. They thought he might be only seriously hurt and could survive until an ambulance arrived.

It was amazing to watch them grab Tiara under his arms and move him slightly away from the body of the helicopter. They stopped. You could see they were timing the swing of the blades, now only about eighteen inches above the street surface. The blades had slowed considerably but could still produce deadly consequences for anyone in their path. As the blade barely passed over their heads with a "whoosh," Walls yelled, "Go!" and the two ran with incredible speed, pulling Tiara with them. They bolted all the way to the curb and onto the sidewalk before they stopped. As both officers knelt to give what aid they could to Stuart Tiara, they looked into the face of horror and death. Much of Officer Tiara's head had been ripped off by the rotor blade. He had been killed instantly.

Meanwhile Dona and Vega had finally freed Brooks's legs and hauled him to safety. Amazingly, they too escaped the scythe of the helicopter blade. As soon as they were out of harm's way, Ron Vega began first aid for Brooks. Victor Comparetto ran to Vega's assistance. He had remained at his original position, believing that he could better serve the situation there in case things turned worse. Both officers freed the air passage of the unconscious Brooks and remained with him until paramedics arrived. It was 7:07 P.M.

A few months later the noise, destruction, and death of that morning seemed far removed as we sat at the Medal of Valor luncheon and listened to the names of Raymond Castro, Noah Walls, Clinton Dona, Ron Vega, Carl Drake, and Stuart Tiara being called out. It was the second time I had sat with the family of Ray Castro on such a memorable occasion. Each officer stood proudly on the stage as his name was read and his heroic deeds were described. Each bowed his head as the blue-and-white ribbon holding a silver-and-blue medallion was draped around his neck—save for one. Stuart Tiara's mother accepted the Medal of Valor for her fallen son.

The following year another officer received the Medal of Valor for heroic actions at the scene of the helicopter crash. Officer Clifford Lloyd had assisted in the rescue of Brooks. Regrettably I had not seen his efforts and therefore had not included him with the other six officers.

IN THE FACE OF ALMOST CERTAIN DEATH some act selflessly to save others. Heroism always involves the element of choice, reflected in an absolute willingness to risk everything for another, regardless of personal consequence. Your marker may be called in at any moment and sometimes is.

"Good morning, Captain. Got a minute? I'd like to talk to you."

"Sure, Mike, come on in."

The captain looked terrible. His face was drawn, and you could tell that if he'd gotten any sleep at all that night, it hadn't been enough. Having just finished morning watch duty, I was glad to sit down.

"I was just wondering what plans you have of doing a 15.7 for Archie and Dewey for the Medal."

"You've written them before, haven't you, Mike?"

"Yes, sir. I'd be honored to do it."

"Why don't you go ahead and get started? They deserve it."

Christmas was only five days away, but that seemed unimportant now. Circumstances during the previous twenty-four hours had changed everything. It seemed as though the luster of life had dimmed, and for most it would be a while before it returned. For some the brilliance would never return. Lives were shattered by events that transpired in only moments, but the effect would be felt forever. Nothing could turn the hands of time back to before that one call on the afternoon of December 19.

A 15.7 is a form, methodically completed after an extensive investigation, that would ultimately be used by the Medals and Awards Committee in deciding whether or not Officers Dewey Johnson and Archie Nagao would be awarded the Medal of Valor. Although I had not been at the scene, I would rely on interviews of witnesses and other investigations conducted by the police department's officer-involved-shooting team to complete this 15.7.

On this December day the city was inundated by a storm that produced intense periods of rain, followed by no precipitation at all. It would rain; it would stop. This pattern continued throughout the morning.

That afternoon two customers were standing at the door of the Lee Wong Jewelry Store on Bamboo Lane. Bamboo Lane is a small side street barely wide enough for one car running between Broadway and Figueroa in the Chinatown district just north of the Civic Center.

When the Lee Wong store was open for business, customers knocked to be admitted. The wood-framed glass door was kept locked at all times to prevent robberies. The proprietors, Lee Wong, and his son,

James, were inside, along with Lee's sister, Mary Lee. Thomas Lin and William Han were both dressed in business suits and peering through the windows on either side of the door. The younger Wong could see that they appeared to be the kind of customers the store welcomed. James Wong opened the door and let the two men in.

"We're looking for an Indian head gold coin," William Han said after gaining entry. Thomas Lin was standing next to him, nodding in agreement.

"We don't keep those out here. I'll have to go in the back to get one," Lee Wong said as he walked through the bamboo partition into the rear area of the shop not open to customers. Cabinets lined the left and right sides at the front of the business. Long glass display counters running almost the entire length of the showroom were in front of them, behind which customers were not normally allowed. Between the cabinets and display counters was a walkway for the owners of the store to service patrons. A break between them allowed the owners to walk from behind the counter on one side of the store to help a client on the opposite side.

In the center of the room stood a waist-high display cabinet. It ran from front to back but was only about half the length of the display counters on either side. Special items of interest were showcased here.

At the rear of the showroom was a bamboo curtain separating the display area from business operations. To the left of the curtain was an additional waist-high glass display counter where cash transactions occurred. Behind the curtain, yet visible from the store, was the cash register. Mary Lee was stationed next to it, a silent observer of what she thought were customers. It was through this curtain that Lee Wong walked to retrieve the Indian head gold coin from his safe that fateful day.

Upon returning the senior Wong looked over the

top of the case to see Thomas Lin and William Han now standing by the rear display counter, but it wasn't unusual for customers to wander about while waiting. Wong held out the coin for their inspection, while Lin and Han made a pretense of businesslike examination. "Do you have a holder for it?" asked Han.

James Wong, who had remained in the showroom area with the customers, came over to help. "Yes, just a moment." He unlocked the rear cabinet and placed some coin holders on the top for them to look at.

Mary Lee joined the four men as they inspected the coin. There weren't any other customers to take care of at the moment, and Mary was curious. It seemed that a routine sale was going to be concluded at the Lee Wong Jewelry Store that day. Suddenly everything changed.

William Han was pointing a semiautomatic pistol at the three startled people. "This is a holdup. If you move, we'll kill you. Get in the back room."

James Wong looked into the eyes of Han, who responded, "You can look at me. I'm not afraid to show you my face. You don't have to worry. You're insured; it won't cost you anything. I'm only going to take money.

"All right, let's go. Get in the back room," Han went on as he waved his gun at the Wongs and Mary Lee, motioning them through the bamboo curtain and into a short hallway. It led past a set of stairs that went to the basement, then turned into a corridor that led past the office to the workshop in the rear. By moving them to the rear storage area, they could proceed to the next phase of the robbery. One of the robbers would keep the hostages corralled at the back while never losing sight of the front of the store.

With everyone removed from the front retail section, the robbers could efficiently ransack the store of its valuables. Han moved without hesitation to the rear workshop, and there was no discussion at any time among the robbers as to the location of anything. William Han and Thomas Lin knew the layout of the store because they had visited before, posing as customers.

The rear workshop was adjacent to the kitchen, and a back door led to an alley not easily approached from Bamboo Lane. There was a second stairway leading to the basement from the kitchen area. It was possible for a person to walk down the first set of stairs into the basement and return to the main floor via the second.

As they were marched to the rear of the store by the robbers, both Lee and James Wong surreptitiously activated their pocket silent robbery alarms to summon the police. The call was routed through a private alarm company, which in turn telephoned the police department, and the call was finally dispatched to a patrol unit. This entire process took an additional eight minutes.

With Han shepherding the hostages, Thomas Lin walked silently to the front door of the establishment and unlocked it to admit accomplices Sam Chang and Lau Ming, being sure to relock the door behind them. Lau Ming immediately went to the back of the store and met up with William Han. Han looked at Ming and said, "Anybody moves, kill 'em." Lau Ming stood silent, a silver revolver in his right hand aimed directly at the hostages.

Han returned to the center of the store and, with the help of Sam Chang, began to smash the glass display cabinets so he could quickly remove their contents. Thomas Lin remained as sentry at the front door while the robbery took place in front of him. From his position he could see everything going on in the store as Han and Chang placed the expensive jewelry in plastic garbage bags.

Wan Sing, his wife, Nora, and their friend,

Mindy Lu appproached the Lee Wong Jewelry Store, stopping to admire items in the display window before entering. Monitoring their approach, Thomas Lin was ready and opened the door with a warm "Come in."

Once inside, he spoke again, in a different tone. "This is a robbery." Lin pointed a revolver at the three frightened shoppers, who were then herded to the rear of the store and placed with the other hostages. In an icy voice Lin repeated the same instructions to Lau Ming: "If they move, kill them." Lin then returned to guard duty at the front door.

In moments another patron came to the front door and knocked. Glenn Song had come to pick up some jewelry. Again without hesitation, Lin opened the door and admitted Mr. Song. Perhaps reflecting his irritation at the constant distractions, he dispensed with pretense and immediately placed a gun in Mr. Song's back. Song was unceremoniously marched to the rear of the business. "If they move, blow their fucking heads off," Lin again told his accomplice. Observing the growing number of hostages, Han and Chang accelerated the emptying of the jewelry cases.

"All Central units. 211 silent, 412 Bamboo Lane." The officers of foot beat 1-Z-22 had just walked into the Chinatown substation at Broadway and Bamboo Lane, seeking refuge from the incessant rain. Officer Dewey Johnson immediately pulled out his portable ROVER radio from his belt to respond. They didn't even have time to remove their waist-length yellow raincoats.

"1-Zebra-22. We'll handle the call."

The robbery was in their assigned area, so partners Dewey Johnson and Archie Nagao would normally handle any calls for police service there. More important, they were only seventy-five feet away from the jewelry store at 412 Bamboo Lane. Quickly they left the substation and strode up the sidewalk to the Lee Wong store.

Reaching the jewelry store, the officers were easily able to see some of the interior from the sidewalk. Dewey Johnson moved in front of the main door and peered in. Archie Nagao also looked in through a side window and saw Thomas Lin. Both officers had seen the owners of the store only a few times and thought Thomas Lin was one of them. Lin opened the door and smiled.

"Is everything OK?" Dewey Johnson asked.

"OK, OK. Come in." Lin stepped to one side to allow Officers Nagao and Johnson to enter, then closed and locked the door behind them.

Mary Lee saw the officers enter and started to wave her hand to get their attention. "Don't say a thing," Lau Ming warned Mary Lee. He then spoke, very quietly in Chinese, to all the hostages for the first time. "Don't move. I'll shoot whoever moves."

"Is everything OK?" Dewey Johnson asked again in a louder voice. "We got an alarm call. Is everything OK?" Johnson walked deeper into the store. Archie Nagao remained standing just inside the door with his back to Thomas Lin.

Lee Wong had now been moved through the bamboo curtain and into the store, accompanied by Lau Ming, who stood to his right. Ming held a chrome revolver in his right hand and concealed it from Dewey Johnson by holding it behind his leg. Officer Johnson asked Mr. Wong directly, "Is everything OK?"

Lee Wong raised his hands to his shoulders and quickly dropped them as he almost imperceptibly shook his head no. Dewey Johnson stared straight into Wong's eyes, realizing for the first time something was wrong, very wrong. Johnson stepped back away from the two men and pulled back his raincoat, ready to draw his .38-caliber police revolver.

Thomas Lin, standing behind Officer Nagao,

quickly removed his revolver at Johnson's action and coolly fired the first shot, striking Archie Nagao in the neck. The bullet traveled through Nagao's neck, nicking his windpipe but miraculously missing the carotid arteries and jugular veins. Nagao heard the shot and instantly felt a burning sensation as the bullet passed through his neck. He was able to draw his service revolver and fired the first of six rapid-fire shots at Thomas Lin.

At the roar of gunfire Johnson whirled and saw Archie Nagao and Thomas Lin engaged in a furious gun battle with perhaps no more than six feet separating them. He must have been able to see an ever-enlarging spot of red on Archie's throat. Johnson took deadly aim at Lin and fired. Dewey paid no attention to Lau Ming, standing to his left about three feet away. As Johnson began to defend his partner's life, Lau Ming also began to act. His revolver was raised and pointed directly at Officer Johnson.

Johnson fired again. Lee Wong ran to the cash register to retrieve his gun. At the same moment Lau Ming fired his weapon. The bullet passed through Johnson's upper left arm and entered his chest. Its deadly path coursed through his left lung, his esophagus, and finally pierced his aorta.

In spite of his wounds Johnson's focus remained on Thomas Lin. He fired a third and then a fourth time. Lau Ming too continued firing. His next bullet struck Johnson in the neck. The bullet traveled directly through the carotid artery and slammed into the spinal column. Johnson collapsed. Ming moved closer and fired a final time, releasing a bullet that would also trace its path through numerous vital organs. Lau Ming fled through the bamboo curtain, down the stairs to the basement, and up the stairs at the rear of the store.

Archie Nagao dropped to one knee and quickly reloaded his revolver. When he stood up to continue the gun battle, he realized that Dewey Johnson was no longer standing where he had been an instant before. Thomas Lin stumbled backward, falling against the counter before he struck the floor.

Sam Chang now began firing at Archie Nagao. Following a quick volley of shots directed at Nagao, he ran toward the rear of the store in an effort to escape. Archie Nagao fired three times as Chang ran across in front of him. Nagao, a Distinguished Expert pistol shooter, struck Chang three times—twice grazing him in the head, once in the body. None of these wounds proved serious, and Chang fled down the stairs leading to the basement.

Thomas Lin was dying on the floor. Three of Johnson's bullets had found their mark, as had five of Nagao's. Nagao began to choke on his own blood, but he was able to hear another gun battle going on in the rear of the store. Lee Wong had armed himself. William Han attempted to flee from the store but had mistaken a closet door for a door leading outside. Lee pursued him, firing continuously until Han no longer moved and Lee believed the robber was dead.

When Ming came up the stairs, he was confronted by James Wong, who had originally been in the work area with the other hostages when he heard footsteps on the stairs. Wong armed himself with a mop, the only weapon he could find, and moved to the head of the stairs to somehow stop the flight of the robbers. The element of surprise was on his side, and Wong was able to hit Lau Ming on the forehead. Ming retaliated by firing one shot at James Wong before fleeing out the back door but missed. Immediately behind Ming was Sam Chang. Mop in hand, James Wong held his ground and delivered a blow to the head of Chang, just as he had done to Lau Ming. Chang also took aim at James Wong and fired, striking him in the chest. Wounded, James Wong retreated to the work area where the other hostages were cowering and managed to dial the Los Angeles Police Department emergency line.

Archie Nagao was afraid he'd lose consciousness in the store and be unable to protect himself. Nagao tried to radio for help, but he was having difficulty breathing and couldn't speak. He staggered over to the front door, unlocked the deadbolt, and went outside, taking up a barricade position behind a vehicle parked in front of the store. Nagao believed the robbers would leave the store through the front, and he alone was prepared to engage them again. Nagao was now choking heavily on his own blood and could barely breathe.

Roberto Gonzalez parked his water delivery truck on Broadway at Bamboo Lane. Bamboo Lane was too narrow to drive up, so Roberto always parked at the corner and walked past the jewelry store to make his delivery. December 19 was no different. Shouldering a water bottle, he had just started down Bamboo Lane when he heard a barrage of gunfire. He wasn't sure where it was coming from, but as he set the water bottle down, he saw Nagao stagger out and realized the problem was inside the jewelry store. Blood gushed from the officer's neck in stark contrast to the yellow raincoat. The rain couldn't clean the coat fast enough. Archie Nagao turned back toward the store with his gun pointed at the door and collapsed in the street. With a superhuman effort, he pulled himself up and stumbled toward a car parked in front of the store.

"Officer! Officer! Are you OK?" Gonzalez asked.

Nagao stopped and shook his head no. His knees buckled. Still clutching his revolver, he fell down again. Gonzalez could wait no longer. He yelled to the crowd, "I need towels!" as he ran toward Officer Nagao. Gonzalez risked his life to save that of Archie Nagao.

"There are two gunmen inside the store," Nagao

whispered as Gonzalez kneeled in the street beside him. Nagao could barely speak as he clutched his own throat. Roberto Gonzalez knew he needed those towels immediately and couldn't wait for someone to bring them. He saw a woman running from a nearby restaurant with a stack of neatly folded white towels. He crawled away from Officer Nagao and grabbed two before she could leave. Gonzalez then inched back to the wounded officer, moved Nagao's hand away, and applied a towel to the wound.

"Call for help. Get me help." Nagao's voice trembled with the effort to speak. He handed Gonzalez his ROVER, his eyes pleading for aid.

Gonzalez held the radio and calmly stated, "Hello, we have an officer down."

A voice answered immediately. "Verify! Verify!"

"We have an officer down on Bamboo Lane." His trial under fire had earned Gonzalez the right to use *we*.

Nagao was battling to stay conscious and keep his gun pointed at the jewelry store door as the first black-and-white patrol unit drove up. Gonzalez crept toward the officers and told them two gunmen were still inside the jewelry store.

One of the officers yelled to the fallen Nagao, "Crawl toward us!"

Archie Nagao struggled to his feet, clutching his gun with one hand and the compress on his wound with the other. As he stood, he spun in a circle and collapsed to the street. Gonzalez realized at that point that if anyone was going to rescue Archie Nagao, it was going to be him. Gonzalez left the two uniformed officers behind and crept to Nagao's side. Gonzalez picked Nagao up by his gun belt, lifted the officer over his shoulder, and prepared to make a run for safety. As he did so, Nagao lost consciousness and dropped his weapon for the first time. Fearing the robbers would retrieve the officer's gun, Gonzalez knelt down, Nagao still slung over his shoulder, and picked the weapon up, shoving it into his own waistband. He then ran toward Broadway, Nagao's limp body slung over his shoulder, past the two officers, and placed him on the hood of the parked car.

There were no suspects inside the store. When Nagao initially left the establishment, he was prepared to do battle with the robbers in defense of his partner and the people inside the store. Unknown to Nagao, the robbers had already fled or been killed, and Dewey Johnson was gravely wounded.

That first calculated act of Thomas Lin launched an intense firefight lasting less than fifteen seconds within the limited confines of the store. Thirty shots would be fired; nineteen of them would find a human target. Inside the store William Han and Thomas Lin lay dead. Dewey Johnson was transported to Los Angeles County Medical Center, where in spite of valiant efforts made by the medical team there would be no miracles, no divine intervention. Dewey Johnson was killed in the line of duty.

It was only one-fourth of one minute, but in that short span of time lives were snuffed out and other lives forever altered. Dewey Johnson and his wife were eagerly awaiting the birth of their first child, but he would never see his daughter. It would have been so easy for Dewey to turn and face Lau Ming in defense of his own life, but instead he chose to defend the life of his partner. That selfless choice ultimately cost Dewey his own life.

Archie Nagao stood fearless, simultaneously exchanging shots with three suspects. When his gun was empty, he knelt and quickly reloaded, returning to the fray. All of this occurred after he was wounded.

Roberto Gonzalez could have waited just a moment, and everything would have been over so he could continue his water deliveries. Instead he responded to an urgent call for help from a fellow human being.

There were arrests. There was a trial for the two suspects who fled. Ming and Chang were sentenced to life without possibility of parole. The two uniformed officers unable to bring themselves to go to the aid of a fallen comrade remained nameless. I probably could have found out who they were through my investigation, but it seemed to me that their exposure would somehow denigrate the acts of brave men.

Dewey Johnson was posthumously awarded the Medal of Valor for heroism. Archie Nagao recovered from his wounds and received the Medal for his own fearless acts. Roberto Gonzalez was honored by the Los Angeles City Council for his courageous actions in coming to the aid of a downed officer.

POLICE WORK IS A CAREER permeated with deadly consequences. Officers are exposed to situations that call for split-second decisions. Sometimes officers are called on to choose a path that exposes them to great personal danger. Other times danger is totally avoidable, and exposure to great personal injury or even death is completely elective. Each of these heroes had choices. Each traveled the far more dangerous path. Each grossly disregarded his own safety "to protect and to serve" others. They had nothing to gain and everything to lose by their actions, but heroes are like that.

Chapter Three

SIEGE MENTALITY

". . . And Remember, It's Us Against Them."

"WHAT THE FUCK IS HE doing over here?"

My partner was watching a lone black male walking east as we turned onto Jefferson from Broadway. The young man didn't appear to be particularly concerned as we drove by him and came to an abrupt halt. My partner immediately retrieved a pair of black deerskin gloves from the dashboard and carefully put them on. I had thought the gloves were intended to keep his hands clean when he handled a derelict or someone particularly filthy. This pedestrian, however, didn't fit into either category. In a flash my partner was out of the car and headed toward the young man. I stepped out on my side and walked to the rear of our car. The young man froze. His arms were held slightly away from his sides, palms open, so we could see he had no weapon.

"Officers, it's cool. I haven't done anything."

As my partner approached the man, the size difference became striking. The young man was about five-foot-nine and slightly built. My partner was six-one and weighed about 250 pounds. Without any discussion or warning, my partner walked up to the pedestrian and knocked him unconscious with a single crashing blow to the jaw. The young man's arms flew in the air as he smacked the sidewalk spread-eagled on his back, out cold. My partner turned around silently and walked back to the car. It was apparent whatever business we had there was finished.

I also got back into the car, and as my partner meticulously removed his gloves one finger at a time, he said slowly, "You can't teach those fucking niggers a thing. Remember, it's us against them."

Had my partner and I been to the same police academy? There was never any tolerance for racism within the academy, or if our instructors did hold racist views, they never revealed them.

ONE INSTRUCTOR TOLD US in a class about officers killed in the line of duty, "When you stop some suspect and he's got a gun, I don't give a shit what color you are or what color he is. He'll blow you out of the fuckin' water for one reason—you're wearing blue, and that's the only color he sees. If you don't believe it, someday we'll be showing your picture in this class."

While in the academy, we watched a movie about a sit-down strike at a lunch counter, the only "training" we had on race relations. In the film the police were busily arresting protesters trying to integrate an unknown restaurant in some unknown city. Everything was very orderly as the officers took one person after another into custody. The narrator was careful to note only the various arrest techniques employed.

Our instructors offered no commentary about the social justification of the protesters. The arrest of the sit-down strikers I found troubling. They were Americans trying to secure rights guaranteed by the Constitution and the Bill of Rights. It occurred to me that it was the owner of the diner who should have been hauled away, not the protesters.

AS POLICE RECRUITS WE WERE SENT out on weekend assignments to give us firsthand experience along with our classroom training. It was a good program because it allowed us to see the practical application of what we'd been taught. It also whet our appetites to graduate and join the troops in the field.

One weekend I was assigned to work with a Wilshire traffic officer. Our first call was to an accident on Hollywood Boulevard, directly above the Hollywood Freeway. It was raining, and one car had broadsided another, causing injury to a twenty-year-old white female who was a passenger in the car driven by her boyfriend, a black male about the same age. The accident was clearly the fault of the other driver.

The injured woman was taken to the hospital and told not to leave before we arrived because we wanted to interview her for the traffic report. While we were investigating the accident, another car slammed into our existing pileup. We now had two traffic collisions to investigate, which delayed our arrival at the hospital. When we got there, the young woman, who had been treated and bandaged, was upset at us for being late.

"It took you guys long enough! Now that you're here, hurry up and ask me your questions so I can leave."

Her boyfriend was standing quietly next to her. My partner looked this young Caucasian woman right in the eye, and the first question out of his mouth was "Ma'am, exactly how long have you been a nigger?"

The woman stood mute, her eyes open wide in shock. Without skipping a beat, my partner then launched into the questions that were part of a typical accident investigation. After we completed our questioning, we returned to Wilshire Station. En route, my partner said, "Sometimes when they act like complete fuckin' assholes, you've got to treat them the same way to get through to them."

IT WAS INCREDIBLE ENOUGH to treat the public in this manner, but it was a real shock when I heard the same words used by one officer to describe another after I arrived at Newton. By then I realized what the situation was regarding blacks outside the department, but we had been told by our instructors at the academy that all officers were the same color—blue. Anyone who didn't believe that should get out. Maybe those teachers hadn't been to Newton.

The Los Angeles Police Department has always promoted sports programs for its officers. In 1967, Newton Division had one of the top baseball teams in the league. I thought it would be a good way to blend in with the other officers and, enjoying baseball as I did, joined the team. I was no one special, but I had a lot of fun, and we won the league championship that year.

Our coach was Sergeant "Red" Davis. The word was that Red would have played professional ball except for one fatal flaw. He was black. His complexion was not dark; in fact he was quite fair, with red hair and blue eyes. Red was one of the true gems in my career as a police officer. He was kind and considerate to young officers and insisted on hard work. When you came in with an arrestee and went into the watch commander's office for booking approval, you'd better know what you were talking about, and the arrest better be a good one. Never once did I see

Red do anything inconsistent with the finest traditions of our police department.

However, I was told right away by other officers, "Be careful talking about niggers around Red, because he's got Negro blood." Many of these officers really liked Red and said those words out of deference to him because they didn't want to have his feelings hurt.

We were playing Motors, which always fielded a good team. This was an important game because if we won we'd get the O'Shaunessey trophy. These motorcycle officers had two pitchers who were dynamite; one had played for the St. Louis Cardinals but washed out due to a bad arm. He may have had a bad arm for the pros, but it was great in our league.

Nobody was a fiercer competitor than Red. Late in the game he made a fairly routine player change. I was in my usual spot on the bench when the officer who'd been replaced returned and sat down next to me. He was extremely angry about Red's decision. He began a conversation with another officer whom I considered one of the most obnoxious people I've ever met. These two "men" were to be longtime partners and proved to be well matched.

"That fuckin' Davis! What a worthless, fuckin' nigger! He really pisses me off."

"Are you surprised? Those fuckin' niggers are all alike." He had found a sympathetic ear. "The only reason he pulled you was so he could put a 'brother' in. Fuckin' niggers!" I was so naive then, it honestly didn't occur to me that racist remarks would ever be directed against police officers by other officers.

I then realized that the officer who had been sent up to bat was black. The change worked well. He got a hit, and we went on to beat Motors because of the rally that officer started. That really gave me an inner sense of satisfaction, because I thought the two officers I had overheard on the bench were losers, and my contact with them on and off over the years consistently confirmed this. They were a pair of racist pigs, who interestingly enough always worked in the black community. You'd think that hating blacks as much as they did they would have transferred to a white area, but then they wouldn't have had power over people they loathed so much.

As a new officer at Newton, you worked a variety of duties on your watch to broaden your experience. One evening I was assigned to work with a desk officer who had more than five years on the job. He was very laid back, and sure enough, up came the discussion of my first homicide.

"Weren't you the kid on that shooting where you gave mouth-to-mouth?" he asked with a smile.

"Yes." I was prepared for yet another onslaught of criticism. Following my attempted revival of the murder victim, things had been difficult. More than once I had had to explain why I had tried to "reinflate a dead nigger."

"Let me tell you something, Mike. Your partner's nothing but an asshole, and just about everyone here knows that. Nobody likes to work with him because he's basically an obnoxious fuck. I heard you got pretty hot the other day when one of the guys asked you about it, and—"

"Look," I interrupted, "I am so sick of being asked about that call. I did what I was taught to do in the academy. They didn't say 'You're going to get down and give mouth-to-mouth only if he's white.' They said that we would do it, no matter what. I don't know; I thought that's what I was supposed to do! I did what I thought was right, and I'd do it again. I don't give a shit what any of these people think. I know I don't know a whole lot about police work, but I did what I thought—"

"Relax! I know you did. What I'm trying to tell you is forget guys like him. They're idiots. I wouldn't give most of them the time of day, but you've got to be cool. If you fuck with them, you know what they'll do? They'll tell the watch commander you're not a good police officer. They're not going to walk in and say 'Hey, Sarge, Middleton jumped on my shit because I'm a worthless racist.' They'll say 'Sarge, I don't know about this Middleton guy. I don't think he has the right attitude.' Or do what your partner did the other day when he came into the watch commander's office. When I'm working this desk, I hear everything going on in that office. Your partner was in there talking about some situation where you guys were looking for an armed robbery suspect, and he said he thought you were afraid to get out of the car."

"Wait, it wasn't like that! We pulled up in front of the Rib House on Avalon to look for a guy wanted in a residence 211. He thought the suspect might be there because it's an asshole hangout. When we pulled up, I thought I should wait and get out of the car at the same time. He jumped in my shit because he said that put us in a bad situation if anything happened. He still had to turn off the car and everything, so I should have gotten out immediately and confronted the guys on the sidewalk. He was right, but I didn't know that was the proper technique. When he told me, it made sense. It had nothing to do with being afraid. That's bullshit, and he's a liar. I can't believe he'd come in and say that to the watch commander."

"Did you ever tell him you didn't give a shit what he thought about giving mouth-to-mouth to that guy? Did you tell him you'd do it again?"

"Yeah! I was sick of hearing about it."

"That's my point. He didn't go to the watch commander because he thought you were afraid. That's just his chicken-shit way to fuck you over because you stood up to him. You've got to cool that, 'cause they're going to fuck you if you don't."

It was my introduction to surviving in a racist environment and what could happen to those who don't conform.

EACH DAY YOUR SHIFT BEGAN with a forty-five-minute roll call, but racism was never a training topic. If you looked for leadership from your supervisors in race relations, you'd be disappointed. Customarily included in roll calls were descriptions of suspects wanted for various crimes. Sometimes the suspects had names; other times they were only physical descriptions. Generally speaking, only suspects wanted for crimes in your division or the neighboring divisions were read off. Los Angeles is a sprawling city, and the Valley divisions were twenty miles away from the inner city. Wanted suspects from those areas were not likely to be found in Newton Division. A typical crime description would involve the name of the suspect (if known), sex, race, age, height, weight, hair and eye color.

One older sergeant would read the wanted suspects listings with a typical description of "Got an armed robbery here. It's a male usual, twenty-five years old, five-nine. . . ." By *usual* he meant a black person, because as far as he was concerned, "everyone" knew that suspects were black. This would be done even if black officers were sitting in the room. I was embarrassed for those men. Of course the suspects were black; so were their victims; so was nearly everyone else in Newton Division.

AFTER THIS INTRODUCTION to what a partner could be like, I was assigned to work with two old-timers. One of them was very good, and I learned a tremendous amount about street police work. His longtime partner was insensitivity personified. I honestly don't think he liked anyone. He gave me the obligatory "us against them" warning, and then he told me, "I don't have any use for fuckin' niggers. Chief Parker was a great guy, but he really fucked up when he integrated, making us work with those fuckin' monkeys. They assigned me to a nigger once; I called in sick for an entire month. I told my sergeant I don't work with niggers."

On one of the first nights I worked with him, he gave me a crash course in race relations, Newton style. We were northbound on Central Avenue when a car pulled out at Twelfth Street directly in front of us. My partner braked quickly, which probably prevented a traffic accident. He turned on our red lights and stopped the vehicle for what I thought was an obvious traffic violation. We got out of the police car, and my partner approached the driver's side. The driver's door opened, and out stepped a black man in his early twenties.

"This is bullshit! Just plain bullshit!" The driver was angry.

Unfazed, my partner responded, "Let me see your driver's license."

"There's only one reason you stopped me."

My partner responded in a voice dripping with sarcasm. "Oh? And what reason might that be?"

"You only stopped me because I'm black." He handed my partner his driver's license.

My partner didn't respond immediately but simply began to write the traffic citation. After finishing the first few lines, he paused, stared through the suspect, and with the same sarcastic tone slowly stated, "No, sir, you're wrong. We stopped you because you are a fucking nigger. By the way, is the address on your license still current?"

WHEN I WORKED WITH THIS PARTNER, we simply went through the motions. He was reasonably friendly to me, but he was lazy. After about four months I was assigned to new, younger partners, finding out at the end of one shift when my old partner told me, "Tough luck, Mike. You're getting new partners next month, the nigger and the spick."

"What?"

"Ford and Arroyo. They're coming to A.M.S [midnight shift], and you're going to be working with them. I'm heading to day watch."

My new partners were Ron Ford and William Arroyo. Ron was a black officer and Bill a Latin. I was to work with them for only a few months, but I always remembered the things they taught me and valued what they had to say. I doubt if my old partner would have given much merit to their thoughts.

So many times I heard the loyalty of black officers questioned. One simple incident illustrates the fallacy of that reasoning. Ron Ford and I stopped a traffic violator on Slauson, east of Broadway. It was my turn to issue the citation, and Ron was closely monitoring my work. The violator stepped from his car, and we were standing on the sidewalk.

"Sir, may I have your driver's license?" I said. "You're going to be issued a citation for making a right turn on a red light without stopping."

The man looked at Ron and said, "Come on, man. You're a brother. Give me a break."

Ron fired back at him, "First of all, let me explain something to you. I am *not* your brother. Second, give my partner your driver's license like he asked." Ron was always a bit more distant with me than Bill was, but it was clear where his loyalty was. He was a Los Angeles police officer.

AFTER GRADUATING FROM THE ACADEMY in the spring of 1967, I was amazed at the racism in the Los Angeles Police Department, but within a few years I had become part of it. My immersion in a very racist environment changed me. I was not strong enough or mature enough to resist it, and I acquiesced, becoming part of it. I couldn't change an entire social order, but I didn't even hold true to my own beliefs. No blame can be assigned to anyone but me for this change. To achieve acceptance, I willingly became part of what had previously shocked my senses so profoundly.

It would be easy to categorize all Los Angeles police officers as racist, but that is not true. It is also incorrect to say racists were bashful strangers in the police department during my early years. Those with racist attitudes could openly express their views without fear of disciplinary action. Dysfunctional attitudes were allowed to grow in the socially homogenous police society. Diversity of thought was sometimes hard to find. You worked with police officers, your friends were police officers, and your leisure activities were usually with other police families.

For racism to function, there can be no great analysis of the target group. Close scrutiny of these attitudes by any reasonable and prudent individual raises too many questions. By the summer of 1969 I had stopped asking those questions.

During those years the racial mix in south central Los Angeles was predominately black. Over the years it would change as the Latino population increased steadily, but at first residents were almost exclusively black. There was a small middle class, but most of the people were lower middle class or below. By and large we dealt with a poor and often uneducated constituency. The suspects we arrested were almost always black. The prostitutes were black, as were their johns; the drug dealers and their customers were black; the victims were black. The people standing at the bus stops were mostly black, as were the clerks in the stores. The real majority was disregarded—those men, women, and children who regardless of their socioeconomic station in life did their best to be law-abiding citizens. We never saw them. I would venture to say we never came in contact with more than 5 percent of the people who worked and lived in our division.

Statistics showed blacks committed more felonies per capita than whites. Similar statistics revealed that people in the lower socioeconomic stratum commit the majority of crimes in society, irrespective of race. However, I didn't scrutinize too closely the real meaning of those statistics during those years, and neither did most of my peers. Nearly all of our arrestees were black. Racism developed when an officer began to label all blacks as criminals. Racism can function only if the exception becomes the rule, and the rule must support this racist construct of truth.

It would be historically inaccurate to think that the views of Los Angeles police officers were necessarily exceptional in society at that time. The difference between the police and the general population was that we were expected to uphold the law and assure equal protection under it for all Los Angeles citizens, regardless of color. The problem was the difference between the ideals of the academy and street reality. I don't remember participating in any arrest that was based solely on the suspect's race, but the attitude toward the citizenry was clearly less than friendly.

WHILE I WAS WORKING SEVENTY-SEVENTH division in 1969, the department developed a community relations program that included the use of bumper stickers stating, "Another Family Against Crime." I had a brilliant idea to alter one. Carefully I rearranged the letters and made a new, quite authentic sticker that said, "Another Family Against Niggers." My fellow desk officers gave me a hearty round of approval when I showed it to them. We thought it was great. I had become very much a part of racism in the LAPD. My disregard for the feelings of blacks went beyond making bumper stickers. Calling suspects "niggers" to their face was a common occurrence for me by then.

I never really had any intention of using my new and "improved" bumper sticker, but I took it home to show my wife. She had remained sane during my racist transformation and was appalled. She insisted I destroy it, which I did.

THE DEPARTMENT WAS CHANGING; now a significant emphasis was placed on education. A great many officers were attending college in their off-duty time because the classroom could provide a key to advancement. My primary goal in returning to college was not advancement. I enjoyed the challenge presented by the college classroom and wanted to better myself intellectually. I went to college to get an education but found much more. Education was to provide the bridge back to racial sanity.

My undergraduate studies were in English literature, and as part of the general education requirement

I took two semesters of philosophy. This proved to be the transitional period for my political and personal philosophies. I was fortunate to have an excellent young professor named Paul DuBois both semesters. He developed an individualized reading list for each student, which for me included *The Autobiography of Malcolm X* and *The Strength to Love* by Martin Luther King, Jr. It was as though the lights came on, and I started on my way back to rational thinking. No longer did I look at blacks as "niggers."

THERE WASN'T ANY WAY I WAS going to change the racial attitudes of others on the department just because I believed I had now "seen the light." However, my own actions as a training officer could influence my probationary partners. On one particular evening, I had a young officer from Kentucky. He really wanted to do a good job because he loved this new business called police work. On East Sixth Street we stopped a heroin addict obviously under the influence of the drug. I let my partner approach him.

"Hey, nigger, get over here." The man stopped and turned around. My partner barked at him again. "That's right—you, nigger."

We could have arrested the man for internal possession of heroin, a felony. We didn't, principally because of my partner's misconduct. I could have reported him to my sergeant but decided to see if it could be dealt with in another manner. My partner had no clue he might have done something wrong. He was a brand-new probationer, and even though he was with his training officer, he felt very free to speak in this manner.

"Excuse me. Did you know that man?"

"No," he replied.

"How did you know he was a nigger?"

"Well, I . . ."

"Are you aware of what would happen if I decided to call a sergeant? Are you aware that the reason we did not arrest him was your misconduct?"

"But, Mike, he was just some old hype!"

"Well, be that as it may, he had your future in his hands, because if he had wanted to make a personnel complaint against you, he could've done it. He could still do it. Do you know what I'd say if asked by the sergeant if you called some citizen a nigger? I'd roll you in a flash. I can't control how you think, but I can damn well control how you act, especially in front of me. You just got a free one, just like the guy we had to let go because of you."

I am not so naive as to believe that this officer experienced an instant awakening regarding his racist views, but he knew one thing for sure—overt racism was not going to be tolerated by everyone. In fact, by the mid-seventies, the "come here, nigger" crowd was a dying breed. Not dead, but dying.

ONE DAY MY LONGTIME PARTNER, Frank Long, and I had to go to detective headquarters to get booking advice involving an arrest we had made. There was a crusty old lieutenant there who had a reputation for always speaking his mind, no matter how rude or distasteful it might be. While we waited for our booking approval, the discussion somehow turned to Nixon and Watergate. It was simple. Nixon was a crook and belonged in jail. To me the arguments that he "only got caught" and "others are doing the same thing" were ludicrous, and I told the lieutenant so. What type of defense that would be for some burglar who said, "Other people are burglars, too. I just got caught."

He looked at me and said, "Well, Middleton, I've

heard about you and your liberal views. Personally, I think you're a commie, just like your old buddy Martin Luther King, Jr. You probably *love* him, don't ya? Your kind usually does."

Looking at him, I uttered the last words ever spoken between us. "Lieutenant, it is very refreshing to know that I did not previously overestimate your level of intelligence." For once he was speechless. Frank and I had our booking approval and left.

In many ways this lieutenant echoed the approach of those who clung to the old racial views. Five years earlier, he simply would have called me a "nigger lover," but now it was just "my kind." The racist could no longer act openly without fear of repercussion.

EVEN THOUGH THE OVERT ACTS of the past were no longer permissible, careful examination of an officer's underlying motives was not always made. While I was working Southwest Division, two of my officers had an uncanny ability to find felons. They continually arrested hard-core dangerous criminals, but there was a problem. A pattern of violence began to surface. A few personnel complaints were taken against them and investigations completed, but initially there was insufficient evidence to prove misconduct on the part of either man.

At first I didn't believe there was a problem with their work. Doubts began to creep in as time passed, but it was hard to put a finger on the source of the problem. It wasn't as though they would have shied away from a fight with a white suspect if that's what he wanted. It was subtle. The intangible factor involving their actions was racism. The lines of acceptable conduct were more tightly drawn for black suspects. It was a lot easier for a black suspect to go outside the lines, and when you went outside the lines with these two, you had a real problem.

Maybe I just rationalized it by thinking about how many vicious criminals this duo put in jail. Socially they were nice guys, but in uniform dealing with black suspects they were totally different men. Maybe I just didn't have the intestinal fortitude to go out on a limb against the system. Regardless of my reasons, I failed to recognize the problem and stop it.

Ultimately both officers ended up losing their jobs as a direct result of excessive force toward suspects. It would be comforting to say that other sergeants, other lieutenants, other captains could have acted to stop them before it was too late. Somebody could have altered their course of conduct and perhaps saved their careers. The fact remains, I didn't.

DURING MY CAREER, RACE RELATIONS made strides. The days of the overt, heavy-handed racist disappeared. They became like the bones of dinosaurs from the La Brea tar pits—relics from another time. The officers who replaced them were better educated and more often came in different colors.

The department never really addressed racism directly during my twenty-one years. We talked around it. When we had a problem officer, we might have said that he was "overly aggressive." We almost never looked at one of the central causes of excessive force by some police officers. Not one time did a sergeant ever ask me questions relative to racist attitudes in a personnel complaint I was the subject of or as a witness officer. This included personnel complaints against blatantly racist officers. Never was a question asked regarding an officer's mind-set toward the minority community.

Not one class in sergeant's school dealt with the

connection between racism and personnel complaints. In the manual for personnel complaint investigation, nowhere did there exist any language that asked the investigating supervisor to address issues of racism as a motivating factor.

It is important to recognize that while arresting various suspects for a myriad of crimes, certain suspects simply refuse to comply with the orders of the officers. It is not possible to take these persons into custody without the use of force, which may ultimately mean using sufficient force to lead to the hospitalization of the suspect.

Classes were taught at the police academy and at roll calls on the "escalation" and "de-escalation" of force. Officers were told to use only that force necessary to arrest the suspect and no greater force. These classes were taught from the premise that force was justified. The police department fell short by not addressing a possible underlying motivation in the excessive use of that force—racial hatred. The fact remains there were officers whose treatment of an arrestee was influenced by the color of that suspect's skin. We never adequately addressed the root cause—not the chiefs, not the captains, not the lieutenants, and not me.

Chief Daryl Gates in his recent autobiography, *Chief, My Life in the LAPD*, either failed to recognize the significance of racism within the department or did not feel its impact was noteworthy. He talked around the issue but never acknowledged the internal problem that existed. It shows a lack of understanding at the upper echelons of the department. They either didn't know what was going on or didn't want to know.

The Watts riots had ended, but their impact was to coalesce the attitudes of many officers against the black population of south central Los Angeles. These riot veterans trained a new generation of police officers who in turn passed on racist traditions. These attitudes were reinforced by continual contact with the criminal element—a black criminal element. Old legacies would come into direct conflict with an awakening conscience in America. Civil rights activism and the Vietnam War protesters were a direct challenge to the long-standing social system. Police officers circled their wagons to repel the inevitable onslaught of change.

Siege mentality. The press, congressional committees, and citizens' groups accused us of it over and over again. We always denied it. These were dirty words. We never really dignified their accusations with in-depth responses. They kept saying it, though . . . and they were right.

We were under siege from an ever-changing society, even as we were sent out to maintain the status quo. The views of many officers became polemic. It was "us against them." *Us* should have been society; *them* should have been the criminal element. It didn't quite work that way. *Us* became the police. We believed no one else really understood the dangers presented by change. *Them* not only encompassed the criminal element but also included law-abiding citizens who wanted equality and justice.

We didn't have to look very far to find some of those people who sought equality and justice. They were right in our own ranks. Maybe their skin was the wrong color; maybe they were the wrong sex. They should have been part of the *us*, but they weren't.

AS A WHITE OFFICER I could be only an armchair observer of what some black officers had to contend with. It would be wrong to imply that black officers were constantly toiling under the yoke of skin color. It would be equally wrong to say that skin color was not a factor in promotion and job assignments in the department. Noel Cunningham was a black captain I worked for who gave me a rare personal glimpse of racism and how it made you feel.

"Mike, I know how you feel about racism, but we have really come a long way on the department. Not so long ago, I wouldn't be where I am now."

"Have you ever had anything so blatant happen that you couldn't believe it?"

"You bet. When I first went to Narcotics Division, I was told that I probably shouldn't attend the Christmas party as it was a whites-only function."

"What'd you do?"

"My wife and I went, and we had a good time, but that was minor compared to something that happened when I worked Wilshire Division."

"What was your rank?"

"I was a brand-new police officer and still in the academy. We lived in Wilshire Division, near the station, nothing fancy, a neighborhood changing from white to black. We didn't even have a car; I'd take the bus back and forth to the academy. One afternoon when I got home, there was a police car out front. I ran into the house, and my wife was crying. She'd been robbed by two black women who strong-armed her and took her purse. I didn't know the investigating officers. One looked at me and said, 'Who the hell are you?'

" 'I'm her husband,' I said. He looked me up and down and says, 'Yeah, right,' kind of out of the corner of his mouth—you know what I mean? Then he asked my wife what she was doing when she was robbed. She told him she was going to the store. 'You sure you weren't workin' that corner?' he asked, his voice dripping with sarcasm.

"This wasn't a one-way street. My wife called to

passersby for help during the robbery, yet the people in the neighborhood also thought she was a prostitute. After all, what else was a white woman who lived with a black man?

"I couldn't believe it. I hadn't said I was a police officer yet; maybe I should have. 'Wait a minute, that's my *wife* you're talking to!' I yelled. He fired right back, 'Yeah, boy, whatever.' I'd had enough. He thought my wife was a streetwalker simply because her husband was black; therefore, I must be her pimp. And you know, Mike, there was nothing worse than a white hooker with a black pimp. 'I'm a police officer, and you're not going to talk to my wife like that! Get out of my house!' I shoved my police ID card in his face. He didn't say a word; just glared at me.

"They finished their report, and on their way out one of them said to the other, 'Christ, they're letting everything on [the police department] now.' I really wanted to make a personnel complaint against them, but I was afraid it would cost me my job. I swore I'd get even with him somehow, someday."

"So tell me, Captain. Did you ever run across him again?"

"As a matter of fact, I did. He worked for me in Narcotics Division some years later."

"You never did anything to him, did you? I'll bet you never even mentioned it."

"How do you know that, Mike? Who says I didn't?" he said with a smile.

"It's easy, Captain. It's not you."

"I really wanted to do something, you know? But you're right. I didn't do anything. It's funny. My wife said the same thing you did. With her accent, she told me, 'You von't do a thing. Dat's not you.' So, you see, Mike, things really have come a long way."

Noel was right, but things came a long way because of supervisors like him. I don't think I ever knew a more concerned or compassionate commanding officer. I remember the first time I met him was just before morning watch started in Central Division. He and his wife had been out to dinner and were on their way home. She was standing in the watch commander's office while Noel was next door in his office. Some of the other sergeants knew her and were talking with her. I was standing nearby, listening to the conversation, noting that she spoke English with a pronounced German accent. Moments later the captain came out, and the couple bid everyone good night. Watching them leave, one of the sergeants commented to me, "Those are two great people." The sergeants could have said anything they wanted. No one else was around, but they didn't see his color. They saw only him.

During this time I was a defense rep [an officer who represents other police officers charged with misconduct] and talked to Captain Cunningham routinely about my cases because he had a good sense of what our mission was—what "protect and serve" really meant. It extended beyond the public; protection and service also included the officers. I think the only color Noel Cunningham ever saw was blue. He was right; we had come a long way—but not nearly far enough.

"OK, GUYS, LISTEN UP. We have a special order here involving the new unisex program. Female officers will now be able to become field certified. Academy classes will include the field certification of *all* recruits, irrespective of sex. Female officers currently on the department who meet the height and weight requirements and wish to become field certified will be allowed to return to the academy for additional instruction. After successful completion of the necessary training, they will be allowed to assume regular positions in patrol."

As the sergeant finished, the Central Division roll call room was abuzz. A new phase of the siege had begun. A different element had been added to the tide of change in 1973.

"Sarge, there ain't no way that I'm working with some fucking bitch. I mean it, Sarge. No way. I'll fucking quit first!" an older officer obviously resistant to this change blurted out.

I was sitting a few rows in front of him and turned around to face him. "Now let me get this straight. If they assign you to work with a police officer who has graduated from the academy, you're going to quit. You're going to give up your profession rather than work with this officer solely because of her sex. Is that it? Even before you know if she's any good? That sounds really swift."

He fired back, "Fuck you, Middleton! Everyone knows you're a fucking bleeding-heart liberal."

"Thank you very much."

The roll call room was definitely quieter after our heated exchange. Officers weren't jumping on the bandwagon to defend their protesting colleague. The reaction, or lack of it, made me believe that the elevation of women to equal status might not be too difficult.

INITIALLY, THE UNISEX PROGRAM required women to meet the same minimum height and weight standards as men—five-foot-eight and 140 pounds. Only 39 of the 164 women on the department met this standard. Patricia Berry had led the way for many women on the LAPD when she became the first female field-certified officer in 1973. This program was instituted in response to directives from the city council, which had become concerned over the fact that a female officer, regardless of her ability, could not advance past the rank of sergeant or detective II. Prior to this time, the department's answer to the women officers who wanted change was to hire no females at all for a period of four years. These were the enlightened years of Chief Edward M. Davis.

A female officer named Fanchon Blake filed a class action lawsuit that challenged the unisex policies. She felt the height and weight requirements mandated by the program were inherently discriminatory and therefore a violation of the federal Civil Rights Act. The courts agreed, and the height requirement eventually became five feet for all police officer candidates. Administratively, women had found equality. Acceptance by their male counterparts in the field was another matter.

LIKE THEIR MALE COUNTERPARTS, some female officers were very good, some were very bad, but most fell somewhere in the middle. One female officer who worked with me on two occasions definitely fell on the bad side of the spectrum. I had the distinct feeling she was there primarily to find a husband.

She was quite attractive but not terribly competent. When around a sergeant, she put on a real performance. It was clear she believed that by waving her ass at these drooling fools she would successfully get through her probationary period. It was something you might have expected from a high school student. It was unfortunate because she fulfilled the sexist's stereotype of female officers.

My view was simple regarding female officers in patrol. If they could do the job, there was no reason to consider them any differently than male officers. From a personal standpoint I wanted to see them succeed. This particular person was not going to become a competent field officer unless she changed her approach to police work. I decided to speak to her directly.

"You'd better start listening more to your training officers and stop paying attention to every sergeant who's trying to get in your pants. Not one of them is going to save your ass if you go head-to-head with an armed suspect."

"Well, I don't plan to go head-to-head with any armed suspects. In fact, I don't think I'll be in this division much longer."

She was right. The next week she was moved to a plainclothes assignment inside Parker Center, the police administration building. In a way it was a blessing to get her out of patrol before someone got hurt. The shame was that some would try to hold her up as the norm for female officers.

IN THE SUMMER OF 1976 I went to Newton Division as a sergeant. At one point on the A.M. watch we had three or four female officers, and I supervised all of them. One morning a sergeant who is a good friend of mine told me why.

"Mike, we figured that because of the way you feel about women in patrol it would be better if you supervised them. They get a fairer deal from you."

I didn't perceive this as punishment and was happy to supervise these officers. It seemed to me that all sergeants should be able to supervise all officers if those sergeants were doing their jobs correctly. At about the same time, there were female sergeants in the neighboring division of Central, and I had a chance to observe their work as field supervisors. It was as I'd expected—just fine. They were accepted by almost all the officers. If those female officers had not been assigned to me, I don't believe they necessarily would have been treated unfairly by other sergeants. There was no question, though, that I had a different viewpoint regarding the status of women in the police department, and in society in general, from my fellow sergeants.

NEWTON DIVISION MORNING WATCH was very active. Police officers who did not want to handle a lot of radio calls or make a lot of arrests didn't belong there. Female officers assigned to that watch were no different from anyone else; some of the finest police officers I've ever had the pleasure of working with were on that watch.

One particular officer had patrol skills second to none. He looked very professional in his uniform and acted accordingly with the public. He treated arrestees with respect and clearly was one of the top officers in the division. His having those skills, I thought it would be good to put one particular probationary officer on his car. In south central Los Angeles all squad cars are manned by two officers. Each two-man radio car actually has three officers assigned to it, one of whom is usually a probationer. While one officer is on days off, the other two are working.

When I told him I was going to put this particular officer on his car, he looked at me and said, "I'm sorry, Mike. I can't do it. I don't work with female officers. You know how hard I work, and I don't want one of them or me to get hurt. I just can't do it."

This wasn't a response I was expecting. The probationer would gain tremendous experience by working with him, and she clearly enjoyed working hard. I told him this, and he simply shook his head. A very easy course of action was at my disposal—simply order him to work with her and, if he refused, complete a personnel complaint against him for refusing a direct order.

No one else knew of my idea to change officers on this car. After discussing the situation with my lieutenant, I told the officer that, given his feelings, he wouldn't be assigned to work with this probationer right away. We would wait thirty days, allowing him time to adjust his thinking. He reminded me of my partner many years ago, who had called in sick rather than work with a black partner.

The following month this officer did work with that female probationer. Later he told her of his initial rejection and how he felt about her as his partner. He also admitted he had been wrong. No one else ever knew of his original refusal. We talked on several occasions during that cooling-off period, and I explained to him that no one was going to hold back the tide of change coming to the police department. Female officers would be working regular positions in the field, and if they weren't good, they wouldn't make it. However, they had to be given the same opportunity as their male counterparts to prove themselves.

IN OTHER DIVISIONS, FEMALE OFFICERS were put in low-profile positions, which ultimately was a great disservice. How would these officers learn to deal with all the tactical situations they would be exposed to if they weren't given the opportunity to experience them? Of course, for those vehemently against female officers in patrol, it was a good approach. Don't give them the training, don't give them the experience, and when they don't do well, point out their ineptitude.

Female officers challenged the traditional role set for them by men. Women belonged in the home or, if they had an education, should be teachers or nurses. I recall on one occasion a police lieutenant saying to my wife, "So when are you going to get a real job? You can't be a writer. The only thing you can do with an English degree is teach."

Not only were female officers competing directly for jobs in the male bastion, but they didn't look like the standard cop. They weren't willing to take a backseat anymore. These women wanted to be police officers. Chief Davis certainly didn't help when he issued inflammatory remarks attributing the rising crime rate in America to women's liberation.

ON ONE OCCASION I WAS TALKING to a female officer following her involvement in a traffic accident. It was a very straightforward investigation, and she would be reprimanded. I took the opportunity to talk to her about her role as a female officer, thinking it would be a good chance to discuss some ideas that might help her improve.

"You know, you have to remember that when some people look at you they're watching your performance and gauging your work as a standard for all females. It doesn't make sense, but some people around here feel like that. The work you're doing now will make it easier for those women who come after you, just as the women who came before you made it easier for you."

She surprised me with her response. "Sarge, I don't care about women's liberation. I don't give a shit about women coming after me, or who came before me, or anything else. I just want to be a police officer. For me, Sarge, just for me. This isn't my social crusade. I just always wanted to be a police officer."

It was a good lesson. I had viewed women's entry

into the police department too much on social terms. It was true that those who had come before made it easier for her and that she would make it easier for those in the future, but it was equally true that it was all right if these were not motivating factors for her.

ROOKIE OFFICERS ON THE LOS ANGELES Police Department had to pass the test of dealing with suspects in the field. Every new officer is closely scrutinized, but there was an extra measure of observation afforded the women on probation in patrol. Carolyn Flemenco was on probation. Her regular partner was off, and she was assigned to work with another experienced officer, J. P. Anderson. She hadn't worked with him before this night. They exchanged idle conversation as they drove along until J.P. posed a serious question to his novice.

"Tell me, Carolyn, do you think you'd have any hesitation about shooting someone if it came down to it?"

"No, not if I had to do it to save my life or someone else's."

"None?"

"No, I don't think so."

Three minutes elapsed.

"Look, that bus has its emergency flashers on," Anderson observed.

"Yeah, I see it." Flemenco was the passenger officer that night and in charge of the radio. "13-A-43, show us code six [out for investigation] on Florence, east of Broadway. We have a bus with emergency flashers on."

J.P. pulled the police car onto the sidewalk. It had barely come to a stop when a passenger bolted from the bus and ran to Carolyn's side of the car. "Hey, there's two guys down on Broadway. Look down there. They're on the corner."

At the same time, the driver of the bus ran over to J.P.'s side of the police car. "I was coming down Broadway and made a left onto Florence when those two guys up there flagged me down." No one knew that these men had just committed an armed robbery and intended to use the bus as a getaway vehicle. "I saw one of 'em had a gun, so I kept goin', and they fired at my bus. Look, you can see where the bullet hit the bus." Using her hand-held spotlight, Flemenco could see where the bullet had hit the first window in the bus.

"Yeah, I was sitting right there!" The passenger pointed out his seat to Carolyn.

"Did you get hurt?"

"No, but look, they're still down there. They're just now going into the alley."

"Can you identify them?"

"Yeah."

"Do you mind getting into the car with me?"

"No." The passenger climbed into the rear seat of the police car, and the trio headed back to Broadway. As they passed the alley, both Carolyn and the witness saw the silhouettes of two suspects.

"There they are!" the witness shouted.

"J.P., I think they're probably a block or two down, maybe to Seventy-Fifth Street by now."

J.P. passed the alley, went south on Broadway, then turned left on Seventy-Fifth Street. Carolyn was readying herself for the confrontation and unlocked the shotgun.

"Carolyn, when I hit the alley, I'm going to light these guys up with my high beams."

"OK."

As they turned into the alley, they could see silhouettes about sixty feet away. One suspect was wearing a black leather jacket. He whirled and fired one round at the police car before both suspects began running south in the alley. J.P. accelerated the police car to catch up with them.

The leather-jacketed suspect turned and fired again at the pursuing officers. Flemenco decided to put out an "officer needs help" call. The mike fell from its clip to the floor as she removed it, and she couldn't find it.

"13-A-43. Officer needs help. Shots fired in the alley east of Broadway at Sixty-Fifth." J.P. had retrieved his own ROVER and put out the help call.

Anderson then took his backup weapon (a gun carried by some police officers in addition to their primary weapon) and fired out the open driver's side window at the suspects with his left hand while controlling the car with his right. Flemenco was desperately searching for the microphone on the floor of the car without success. She decided to use her ROVER but couldn't get it out of the holder. It was jammed between her body and the seat of the car. She realized that in the excitement J.P. had inadvertently indicated they were at Sixty-Fifth and not Seventy-Fifth Street. Backup units had to know exactly where they were so they could help. Carolyn keyed the ROVER mike so she could speak without taking it out of the holder and screamed, "We're at Seventy-Fifth! Seventy-Fifth!"

One suspect jumped a fence on the west side of the alley into a salvage yard and escaped. Carolyn removed her revolver and was holding it in her lap as J.P. closed in on the primary suspect. Suddenly the man in the black leather jacket was in full view of the police officers. He had just finished reloading his weapon. J.P. slammed on the brakes, and the police car slid to a stop. The suspect looked Carolyn in the eyes as he raised his weapon and deliberately fired one round at her. She watched his gun belch fire as it discharged and at that instant threw herself onto the seat below the dashboard line. Immediately after the shot was fired, she sat up. The suspect was standing so close to her that she threw the door open in an attempt to knock the gun from his hand. She missed.

The muzzle flash blinded Carolyn for an instant, and she threw herself back down on the seat to give her eyes a chance to focus so she could see her target. Click. Click. Click. She could hear the suspect's gun as it misfired. Backing slightly away from Carolyn, he stood next to the right front tire of the police car and fired again.

J.P. left the police car. Carolyn wasn't able to tell where he was but could hear the discharge from his weapon as he fired at the suspect. She maneuvered herself in the seat so she could see the suspect's legs and fired one round at them through the still-open door. After firing, Carolyn pulled herself up in the seat, and the suspect immediately shot at her again. She dropped back down.

No longer could she remain in this vulnerable position. Carolyn pulled herself back up, and her weapon accidentally discharged through the open door into the air. The suspect again returned her fire. The muzzle flash once more prevented her from focusing on her target. The suspect's weapon was empty, and he moved closer to the front of the police car to catch some of the light from the vehicle's bright beams. Seemingly unaware of the danger, he began to reload, making no attempt to conceal himself. Carolyn took deliberate aim and fired one round. She could see his jacket bulge as the round entered his body and watched him draw his left arm in close as though he were clenching something between his arm and his side. He continued to reload.

The suspect seemed invincible. Carolyn decided to use the shotgun. Each round from the shotgun contained twelve .32-caliber pellets. No one can withstand the incredible force produced when its load slams into the body. Reaching out with her left hand, Carolyn was unable to retrieve the weapon; it was entangled in the cord of the hand-held spotlight. She threw it back onto the seat. There was no time to get it free. Up to this point the suspect's shots had missed her, but she believed that he would step forward and kill her with a single shot. She started to pray aloud.

The witness was still in the back seat. After each shot by the suspect, Carolyn yelled to him, "Get down! Get out of sight! Lay flat!"

Mentally she responded to the intense training she had received. From the perspective given to me by my own shootings, this is exactly what happens. You become very analytical and are thinking only of one thing—stopping this person from doing whatever he is trying to do. In Carolyn's case it was to prevent the suspect from killing her, her partner, and the witness.

She positioned herself between the door and the car frame, her right knee on the ground as she sat on the floorboard of the police car, firing at the suspect. It was imperative to neutralize the suspect before he reloaded. Taking careful aim, she fired a fourth time, a fifth time, and a sixth.

The suspect turned away from her and started walking slowly along the edge of a building in the alley. As he reached the far end of the structure, he disappeared.

Her gun now empty, she retrieved a Speedy Loader (a device that usually holds six bullets, which allows an officer to load a revolver with greater speed) from her Sam Browne (equipment belt) and promptly dropped it. Worried that one of the rounds might be damaged, she picked it up from the pavement and put it in her left front pocket. No such problem occurred with the second loader. She resumed her position between the door and the car, certain the suspect would return.

Out of Carolyn's sight, he was continuing to try to reload his own weapon. However, the wounds he had sustained were fatal, and he collapsed on the sidewalk, his gun in his right hand and cartridges in his left. Carolyn never found out whose shots were the deadly ones. It was of no interest to her.

Help was now arriving. Some officers had actually run from Seventy-Seventh Station, only two blocks away. The alley Carolyn and J.P. were in was adjacent to the station. Carolyn looked to her left and saw J.P. had successfully retrieved the shotgun. He too was prepared for the suspect to reemerge into the alley. Miraculously, neither officer was struck by gunfire.

When the danger was past, the witness excitedly jumped from the car. He walked between Carolyn and J.P., putting an arm on each of their shoulders. He too had shared in the danger and the emotional rush you get when you realize you've lived through it and your life would not be taken.

"Man, I'm gonna tell you guys somethin'. I've lived here in this neighborhood all my life. I seen a lot of police do a lotta things, but I want to tell you, I ain't never seen police do what you guys did. And I am never gonna bad-mouth the police as long as I live!"

UNFORTUNATELY, IF A FEMALE MADE a mistake, some officers viewed that as a mistake made by *all* female officers. It would have been nice if the same formula could have been applied to the heroic acts of Carolyn Flemenco.

I remember discussions with friends of mine in

Newton Division where the topic of women's ability to do street police work came up. On one occasion the perceived failure to act by one female officer caused a friend of mine to rail against the use of women in the field.

"Mike, they just can't do the job!"

"Well, what about Carolyn? J.P. sure as hell thinks she can."

"That's different! That was her."

"That's exactly right, and that's my point. These are individual officers, and it's not any different from when we're talking about male officers. Some men are better than others; some females are better than others. To make a blanket statement 'They just can't do the job' is ridiculous."

Shortly after her shooting incident, Carolyn completed her probationary period and was transferred to Southeast Division, an area much like Newton. She'd been there a few weeks when I called Southeast Station and happened to talk with her. "Hi, Carolyn, how's it going down there?"

"Great, Mike, but I have to tell you what happened the other night. I'm working with another P-II who graduated from the academy a class or two after me. Not that my seniority over him is any big deal, but this guy was an asshole. It was the first day of the deployment period, and we'd been assigned to work together. After we checked out the car keys and got our shotgun, we walked out into the lot. He sat down in the driver's seat and said, 'I'll drive for a while till I see how you are in the field.'

"I looked at him and said, 'What did you say to me?'

" 'I don't know you, and I make it a policy to always drive when I work with females till I see how they are.'

"I told him, 'Let me set this straight. *I* am senior

to you, so *I* will drive. We'll see how it goes with *you* in the field, and as far as how *I'll* do in the field, maybe you can ask me that question after *you've* been in your first shooting. So get your books and move your butt over to the passenger side.' He was speechless! Honestly, Mike, his comments weren't any surprise. The first time I encountered this guy, he told me that there might be places for women on the job, but it certainly wasn't in patrol. Then he said the most incredible thing. 'You better hope you don't ever need help or backup, because I don't respond to calls by females.' "

"What'd you say then?"

"I told him, 'I wear a blue uniform just like you do. God help *you* if I need backup and you're supposed to respond and you don't. You better hope I don't survive, because if I do, I'm coming after you next.' "

We had a good laugh over it. Carolyn is a very independent and strong person, but there wasn't anything funny about this situation. The bottom line had changed very little. Female officers still had to prove themselves one watch and one partner at a time. Their male counterparts were not exposed to this attitude. This is not to say if a male officer was a substandard performer he wouldn't receive similar treatment, but for women it had nothing to do with individual performance. As far as many male officers were concerned, if you were a female officer, you already had a track record—and it wasn't good.

AS A SPECIFIC RESULT OF the Fanchon Blake lawsuit and subsequent federal court ruling, the department was forced to work toward parity involving the promotion of females to the rank of lieutenant, a position previously held only by male officers. All officers must take both a written and an oral test to advance in rank. Those who pass both successfully are placed on a promotion list in the order of their final scores. Also added to their final scores are points for seniority to give an additional advantage to officers who have more time on the job. The lieutenant's list, on a onetime basis, implemented a different formula in the early 1980s. The top five women were moved to a separate pool. The first ten lieutenant promotions would be made alternately on the basis of sex until these five women had been advanced to lieutenant's rank.

The response among the overwhelming majority of male officers was very predictable and negative—"they're not ready." It was the same type of argument previously used against blacks, and now was being dusted off to be used against women.

One of the new female lieutenants off this unique promotion list was sent to Newton patrol. On her first night in charge she explained her feelings about the "dual" promotion list when she addressed the morning watch roll call. The room grew quiet as this tall, striking woman with fiery red hair began to speak.

"You probably already know who I am, but for those who don't, I'm the new morning watch lieutenant. I know this list thing is very unpopular. I didn't start the lawsuit against the department, but I didn't disagree with it either. For many years I was ineligible to take the lieutenant's test even though I had a sufficient amount of time as a sergeant. It's true, I hadn't worked as a field supervisor, but that wasn't my choice. Just consider how I felt being denied promotion when men who had less time on the job were able to promote. I have a family, too, and wanted to better myself, but I wasn't allowed to. Think about it. Now, I don't have field experience, so I'm going to rely on my sergeants in that area, but being a lieutenant is really being a personnel manager, and I know about dealing with people. All I'm asking for is a fair shake. If I'm not any good, I'll fail. Give me the chance to make those mistakes first before you judge me. Does anybody have any questions?"

The room was silent, and I noticed many officers with approving looks on their faces. The lieutenant would get her chance, and she would not fail. She was right. She knew how to deal with people, and she consulted the sergeants in unfamiliar areas. From that first night everyone seemed to be on her side; I know I was. She was one of the best lieutenants I ever worked for.

Some opposition to women in patrol came from an unexpected quarter. The wives of certain officers were less than enamored with the idea of their husbands spending so many hours sitting next to a female partner. Time spent with partners added up to much more than time spent with wives and families. These wives felt threatened if that partner was female. On more than one occasion my wife had conversations with spouses who were vehemently against women in patrol because of the potential threat it posed to their home life.

There were even a few telephone calls to the watch commander's office from wives asking that their husbands not be assigned with a particular female officer or sometimes just in general asking that their husbands not work with women officers. I personally had conversations with officers who asked to be changed from their female partner because of the problems it was creating at home. The requests weren't made because of anything that had occurred but were the result of a perception that romance might develop.

BROAD-BRUSHING INCIDENTS of racial and sexist misconduct by members of the Los Angeles Police

Department is easier than delivering the complete picture. Were there significant elements of racial and sexist attitudes and actions during my years? Absolutely. Initially they were quite blatant in both areas. As time went by, attitudes began to change. Diehards lost their freedom to act with impunity, and younger officers didn't have the same level of discriminatory feelings.

Were racism and sexism the driving forces behind the LAPD? The answer is an unequivocal no. Did they have a significant impact on police operations where I worked? Yes.

Police officers in south central Los Angeles are constantly immersed in a high-stress, high-crime environment. White officers are constantly dealing with ethnic minorities in negative situations. This environment, coupled with the closed police society, makes it easy for an officer to see only part of the racial picture. When only a portion of the picture is examined, stereotyping becomes very easy.

The leadership of the police department fell woefully short in tackling racism and sexism. Only the most cursory attempts were made to address the problems. This is apparent in policies involving internal investigations. It is supported by inflammatory statements by former chief of police Edward M. Davis. Even retired chief Daryl Gates gave issues of racism incredibly short shrift in his own recounting of significant events during his tenure.

My hands weren't clean either. I erred through acts of commission and omission as well. The siege mentality exacted a significant toll on our police department. A longtime friend of mine, a retired black sergeant, summed up race relations within the department when he told me, "Police officers I knew lived in either the past or the future but never understood the present." He was right.

Chapter Four

DRUGS

". . . Coon Can! Come On, Open the Door!"

SMACK, SHIT, HORSE, SPOONS, coke, rock, speed, meth, dust, Super-Kools, acid, thirteen, Mary Jane, dexies, reds, eight balls. It doesn't matter. They're either gettin' down or gettin' straight, just trippin', on the nod, geezin', skin poppin', chippin', doin' lines, or basin'. They're acidheads, strung out, dusters, pill heads, or potheads. It's all the same, and it's all drugs. You saw it every day. You saw the sellers, the buyers, and those whose lives were crushed or ended by the single greatest factor in inner-city life. Drugs are everywhere in America, but I wasn't everywhere. For most of my career I was a cop in the inner city, a ghetto cop, and nothing influenced lives on the streets of south central Los Angeles like drugs.

I'D BEEN AT THE POLICE ACADEMY for several weeks when the most dreaded words a recruit could hear were uttered as the rear doors to the classroom opened and an instructor bellowed, "Middleton, get your hat and books!" This could mean only one thing—I was history. You never knew when you were going to be axed. Quite frankly, I believed it could come at any moment. I scooped up my things and took one last look around as the instructor issued his second command: "Get your ass in gear, Middleton! I haven't got all day." I left the room at a semitrot.

There were 150 of us in the only classroom for recruits. It was on the second floor, while the administrative offices were on the first floor. I walked down those stairs with the instructor, and my worst fears were realized. We stopped in front of the door of the training division commander's office. "Wait here," I was told. I stood at attention beside that door with thoughts racing through my head, trying to figure out exactly what I had done to wash me out of the academy. I didn't know what would happen when I went into that room, because when other recruits washed out you never saw them again. It was as though they'd been dropped into a great abyss, never to be seen again.

The door opened. "Middleton, get in here!" I ran in and stood at attention again in front of a desk with three men sitting around it. They weren't in uniform, which seemed strange to me. There was a chair directly in front of them, and one of the men motioned for me to sit down as he smiled and said, "We're from Narcotics Division, and we'd like to talk to you about working with us after you finish the academy."

Thank God, they weren't firing me! I must have been smiling, because one of them asked me what was wrong. I told them I thought I was being terminated. He laughed and responded, "No, no. It's nothing like that. We have a new program starting, and we'd like to interview you for a position as an undercover officer in Juvenile Narcotics. It's a brand-new concept. Are you interested?"

It was the first time since I had joined the police department that anyone had asked me if I wanted something. "Yes, sir, it sounds great. When I joined the police department, I wanted to work narcotics. I'll do whatever I can to help."

"Well, Middleton, this assignment is a little bit different. Normally, an undercover officer works with a snitch, but you wouldn't have one. Usually the officer has some money to throw around so he can buy drugs, but you wouldn't have much. You see, Mike, if you're accepted, you'll be going back to high school."

They explained that I had been chosen because of my youthful appearance. I was twenty-one, but looked more like a seventeen-year-old. After that interview I heard nothing for about three weeks. We had about a week left at the academy, and again the doors to the classroom opened and I was ordered to get my hat and books. It was different this time; all of our tests were finished, and while I knew I could still be washed out at any time, I wasn't particularly worried. As we descended the stairs, the instructor spoke to me without looking back. "You got the job."

Again I waited outside the commander's office at attention. Even though we were close to graduation, some things didn't change, and standing at attention until you were summoned was one of them. Basically you were treated like shit at the academy, but you definitely knew what taking orders without question was all about. The discipline instilled in the academy helped carry you through some very difficult times on the streets. I was never above questioning authority in the course of my career, but I also knew where the line was drawn.

I was summoned into the room. "Mike, we'd like you to come and join us in Juvenile Narcotics. Don't discuss this with anyone, including your classmates. When the divisional assignment list comes out next week, your name won't be on it. If you're asked about it, tell them it must be an oversight and it's being looked into. The Sunday after graduation you'll receive a telephone call at home, and you'll be told where to meet the officers who will be your supervisors for the duration of your undercover assignment. You're not to associate with any other officers, including your classmates, after graduation night. The press will be around on graduation day, but you are not to be interviewed by them. If they photograph you as part of the group during the ceremony, that's fine, but don't pose for any pictures and don't talk to any reporters. You'll be told where you're going and what you'll be doing by the officers handling you. Any questions?"

"No, sir."

He shook my hand. "Welcome aboard."

I really was going to be an undercover narcotics officer, and it felt great.

The Sunday after graduation arrived, and true to the instructions I'd been given, the telephone call came. "Mike Middleton, please."

"Speaking."

"This is Officer Middleton, right?"

"Yes, sir."

"Don't call me sir. I'm only a sergeant. You live in El Monte, right?"

"Yes, sir . . . I mean, yes." Habits from the police academy die hard.

"Tomorrow morning at nine o'clock, be at the restaurant at Rosemead Boulevard and Las Tunas. I can't remember the name of it, but it's on the northwest corner. Know the one I mean?"

"Yeah."

"I want you to sit in one of the empty booths along the window on the east side of the restaurant. I want you to face away from the door. Don't talk to anyone, and sit alone. Do you understand that?"

"How will I know who you are?"

"You won't, but we know who you are, and we'll

sit down with you and have breakfast. Make sure you order breakfast when you get there. Remember, nine o'clock sharp."

Monday morning I drove my '54 white Ford station wagon up Rosemead Boulevard and parked in the restaurant lot. I'd never been there before, but I'd driven by it hundreds of times. Fortunately, most of the booths by the windows were empty. I ordered breakfast, and about five minutes later two men sat down at the booth with me.

"Hi, Mike. How're you doin'?"

They introduced themselves to me, and the older of the two began to explain my job.

"We're going to try something new. You're going back to high school as a student at Canton High. They think you're new in the area, dropped out for a while, and now you're going back. That way it makes sense if someone thinks you look older. Only the principal knows who you really are. In a while we'll go for a little ride. Our car's out back."

After finishing breakfast we drove about forty miles from the restaurant to the area where Canton High was located.

"This is it. Most of the dopers hang out along the side of the school. Here's a list of their names," the sergeant said, handing me a typewritten piece of paper with six names and the class schedule for each person. "Here's your schedule, too. You have classes with most of these guys. The principal had some of their schedules changed to make sure you'd be close at hand. We think your two best opportunities to make contact are going to be in audiovisual class, and at phys. ed."

"What's audiovisual?"

"Those are the guys that run the movie projectors. We think they're dealing drugs right out of that class. You know how to run a projector, don't you?"

"I'll catch on."

"OK. Look at these photos. This is your group. I want you to pay particular attention to this kid. He's probably responsible for most of the drug dealing that goes on. We've tried to make buys from him using undercover officers from Narco Division, but he won't touch 'em. He only sells to kids he knows. The problem you have is getting him to trust you so you can make a buy."

As we drove back to the restaurant, they continued my indoctrination. "Don't carry a gun at any time. If you want to keep one in your car, that's OK, but keep it well hidden and don't take it to school. The last thing we want is for you to blow up some asshole in front of the English teacher, and you'd end this program for good. At no time do you go into any police station. We'll meet with you next week and show you how to go into Parker Center. The only time you'll go there is when you need to book narcotics into evidence. Keep your ID card hidden in your car; don't carry it on you. If you get arrested, just go along with the program. Go through the booking process, and when you're in a cell by yourself, you can have the booking officer call us. If you're not alone at any time, wait until you're allowed to make a phone call and call us. Then relax, because you'll be there awhile. You won't get bailed out any faster than the people you're arrested with. If you get thumped by the arresting officer, that's too fuckin' bad. You don't make a personnel complaint against any police officer for kicking your ass. That goes with the territory."

It was decided I would use my own name, and I was given an address on the border of the area covered by Canton High. It was an apartment house, but in reality I'd commute back and forth from my home to school every day. Bright and early the next day, I parked three or four blocks from the school and walked to the campus.

It didn't take long to find the spot where the dopers and dealers hung out. They were sitting on the retaining wall on the south side of the school and included a couple of the young men I had seen in the photos. Carlos was a seventeen-year-old, somewhat overweight Latin kid. Steve was a too-thin, blond Caucasian who later told me he dropped a lot of pills. Most of the people in the group were smoking, and I too lit up a cigarette as I sat down on the wall. Not knowing anyone, I said nothing but waited for an opportunity to enter the conversation. A fortunate turn of events was about to occur.

"Watch out. Here he comes."

Suddenly I was the only one still smoking. I stood and turned around to flip my cigarette into the street and in doing so came face-to-face with the boys' vice principal. By sheer chance I flipped the cigarette so that it barely missed his right ear.

"How's it goin'?" I said, walking past him. His hand was instantly on my left arm.

"Just a minute, mister. What's your name?" he demanded.

I stared him right in the eye, looked at his hand on my left biceps, and then returned an icy stare to his face. "Mike. Why do *you* want to know?"

"Are you a student here?"

"Yeah."

"I don't know you."

"So?"

His anger was clearly increasing as this exchange went on. "Just give me your identification."

"I don't have any."

"What's that?" he asked, pointing at the left rear pocket of my jeans.

"A wallet."

"OK. Get out your ID."

"I already told you. I don't have any."

"What's your full name?"

"Michael Middleton."

"I'm sure you know smoking is a violation of school rules. You're lucky you're standing on the sidewalk and not on campus. Your smart mouth is going to get a letter sent to your mother."

"Well, I can't tell you how much that worries me."

He said nothing else as he wrote down my name on a pad he retrieved from his jacket pocket. He was absolutely furious. I admired him for not doing what I probably would have done—punch me out.

Amazingly enough, he didn't take me to the office with him, but abruptly turned and walked away. As soon as he was out of earshot, the group was buzzing.

"Man, that was cool. You know who he was?" The person who appeared to be the leader spoke as the group closed in around me.

"No."

"Man, he's the boys' VP. He's always on us."

"Fuck him. I'll see ya later." I walked away from them and onto campus to my first class. I was absolutely elated at the turn of events. It couldn't have gone better if it had been staged.

My first class was English, and I found an empty seat in the back row. Steve came in a few minutes after the tardy bell rang and sat down near me. The teacher immediately announced to the class that there was a new student and they were all to give me a big Canton High welcome.

"Mister Middleton, please raise your hand so we can all see you."

I did nothing; simply stared straight ahead, not smiling, not acknowledging her.

"Come now, Mr. Middleton, don't be shy."

I raised my hand slightly and cocked my head to

the side. Still I said nothing but looked very sullen and inconvenienced.

Following English was audiovisual and my first chance to talk with the two principal characters believed to be involved in drug dealing at the school. There were only four of us in the class. One guy was totally straight, complete with pocket pen protector and coke-bottle glasses. The other two were on my hit list. Steve was openly suspicious of me and said very little, but I became friendly with Carlos. In time I would make narcotics buys from both of them.

It's difficult working undercover narcotics with juveniles because they've had the same circle of friends for many years and might deal only within that group. Anyone coming in from the outside is viewed with great suspicion. Since narcotics use by undercover officers is forbidden except in a life-or-death situation, I would have to prove to these young dealers I was trustworthy without doing drugs with them. In adult narcotics a snitch is used as a reference and will often introduce the undercover officer to the dealer, but no such system was available for juvenile narcotics. The juvenile legal system didn't allow for a minor arrested for possession or sale of narcotics to work his case off by acting as an informant.

During the next few weeks I just went to my classes and kept a low profile. With Carlos I was definitely making inroads. We would talk about using drugs and things we liked to do. I had confided to him that I was a burglar.

"Man, that's cool! I want to go with you sometime. I've hit some places myself, but not houses like you do."

"You're not going anywhere with me. I shouldn't have even told you. For all I know, you might be a fuckin' cop."

"I'm no fuckin' narc. You're the one that's new.

I've been around here all my life. Everyone knows I'm no fuckin' narc."

"Yeah, so you say. I don't know you. I don't think you're a narc, but I don't know you. Like I said, I've already been busted, and I'm not doing another YA stretch. I've already got a tail, and my PO doesn't like me."

YA was the California Youth Authority, a prison for youthful offenders that includes forestry camps. I had told Carlos I was already on probation and not on good terms with my probation officer.

"Come over to my place after school. We can smoke a joint and kick back."

"I told you before, I don't blast off with anyone I don't know. A couple weeks ago my PO told me that he thinks I'm rippin' off houses. He thinks I'm a smart ass and told me that if he had anything to stick on me he'd do it, and I'd be back in camp in a flash. No thanks, man. That just doesn't seem too appealing to me."

One afternoon Carlos and I drove around so I could show him a few houses I'd supposedly burglarized. He admitted that he had burglarized a couple of stores and robbed a guy on the street one night at gunpoint. He was most proud of the high school girls that turned tricks for him.

"I make good money on those bitches, and I don't have to do a fuckin' thing."

"If you're making so much money off these whores, what're you doin' at school every day? I'm only here because my PO says I have to be. It's here or YA, and this is still slightly ahead."

"My old man, he told me if I don't go to school he'll kick my fuckin' ass—again. That son of a bitch is mean. Sometimes I could kill that motherfucker, but then I'd just fuck over myself. In a couple years I'll be gone anyway."

After about three weeks I complained one day in audiovisual that I was out of grass and looking to buy some. I told Carlos I'd fenced some jewelry from a burglary for a kilo of marijuana, but it was all gone, and so was my connection, who was in jail. He told me that he didn't have any right now, but Steve did. Steve was out picking up a projector from a classroom, and when he came into the room he had the strangest expression on his face, like he was there yet really wasn't.

"What's wrong with you?" I asked.

"Last night somethin' really weird happened. I'm tellin' you, I ain't droppin' no more fuckin' acid. I don't know, maybe it really happened. It was real, man! I don't know. It was like I was spinning over my house, and I could look down. There was no roof, like a dollhouse, only all the colors kept changing everywhere. Then my mom and dad started yelling at me. It was the coolest thing—they just dissolved into a pool and ran down into the gutter. I mean, it was no dream! It really happened! This morning when I got up, it was like everything was happening around me, but I wasn't really there! Do you think I had some kind of weird experience? You know, like when you think Martians are comin' to take you away or somethin'? Carlos, what do you think?"

"You fuckin' idiot. I think you've been droppin' too much acid. You know I heard that shit stays in you forever. When was the last time you took any of that shit?"

"It's been a couple of weeks, but I did a lot. Maybe you're right."

"I don't see why you guys drop that shit. It just fucks you up. I stay strictly with grass; it's safer. Think about it. How do you know what's in one of those pills? I mean, grass is grass. You look at it, and you know what it is, unless some fuck stiffs you with oregano."

"Hey, Steve, Mike needs to score some grass," Carlos broke in.

"I don't know." Steve was wary. He'd never really trusted me, and I felt at that moment I needed to do something to swing him one way or the other. I figured if he refused to sell drugs to me that would improve my relationship with Carlos. If he did sell, I'd nail him, too.

"Just fuck you. What do you think, I'm one of the cops or something? Look, everybody knows you sell grass. I don't want to be your best fuckin' friend. I'm just lookin' to score. Do you want to sell or not?"

"Not here I don't. You know where the hot dog stand is at Robinson and Pico? Be in the alley behind it at five o'clock, and I'll deliver. Give me the money now."

"Two things. How do I know where in the alley you'll be, and how do I know you won't stiff me?"

"I've got a reputation for delivering the goods. Just ask anybody. The drugs'll be there. I'm gonna put 'em myself right next to the first telephone pole in the alley on the right side. I deliver drugs there all the time. The pole is right next to the building, and I'll put 'em in a bag on the ground by the pole."

As I handed him the money, I warned him. "Stiff me, and I'll kick your fuckin' ass. Got it?"

"Yeah, yeah. The drugs'll be there. Don't worry."

"Mike, you got Steve all wrong. He ain't gonna stiff you. He's good for his word. I don't know why you don't like him. He's cool, man. I've known him a long time."

"I don't like anyone who treats me like some fuckin' narc," I said, staring sarcastically at Steve.

"Steve, relax! He's OK, I'm tellin' ya."

"Carlos, I've never been arrested, and I never will, because I only sell to people I know. You'd better be right about him. I'm not fuckin' kidding."

Since Steve told me the narcotics would be there at 5:00, I staked out the alley from 3:30 on and did what narcotics officers do most—waited. I'd already checked the telephone pole to make sure nothing was there because in court I'd have to testify that I had inspected the area for narcotics and kept the location under constant observation prior to the drop being made. Otherwise a defense attorney could simply raise the issue that it was impossible to know whose drugs were there.

Robinson Boulevard is a large north-south street, and the alley ran east and west, crossing Robinson. The telephone pole where the narcotics drop was to be made was on the west side of the boulevard. My position was in the alley east of Robinson because it would be unlikely that the car delivering the narcotics would come down my part of the alley. If it did, I had an escape route through a gate and into a backyard so I wouldn't be seen. My own car was in a supermarket parking lot a few blocks away. I'd seen Steve before in a white Chevy as a passenger; I'd never seen him driving, so I didn't know what car would be pulling in. Finally the same white Chevy appeared. It made one pass northbound on Robinson. A few minutes later the car came through the alley without stopping and turned out onto Robinson again. About ten minutes later it came back. Steve jumped out of the car on the passenger side and, after looking both ways, quickly placed an object next to the pole. The car then drove slowly up the alley and out of sight. After watching the scene to make sure no one else arrived, I walked out of the alley a few minutes after 5:00 and picked up the package of marijuana. I'd just made my first buy.

I remained a student at Canton High for another month and made more buys from Steve and Carlos. One day I received word that I was being shifted to the (San Fernando) Valley, working a similar assignment at Rosedale High School. After I was transferred, Juvenile Narcotics Division came to Canton and placed Steve and Carlos under arrest for selling narcotics. When Carlos was arrested, he was crushed that I had turned out to be a police officer. "I can't believe it, man. I thought he was cool."

A sullen Steve bitterly announced, "I knew he was a cop all the time."

My sergeant looked him in the eye and said, "If you knew he was a police officer, what the fuck did you sell him drugs for?"

Steve shook his head slowly and said nothing more.

Carlos looked at his partner and laughed. "You didn't know shit, man."

I SPENT ONLY A MONTH AT ROSEDALE, but I found out right away it was a different drug scene. I struck up a friendship with a seventeen-year-old named Eddie. His parents were divorced, and he had too much unsupervised time on his hands. He wanted to be a drug dealer and make the big bucks. It was all he talked about—what he'd have after he made the big time.

There was a hamburger stand called Paul's Pup Shack located on Ventura just east of Wilson. It was a popular place for motorcycle gangs, drug dealers, and high school students since it was only a block away from school. Eddie was supposed to meet me on a Friday night at the Pup and sell me some "meth." What I didn't know was that the Valley Narcotics Division had plans of its own, and they swooped in at about nine o'clock. Eddie was holding, and he was worried. If he tried to throw away the vial, he knew the narcotics officers would see it, so he decided to take a chance and hold on to the dope.

"Mike, watch out! It's narco. These fuckin' guys are mean."

They were in two or three unmarked cars, but the officers were in uniform. I didn't see all of them, but there were at least six. I was standing in a group of about ten guys, and everyone froze, including me.

"All right, assholes, line up. Get your hands out of your pockets, out where we can see 'em. Turn around and face the wall. Put your hands behind the back of your heads."

I knew exactly what stance we had to assume. We'd done it hundreds of times at the academy as we practiced searching and handcuffing techniques.

"Ugh! My hands!" I exclaimed as an officer grabbed my interlaced fingers and squeezed, pulling me backward and off balance. We had done this maneuver at the academy, but never with this amount of pain.

"Shut the fuck up. What're you doin' here?" he demanded as he started to search me.

"Nothin'. Just hangin' out. Is there anything wrong with that?"

"What're you, a fuckin' smartass?"

"No, but we're not botherin' anyone."

He pushed me back, and another officer appeared in front of me.

"Let's see some ID."

"I don't have any." I'd left my wallet and all my identification in my car.

He began filling out a field interview card with my name and new false address. By now everyone had been searched, and we were allowed to put our hands down by our sides. An officer approached me and began asking questions about what I was doing and where I'd come from that night. I looked straight at him and said nothing. Then I looked at the ground and spat directly between his shoes. My hope was if I diverted enough attention to myself, they wouldn't find the vial on Eddie. I wanted to make the buy, but if he was arrested, I wanted to make sure I went to jail with him. This would help my credibility immensely.

I immediately got all the attention I needed. The officer's baton was out of its holding ring instantly, and he drew it back, preparing to deliver a crashing blow.

"You asshole!"

I could feel the pain already, but his partner stepped between us.

"Don't, man. This shithead isn't worth it. There'll be another day for him."

I never learned that officer's name, but to this day I thank him for stopping his partner. One of the guys I didn't know in the group was holding and arrested. Eddie wasn't taken into custody because the vial of "meth" was never uncovered during the search. The officers finished their interrogation and left. Eddie and I also decided to leave.

"Let's get out of here. My car's in the market parking lot. You still got the stuff, right?"

"Yeah, but I'm not doin' anything here."

We got into my car and pulled onto Ventura Boulevard. Lo and behold, one of the Valley narcotics units hadn't gone very far. Instantly the red lights were on us. I pulled my car over, as it turned out, directly across from Paul's Pup Shack.

I thought if I could get them to take me out of my car and away from Eddie, I might be able to explain that I was working undercover, and they'd leave us alone so I could make my buy. I decided to say something that would ensure I'd be taken out.

"What the fuck did you stop me for?"

"What did I stop you for? I'll show you, asshole!"

He reached into my open window and began to pull me out of it. I cannot tell you how difficult it is to get your legs out from under the steering wheel when exiting a car in this manner.

"Come on, fuckhead! Out of the car! I'm gonna show you just why I stopped you."

I had clearly made a serious tactical error. It was the same officer I had so carefully aimed my spit at. This was "the other day" his partner had referred to. Once I was out of the car, he slammed my face into the hood of my car, splitting my upper and lower lip. I could see the blood smear on the white paint of my car.

"OK, shithead. Any other questions?" Down went my face again. "Anything else you want to say to me?" His face was next to mine.

I spoke very softly. "Yes. I'm an undercover narcotics officer." His grip on my neck immediately relaxed. "Don't stop now. Just finish up with us. This guy's carrying, and I'm trying to make a buy."

The officer played his part well. "Stand up, asshole. You better have some ID this time." He watched me as I retrieved my wallet from the car, and then he pretended to run a record check.

The narco officers released us, made a U-turn, and drove off. At last I was going to make my buy.

"Man, let me off at the corner. I'm outta here. It's too hot tonight. I ain't sellin' shit. It's not you, man, but there's too many cops around. See you tomorrow."

Sometimes you just can't win. There was some justice, though. I did buy from him about a week later. True to my instructions, I never discussed the actions of that officer with my sergeant.

When my assignment at Rosedale High School

was finished, I was sent to a patrol division. You had to spend time in patrol before going back to a specialized division like narcotics. An officer might do a short tour of duty undercover, but it would be four or five years before he would be able to transfer back on a permanent basis. As it turned out, I never returned to Narcotics Division but chose to stay in patrol. It was where it all happened first. You were there when things were going down. I joined the department to work patrol and that never changed. Others wanted out of uniform, but I chose to stay.

FOR SOME YEARS I WORKED patrol in Central Division, which includes the Skid Row district. On the west side of Central Division, Sixth Street cuts through the financial district, but six blocks away it becomes East Sixth Street, and you enter a different world filled with down-and-outers. It's a world filled with pimps, whores, dope dealers, and drug addicts, particularly heroin addicts. My partner and I concentrated on arresting heroin dealers and addicts.

When it comes to heroin, if you're not dealing, you're stealing, or in Desi Taylor's case, turning tricks. Desi was an outlandish streetwalker from the way she dressed to the way she talked. She was strictly East Sixth Street material and tricked with guys who were only slightly above her station. Desi was hopelessly strung out on smack. She was a white girl with reddish-blond, strawlike hair and a heavy New York accent. Desi was Jewish and proud of it and didn't mind telling you so, frequently.

"Desi, what's up, babe?" You always got further with Desi if you were nice to her and treated her like a friend.

"Nothin'." I had never seen Desi Taylor more down on [under the influence of] heroin. Her steps were exaggerated, as if she was stepping over invisible logs on the sidewalk. One shot with the flashlight, and you could see her eyes were constricted to about one millimeter.

"Desi, when'd you last geez [inject heroin]?"

"Huh?"

"You remember, fix; you know, inject heroin into your body?"

"Honest, Mike, it was yesterday. I ain't been able to score today. Business is bad."

"Well, Desi, it's about to get worse, 'cause you know we could bust you right now for internal possession."

"Come on, guys. I always helped you in the past."

"Desi, you've never given me shit."

"But I helped your partner there. Didn't I, Jerry?" I swear Desi knew every police officer in Central Division by his first name. "You told me you busted some dude 'cause of what I told ya."

"Yeah, Mike, she did. I think it was last week. You were off that night."

"Well, Desi, that's cool, but this is today, and I'm the one talking to you. Now, what can you tell me?"

"Mike, you can't say shit about where this comes from 'cause this motherfucker'll kill me. He lives in the hotel at Stanford and Sixth on the third floor. I don't know the room number, but it's on the left side of the hall, and it's three doors from the end. I know which one it is 'cause I've scored there lots. Everybody calls him Coon Can."

"OK. So what do I do? Go up and ask him to please open the door so we can arrest you for dealing? Desi, this ain't shit. What is he, some guy with a couple of balloons? Big deal."

A balloon is a common method of packaging heroin wherein a small amount of powdered heroin is placed inside the end of a balloon, which is then cut off and knotted into a package about the size of a dime.

"No way! He's been down twice for dealin'. I don't know what he's got tonight, but I've seen a hundred balloons in there on the table before."

"How do you know what's in the room? Does he let you come in?"

"Well, you know, we kinda had a date, and I was in the room with him and saw—"

"What'd you do, fuck him for some shit?"

"Yeah."

"OK, Desi, here's the deal. We'll take you to the station and then check this dude out. If he's there and we bust him, everything's cool with you."

"That ain't fair! What if he's there and he ain't got nothin'? It's not my fault. I don't know what he has, but I know he's supposed to be the big dealer on the street."

"OK. If he lives there, we'll cut you loose no matter what happens."

"If you make a good bust, you'll remember me, right, Mike?"

"What do you want, Desi, a get-out-of-jail-free card? I'll take care of you. I'll remember."

Coon Can's hotel was at the northwest corner of Sixth and Stanford, a rat-infested dive with hallways that reeked of rancid garbage. Sometimes when you walked down the halls of places like this, it was almost impossible to keep from gagging. After we located the door, we listened and could hear music playing inside.

"Mike, how're we going to get this guy to let us in? Got any ideas?" Jerry whispered.

"Yeah, I'm going to ask him to open the door, and he's going to do it. Then, if he's dirty [guilty, in this instance of possession of narcotics], we'll arrest him, but remember, no laughing."

I rapped three times on the door, and with my best white boy impression of black dialect, I began.

"Hey, Coon Can." No response.

I knocked again. "Coon Can, op'n d' door. Com' on."

"Who is it?"

I wasn't prepared for this question but fired back the first name that came into my head. "It's Willie, man. Com' on. Op'n d' mufuckin' door. Don' play no game, Coon Can."

"Willie who?"

He might have me now, but no. Inspiration continued. "Willie from Main Street, man."

I figured he must know a hundred Willies. I knocked again, more impatiently. "Com' on, man, I'm hurtin'. I gots to get right, man. Op'n d' door."

At that moment Coon Can opened the door. He stood in full view with his left arm tied off at the biceps with a handkerchief and his "fit" [hypodermic syringe and needle; short for *outfit*] stuck in his arm. No one ever looked more surprised than he when I said, "Hey, Coon Can, what's up, man? It's Willie, and you be under arrest."

Coon Can was no chump change dealer. Several balloons of heroin were on the table, plainly visible when Coon Can opened the door. The syringe in his arm was filled with a water-heroin solution. Coon Can not only dealt but was also a heavy user. Desi was right; he had served two prior stretches in state prison for selling narcotics and received a life sentence for his third offense. In the month following his arrest, burglaries in the surrounding area dropped significantly. The connection is simple. The hype [heroin addict] steals to support his habit, fences the goods, and pays dealers like Coon Can with the proceeds. With Coon Can gone, the hypes had to find new territories closer to other drug dealers and away from Sixth and Stanford.

I never arrested Desi Taylor again. About eighteen months later I was told she had died of hepatitis, undoubtedly a direct result of her heroin addiction.

OF ALL THE DRUGS I SAW as a police officer, PCP [phenyl cyclohexyl piperidine], often called *angel dust*, had to be the standout. It was so different from the rest in just about every way. The product of local commerce, it was often made right in the same neighborhood where it was sold. The only thing you could depend on when you came in contact with a "duster" was that you couldn't depend on anything.

PCP contains a powerful psychedelic drug known as phencyclidine hydrochloride, a tranquilizer when used with animals, but all bets are off with humans.

I was assigned to Newton Division as a sergeant when a radio call came out. "All units in the vicinity and 13-Adam-43. 415 man. Be advised he is in the residence and possibly under the influence of PCP. . . ." The dispatcher then gave the address where a man was purportedly disturbing the peace, and I began to roll to the location.

Two units had arrived before me, and the four officers were standing at the doorway of the duplex where the man lived.

"What's up, guys? Is he in there?"

"Yeah, Sarge. He's sitting in the front room. Looks like he's alone. We've called out, but no one else has answered."

"Is he in custody? What's going on?" I was a little bewildered since the officers seemed to be just standing around waiting.

"Well, he wants to clean his teeth before we leave,

Sarge, so we're letting him. Take a look."

I peered through the door and into the room. Every piece of furniture was broken except the chair this man was sitting in. The telephone was smashed, and I noticed the phone cord. It was a newer type of telephone wire, relatively thin and covered with a clear plastic. He had the cord in his mouth and was flossing his teeth with it. The cord was between his bicuspids and molars on each side of his mouth, cutting deeply into his gums. Blood was running down his chin and onto his shirt as he moved the cord forward and back, much as one would do when flossing in the traditional way. He made a growling sound as he performed this bizarre dental hygiene.

"How's it going tonight?" I asked him, still standing at the threshold.

"Grr-r-r." He continued flossing, staring at me with blank eyes.

We had been taught that when arresting a PCP suspect, if you spoke softly while handcuffing him, problems might be minimal, but the telephone cord presented an unusual obstacle. I told the two officers originally assigned to the call that I wanted to walk in quietly, with one officer on his left and one on his right. On command we would grab his arms, pull him from the chair, and lay him prone on the floor, face-down, with his arms behind him. The other two officers would stand by, and as soon as we pulled him from the chair, they would also enter the room. However, I wanted only two officers to go into the room at first to prevent him from becoming alarmed and fighting. If my idea worked as planned, the officers would enter the room, grab the man, and put him on the floor all in one motion.

The officers entered the room and moved into position as I spoke to him in an effort to divert his attention.

"We got a call from one of your neighbors, and so we just thought we'd stop by and make sure everything's all right. You seem like you might be a little upset tonight. Maybe we can help you out."

Out of the chair he came with one officer on each arm. Losing his balance as he was pulled forward, down he went, and the struggle began. It always amazed me that a person on PCP could seem so strong. One effect of the drug is to block any pain that occurs when a muscle has reached the point of defeat. A person not under PCP's influence wouldn't be able to go any further because of the pain associated with muscle exhaustion, but the duster sails right past the pain threshold. This causes the seemingly superhuman strength so often referred to with persons under the influence of the drug.

The man reacted too late. Instantly his hands were forced to the small of his back, and the handcuffs were snapped on. He was lifted to his feet and searched for weapons. As he stared at one officer standing to his right, you could see his pupils "bouncing," the most common symptom of PCP use, more formally known as *lateral nystagmus*. The telephone cord still hung loosely from his mouth, the wires dangling like plastic spaghetti. He was no longer growling, but he was not acknowledging our presence either. Off to the hospital we went, where the doctors did the preliminary work on what must have been major reconstruction of his mouth. He was eventually booked on a misdemeanor charge of disturbing the peace.

"ANY UNIT IN THE VICINITY of 525 South Grand. 415 man on the front of the hotel."

The first clue that there was something different about this Central Division call was the fact that it was a man "on" the front of the hotel. Another sergeant, James Costello, and I responded along with every available police unit and the Los Angeles Fire Department. The fire department brought a hook and ladder. When I arrived, there he was, and sure enough, he was "on" the front of the building. He had climbed up the architectural detail on the front of the Windsor Hotel and was now perched on a small gargoyle above the entryway arch, at least twenty feet in the air. It was about 7:00 in the morning, and a crowd of pedestrians on their way to work stopped to watch. He was hissing at the crowd like a cornered animal.

Sergeant Costello and I had been friends for many years and responded to numerous calls together as police officers and sergeants, but never one like this. When I parked my car and walked over, Jim was standing near the archway on the sidewalk, talking to the man.

"Hi, Jim. Friend of yours?"

"Real funny, Mike."

"Well, I just thought the way you were talking to him, perhaps you knew each other."

"No, I've never seen him before. Sir, you're going to have to come down. We're going to put a ladder next to you so you can climb on it and get down. We're not leaving until you do."

The only response from the man was another hiss directed at us.

"Jim, I think he's declining your invitation."

"Tell you what we're going to do, Mike. We'll put the fire department ladder over and see if he'll climb onto it. If he doesn't, I'm going to zap him with the taser. What do you think?"

The taser is a device that shoots two darts attached to thin wires, delivering a jolt of electricity designed to cause general muscle failure to the person shot.

"Sounds good to me. Tell you what. If you have to go up the ladder, I'll go up with you. That way, you can 'tase' him, and I'll grab him."

The ladder was moved into position. Jim had instructed the fire fighters to put it directly under the man so he could easily step onto it and come down. If the climber had to be shot with the taser, it would minimize the chance of his falling. One thing Jim and I knew for sure: we weren't going to climb up the ladder and wrestle with him. If anyone fell to the pavement, it would be him, not us. Jim climbed onto the fire truck and up the ladder.

"Come on, sir. Come on down. Everything's going to be OK." If anything, the man's hissing got louder. The crowd was growing. We wanted to make sure we gave him plenty of opportunity to come down on his own. After all, any one of the people watching the events unfold could make a personnel complaint against us, saying we didn't give him enough opportunity to come down, thus appearing to overreact.

After about five minutes of the "Come on down, sir" routine followed by more hissing in reply, Jim called out, "That's it, Mike. I'm going to light him up." I climbed up the hook and ladder to join Jim, who had moved within six or seven feet of the suspect. Once more Jim asked him to come down.

Just about the time the man started to hiss, Jim let him have it with the taser. It was a perfect shot. One dart entered the right side of the man's chest, the other the left. He was tased but unfazed. He opened his arms wide, fists clenched, and let out a yell. All I could think of was the scene from the movie *King Kong* where the gorilla is on top of the Empire State Building, waving his arms in anger.

"Jesus, Jim. I think he likes it."

"No shit! I'm going to give him another dart. Maybe I don't have a good connection." The taser gun holds two cartridges and Jim still had one left.

Bam! This time the man's knees buckled slightly. Jim shut the taser off, handed it back to me, and lunged at the man, pulling him toward us. We each had a hand on his jacket and went back down the ladder as quickly as we could, pulling him with us. Jim had both hands on the man, while I had one hand on him and the other on the taser. When we got to the platform of the fire truck, two officers climbed up to help, and the fight was on. We could not get him cuffed. There were four of us trying to wrestle his hands behind his back. He was big anyway, but with dust in his system, he was incredible.

About a year before, the use of the "bar-arm control" to subdue suspects had been prohibited. This technique involves an officer positioning himself to the rear of the suspect, placing his arm around the suspect's neck, with the officer's wrist against the suspect's throat. The officer's fist is clenched, and with his other hand he holds the fist and pulls with both arms. Simultaneously the officer presses his shoulder against the back of the suspect's head, forcing it to cantilever forward, shutting off the air passage, and rendering the suspect unconscious. The police commissioners, who had never confronted a fighting suspect, ruled that the bar-arm was too dangerous to the suspects. There had been some cases of people on PCP who had been choked unconscious by use of the bar-arm, suffered respiratory arrest, and died. The bar-arm was replaced by the similar carotid and the modified carotid holds, but these involve the officer placing his arm around the suspect's neck with the crook of the elbow at the suspect's throat. The officer squeezes the suspect's neck from both sides and presses his arm against the suspect's neck, shutting off blood to the brain, resulting in unconsciousness. Neither one of these holds sounds or looks very pretty, but the bottom line for an officer involved in a fight with a suspect is subduing that person with minimal danger to both parties.

We weren't winning against this guy. I told Jim, "That's it. I'm choking him out." I grabbed hold of the suspect's neck and bar-armed him out cold. I had not been taught the carotid hold when I went through the academy, and while I had seen it used, I personally had no confidence in my ability to apply it successfully. The suspect was handcuffed and lowered down to the officers standing beside the truck. The platform on the hook-and-ladder truck was about eight feet above street level. Fortunately no officers had fallen off the truck during the struggle.

The man was taken to the hospital, where the diagnosis was "under the influence of PCP." He suffered no injury from the tasing, where each taser dart has a fish-hook-like barb on the end and is about three-sixteenths of an inch long. However, when a suspect is shot with a taser, the darts must be removed by a physician. All four of Jim's darts found their mark and were taken out by a doctor at Metropolitan Hospital. It's probably a good thing he was tased twice; no telling how he would have been without it.

"Hey, Sarge, how do you want me to write the part where you choked him out?" one of the arresting officers asked.

"I want you to write it exactly the way it happened. I did what was needed, and that's the way it is."

"Are you sure? You're going to get in trouble."

"I don't think so."

I was wrong. About a week later Captain Noel Cunningham called me into his office. "Mike, Personnel and Training Bureau wants to convene a use-of-force board against you. They told me to write a preliminary report on what you did. Nobody questions what you did as far as taking the guy into custody. I've talked to the fire captain, and he said he didn't see any way you could've done anything differently. I'm sure you did the correct thing, but there's a question about the hold you used.

"You know, Mike, this could be very serious, and I just wanted to make sure that the arrest report accurately reflects what you did and your sergeant's log entry is correct. When you came on the job, you were taught the bar-arm control hold, and you know that's been outlawed. I was wondering if you didn't mean to put down *modified carotid* instead of *bar-arm* to describe your actions."

"You're right, Captain. I always call it the *bar-arm*." I then described a modified carotid as the hold I had used. We never discussed it after that. No use-of-force board was convened, and the matter was laid to rest.

BY THE MID-1980S the drug picture had changed. Marijuana, heroin, and PCP had taken a back seat to "crack." Cocaine was most often inhaled until some backyard chemist figured out how to put it into pellet form. A whole new drug market opened up, and the word *crack* became a lot more than a line on the sidewalk.

When you look at it, crack seems innocuous. It always reminded me of little chunks of slightly soiled white soap. It was meant for street dealing. Each piece is a "rock" approximately a quarter of an inch in diameter. It's easy to "rock up" inventory right in the kitchen. A little baking soda, a kitchen stove, some crystalline cocaine, and presto—you're on your way to becoming a rock seller. You could hold $100 in $10 rocks in your hand and, if you had to, easily scatter them if a police car pulled up to the curb.

The great cocaine organizations of South America, such as the Medellin cartel in Colombia, often placed their own people in distribution positions inside American cities such as Los Angeles. This was different from the distribution system for heroin, which was usually imported from China or Mexico but didn't come with a sales team. It was surprising when we began to see evidence of South American drug dealers at the street level because I thought these people would be one step removed from wholesale to street dealers.

While I was working Central Division mid-P.M. watch, my officers informed me of a cocaine connection at a large hotel. Uniformed officers began making a significant number of arrests of people with crystalline cocaine in their possession in the immediate vicinity of this hotel. Finally one of the arrestees gave us a small piece of information leading to a Colombian national who lived in the hotel.

When the young officers under my supervision approached me with the details, I believed it was going to be a relatively simple problem to solve.

"Have you contacted Narcotics Division?"

"Yes, Sarge, but they're not very interested."

"What do you mean, not very interested? They're not interested in arresting Colombian drug dealers? Since when?"

"Well, that's not exactly it. They told me they'd get to it when they could, but they're swamped."

"OK. Looks like it's ours then, doesn't it? How's this guy dealing?"

"Near as we know, he works from a room in the hotel, and he paid off the hotel staff to help him. We think some of the staff's transporting the drugs out of the hotel and making the deliveries to the dealers. We've seen them come out and talk to peds [pedestrians], then go right back in."

"Have you guys been staked [running a surveillance operation] on the place?"

"Yeah, between calls. We use binoculars, and we don't think they've noticed we're watching them."

"Has anyone seen this Colombian character with any coke?"

"No. He comes outside the hotel and stands in the same spot. People come up and talk to him, but nothing ever changes hands. He's definitely the one running the show, and he's got a bunch of guys in the hotel handling all the coke."

"How do we know he's the one?"

"Guys we've arrested have fingered him, but they've never had him put any coke in their hands."

"Does he ever talk to any of these guys you've arrested?"

"That's just it, Sarge. He does. He'll talk to them, hang around down the block, then go back inside the hotel for a few minutes, come back out, and stand in the same spot. He's always in the same place. Next thing you know, the guy he was talking with disappears into the alley behind the hotel. It's happened where the guy'll come back out, we'll follow him and stop him a block away, and boom—he's holding."

"Has anyone given you information about any conversation with this guy?"

"Only in a general way. They're scared shitless of this dude. He's supposed to be a real mean asshole."

"Well, we'll see about that. I want you to continue to work him. Let's get everybody on the watch involved. I don't want this discussed with anyone stopped on the street. Just act like we have no idea what's going on. Just keep doing what you've been doing until somebody gives us information or sees this guy with money or coke in his hands."

A month went by with no results. Arrests were continually being made by my officers in the vicinity of the hotel, so I decided to call Narcotics Division myself.

"I really think this problem is one for you guys to work on. We need undercover people placed in the hotel. We can only do so much in uniform."

"I know, Sarge, but we just don't have anyone we can assign. We're not just sitting around up here either. I'm sorry. We'll get to you when we can."

That evening I radioed the two officers who had uncovered the problem in the first place and done the most work on it to meet me in the parking lot at Fourth and Main for coffee.

"Do we have anything as of this moment that can put this asshole in jail?"

"No, Sarge, nothing, but he's still out every night. We just came from there."

"Is the traffic increasing over there or staying about the same?"

"About the same. I think he's got a certain number of dealers he's working with, and that's it. We hear he's pushing over a key [kilo] a day out of there."

"OK. Here's what's going to happen. Don't say anything about this to anyone. I'm going to put that fuck out of business immediately. What time does business slow down over there?"

"Usually after midnight."

"OK. The next time you see him outside the hotel after midnight, I want you to stop him, hold on to him, and let me know. Get me on the radio, and I'll be right over. Don't say anything on the air that'll cause anyone else to respond. I'm going to see if I can't convince him to move."

Another day went by. Sure enough, I got the call.

"1-L-50."

"50 go."

"OK. We got him."

"Same place?"

"Rog."

By now I recognized this Colombian character, having seen him several times. He had a cocky look on his face that made you immediately want to punch him out. He knew we had nothing on him, and he was styling. I got out of my police car and walked up to him.

"Thanks, guys. Let me talk to him for a minute. Well, well. We finally meet face-to-face."

He stood there, wearing what appeared to be an expensive silk suit and a full-length black leather trench coat. He said nothing, just gave me a smirk, and nodded his head slightly in agreement.

"Listen, fuckhead. You're out of business." I grabbed him by the collar of his coat and threw him onto the hood of the police car. He bounced off and rolled off into the street. I grabbed him again, pulled him to his feet, and walked him back onto the sidewalk and against the wall. Holding his coat, I looked him straight in the eye and told him, "This is your last fuckin' night here, 'cause I'm going to come back every night and kick the shit out of you until you're fuckin' gone. You and your asshole friends are poisoning the streets, but not here anymore. You fuckin' got it? You understand what I mean?" I shook him as hard as I could. "Do you understand me, asshole? You think I'm fuckin' kidding, try me. I'll tell you what you're going to do. Get your shit out of your room and be gone. Right now. Tonight. My guys are going to be waiting until you come out with your suitcase. You don't come out, I guarantee you, I'll be back."

I pulled him to me, then pushed him away as hard as I could.

"Get out of here, asshole."

He stood up and stared at me.

"Don't even look at me. Don't you even look at me!"

He turned and walked hurriedly into the hotel.

"Just stand by here and let me know if he leaves."

I left, and about ten minutes later my unit got me on the radio.

"Sarge, you won't believe this. He just left. Got into a taxi with his suitcases and headed east on Fifth Street."

We never saw him again.

WITH THE COMING OF PCP AND crack, a new element was introduced into the narcotics picture. It wasn't just Los Angeles; it was in every large city. Both drugs were ideal for distribution by street gangs, who took advantage of the booming business. There was a ready market in the neighborhood as well as the proverbial "whiteboy in the Beemer" fresh in from the Valley to buy some dope.

PCP was being made in clandestine laboratories in south central Los Angeles. Seventy-Seventh Division, Newton Division, Southeast Division, and Southwest Division all had labs turning out dust. A small vanilla extract bottle would produce a few dozen "sherms" or "Super-Kools" at $10 each. The dust dealers would simply dip a Sherman cigarillo or Kool cigarette in the liquid PCP in exchange for $10 each. It was quick and the bottle easily concealed. If the police came up, you gave the vanilla bottle a toss and thus disposed of the evidence. This method of evading arrest became so popular it even had a name: "busting your dust." Street gangs would sell PCP in their own territory, producing cash for a variety of things, including guns.

Cocaine was the same, except the raw product in crystalline form was imported. Usually it was "rocked up" right in the neighborhood and sold on the streets by gangs. Sometimes a brand-new method of distribution was used, the "rock house." They seemed to spring up overnight and were conspicuous because all the windows and doors had bars on them. The windowpanes were either covered or painted to block any view, and the front door would have a telltale slot for conducting sales. This prevented rip-offs by rival gangs, and rock houses were usually as heavily armed as they were fortified.

The manner in which robberies were committed, cars were stolen, and homes burglarized did not really change in my twenty-one-year career. There were constants in police work, but not when it came to narcotics. Drugs had become a "cash crop" for south central Los Angeles. Every major street gang was involved in narcotics dealings. The violence that came with this new "prosperity" was staggering. Statistics had begun to show that Americans were using drugs at a lower frequency, but in south central Los Angeles where I worked, you really couldn't tell. Drugs, gangs, and murder had become synonymous, and we seemed powerless to stop it.

Chapter Five

GANGS
Competition for the Streets

". . . AND YOU SEE, CLASS, it's all a matter of territorial imperative when it comes to gangs. . . ."

"God, this guy's boring! He wouldn't know a gang member if one slapped his face."

The instructor was a retired Los Angeles police inspector. He might have known a lot about police administration, but what he knew about gangs could have fit in his handcuff case—if he had one.

Maybe it was because I had already taken a class in gang recognition on the streets of East L.A. I came from White Fence territory, where it wasn't easy being a white boy. White Fence was the powerful Latin gang that ruled the streets along Whittier Boulevard in the 1950s. They fought with other nearby gangs like Happy Valley, Varrio Nuevo, Clovers, 18th Street, and Clanton (pronounced clan-tone).

They fought about neighborhoods—simple things like looking wrong at someone's girlfriend, being seen walking or riding in another gang's neighborhood, or maybe insulting a "veterano" [retired gang member]. These transgressions must be avenged, usually by fighting, and sometimes the ever-popular zip gun [a crude homemade pistol popular before the days of the inexpensive Saturday night special] would come into play. A few of my friends had zip guns, and I had handled them. I never fired one because they just didn't look that safe. If my grandmother found out I'd even touched one, there would have been big trouble. She was more formidable than any gang member I knew, and I had to live with her.

The toughest guy I ever knew from the neighborhood was Tony Mendez. By the time we got to high school, he'd already been shot once by the police. One time a guy cut in front of Lalo, Tony's little brother, to get on the bus, so Tony and his gang showed up after school and beat this guy senseless. Tony would have fit well into the present inner-city gang picture. He was ruthless and extremely dangerous. He told me many stories of shoot-outs between his "homies" and rival gangs. For some reason Tony and I always got along. Society eventually caught up with Tony and Lalo. Tony murdered a police officer and was sentenced to life in prison. The last I knew of Lalo, he was doing a twenty-year stretch for armed robbery.

When I was transferred to south central Los Angeles from undercover narcotics, there was one noteworthy black gang, the Businessmen. They had a senior group, a junior group, even a baby group—and, not to be sexist, the women had their own branch, too. From time to time we'd arrest some of them, but they were not a direct force on the street. They might commit crimes or fight with other gangs, but they were strictly lightweight compared to what was to come.

The first significant street gang to impact my police work was the Black Panthers. The Panthers were quick to say they were not a street gang, and writers like Gene Marine, magazines such as *Ramparts*, and attorneys like Charles Gary would emphasize the Black Panther militancy as a desperate act to cast off the bonds of slavery. I have no doubt that the elements of a social movement existed in the Black

Panthers, but maybe I just arrested one too many Panthers with narcotics in their possession or saw evidence of enough armed robberies to finance "the movement" to make them anything more than a street gang.

The Panthers I saw in south central Los Angeles were really not much more than common street hoodlums running in a pack who sought to justify their actions by cloaking them with pseudosocial consciousness. They mirrored the standards set by their founder and leader, Huey Newton, who was convicted of killing a police officer in Oakland, California, and sentenced to prison. This conviction was eventually overturned and Newton released. However, his life ultimately ended in a narcotics transaction gone bad when he was killed in a drug-related dispute.

Confrontations with Panthers on the streets in Seventy-Seventh Division were commonplace. They were easy to spot in their black berets and black leather jackets. It was a regular uniform. Their berets would be adorned with a variety of buttons, sometimes just a Black Panther Party emblem or maybe one with the popular slogan "Free Huey."

MY PARTNER AND I WERE TRAVELING southbound on Figueroa at Seventy-Seventh Street in a black-and-white when a young black man wearing a black leather jacket and black beret flagged us down. On the side of his beret was a Black Panther Party button.

"Officers! Officers!"

I hung a quick U-turn and pulled up at the curb next to the man. My partner was closer to him and asked through the open window, "What do you need?"

"Well, I just wanted to see what a couple of motherfucking pigs looked like up close." It was customary at the time for the Panthers to refer to the police as pigs.

"Sir, you're in luck because I'm going to show you." My partner stepped from the police car and flattened him with a single punch. My partner was a weight lifter who was exceptionally strong, and his punch actually hit the Panther in the sternum, knocking the wind out of him. He was gasping for air and probably thought he'd just been hit by Superman.

His beret took flight. I walked over, picked it up, and inspected the buttons on it. By now this guy realized he'd committed a grievous tactical error. I don't know what he thought we would do, but I felt sure he had grossly underestimated our response. I wasn't sure if he was gutsy or just plain stupid. My partner resolved the situation.

"Have you seen enough of the pigs up close?"

"Yeah."

"Is there anything else you want to say to us?"

"No."

"Then get your hat and get out of here, asshole." We got back into our police car and drove away. No arrest, no report, no log entry.

CONFRONTATIONS OF ONE SORT or another with the Panthers occurred nightly. Several times Black Panthers attempted to shoot police officers. Probably the best known was their shoot-out with the police at the corner of Adams and Montclair.

Officers Rudy Limas and Norman Roberge were involved in an incredible firefight with a group of Black Panthers who had come from Oakland specifically to kill a Los Angeles police officer. Both officers were wounded several times, and four Panthers were killed. Chief of Police Thomas Reddin went to the hospital and interviewed the officers for a videotape made about the shootings. They spoke from their beds about the shooting and what they had done. This powerful video was later used as a training film at roll calls throughout the city. Watching that tape, you knew it could have been you; you could have stopped that car, and you could have been the one in that hospital bed—or worse.

These were violent times in south central Los Angeles, and inner-city streets had become more and more like a war zone, a war that never ended. The players changed; the gangs had different names; we had competition for the streets.

I was assigned to Seventy-Seventh Division for eighteen months, and eight police officers were shot during that time. Not all were shot by the Black Panthers, but some were, like Conway Walker and Gary Dino.

There had been a rash of 211s of fast-food restaurants so Walker and Dino were assigned to stake out one such location. Across the street from this restaurant on Manchester Avenue was a recently burned-out building set back from the street with room to pull the police car inside the shell. The officers were staked out on the restaurant for robbers, and a would-be Panthers hit team was staked out on them. The hit team had one purpose—the assassination of two Los Angeles police officers. Maybe the Panthers were still smarting from their failed attempt on Limas and Roberge and wanted to settle the score.

Gary Dino and I had worked Central Division together. He was what you'd call a street-smart cop, the kind of guy who could assess a situation quickly and accurately. As it turned out, those skills saved both his and his partner's life.

Walker and Dino had been sitting for several

hours in the dark, watching the restaurant. At about 10:30 P.M. two Panthers parked their car in an east-west alley just south of the officers. The would-be assassins made their way into the burned-out building and were now only a few feet from their targets.

Snap! One of the Panthers stepped on a piece of wood left over from the fire, and Dino was immediately on the alert. Glancing in the rearview mirror, he saw a shadowy figure. Instantly the police car doors flew open, and a fierce gun battle began. Conway Walker was struck by a shotgun blast in the chest. One of the Panthers was felled by the officers' gunfire; the other ran south to the alley and fled in the getaway vehicle. Walker and the wounded Panther had emptied their weapons and were lying only a few feet from each other. They were in the process of reloading, but Walker finished first and fired the final shot into the head of the Panther, killing him instantly.

As these events were unfolding, I was standing in the watch commander's office and heard Dino issue the most dreaded of all calls: "Officers need help. Officer down." Events like this couldn't help impacting the way you dealt with the Panthers on a nightly basis. You knew some of them were just wanna-bes and others would kill you if they had a chance.

"ALL RIGHT, MEN. WE HAVE A thirteen-car plan tonight, and—" The watch commander's opening was cut off when an explosion rocked the 77th Division roll call. Thirty or so other officers and I poured out of the roll call room. I didn't immediately associate it with a bomb blast and went out of the north side of the station. There was smoke in the air along with the acrid smell of burned powder. The cloud was most intense above the Detective Bureau's portion of the building.

Inside the Detective Bureau you could plainly see what had occurred. A large pipe bomb had been thrown onto the roof and exploded, blowing shrapnel through the roof, through the desks, and into the concrete floor, causing massive destruction. The bomber was a well-known Black Panther. The explosion occurred at the morning watch roll call, around 11:00 P.M. If it had happened during the day, no doubt many officers in the Detective Bureau would have been killed or injured. The bomber was later arrested and convicted of the attack and served time at San Quentin prison.

Some Panthers were fascinated by explosives, but not as skilled. One group of Panthers decided to bomb the nearby Compton police station. A witness observed a man throw an object two or three times onto the roof of the station, but each time it rolled off. Before he could throw it back for a fourth try, the bomb exploded in the hands of the would-be bomber, killing him instantly.

"ALL UNITS AND 12-ADAM-5. See the man regarding possible explosion. . . . Handle the call code two."

"Shit! We can forget getting off on time." End of watch in Seventy-Seventh came at 7:30 A.M., and we got the call at 7:25. Normally, day watch would pick up the call, but apparently there wasn't anyone who could handle it, so we were stuck. Code two meant we were to respond as quickly as possible without the use of emergency lights and siren yet obeying all traffic laws.

"12-Adam-5, be advised an additional ambulance has been dispatched to your call." It was dangerous enough responding to a call when one of the units, in this case an ambulance, was en route code three—using emergency lights and sirens with the ability to disregard certain traffic laws—let alone two vehicles responding code three. We would have no way of knowing which fire station they had come from or what direction they'd be coming from and therefore would have to exercise more caution at every intersection.

"12-Adam-5, roger." Any thoughts that this call might be a phony had just evaporated. I really wanted to get off on time that morning since I'd been in court two days running and when you work morning watch—11:45 P.M. to 7:30 A.M.—court cuts directly into your sleeping time.

As we pulled up to the two-story stucco building, both ambulances were already at the scene. We parked our police car, and by the time we got out both ambulances had left for the hospital. Unless there was an urgent need to get to the hospital, the paramedics normally waited to speak with us.

The first floor appeared to be some sort of business, although we couldn't tell what it was since there were no signs outside and it was too early for it to be open. There was glass all over the sidewalk, as well as bits of wood and a fair amount of blood. Looking up, I could see what seemed to be double French doors. Originally they had had glass in them, but not now. Hanging in the air was a smell similar to what you'd encounter at the pistol range.

"Mike, someone's fired a hand-held rocket launcher or something like it. I smelled hundreds in 'Nam."

"Go on. You've got to be kiddin'."

"Nope. You'll see." And up the outside stairs leading to a second-floor apartment my partner went, with me behind him.

As we walked into the one-room apartment, we could see the place was a mess. On one of the walls were scorch marks, and smoke was literally still hanging in the air. Strewn about the floor were several copies of the latest edition of the Black Panther newspaper, as well as various pamphlets and fliers promoting the Panthers. A large poster of Panther cofounder Huey Newton sitting in a high-backed bamboo chair wearing the customary black leather jacket and beret with a spear in one hand and a rifle in the other was prominently displayed. Whatever had happened in the room had also gotten the poster, because Huey appeared to have taken a shrapnel hit.

"Told you, Mike. Here it is." My partner was triumphantly holding an olive-drab tube with markings designating it as a rocket launcher. It was basically all Greek to me, but my partner was quite familiar with this weapon. "That's not all. They had another one that's still unfired. Look, you can see it's still got—"

"Is that thing dangerous?"

"Jesus, Mike, you can be such a wimp. It's not dangerous until you remove the protective covers and pull the trigger. Then it gets *real* dangerous. These two idiots, whoever the hell they are, are lucky they're still in one piece—if they are."

The rocket itself had left the room, and our later investigation revealed that no one had been killed on the street. It apparently malfunctioned when it was fired and rattled around in the room before blasting through the wall.

"While you finish up here, I'll go downstairs and see if anybody saw this whole deal."

"OK, Mike. I'll be down in a minute."

When I got down to the sidewalk, an elderly black woman approached me. From the look on her face, I knew she'd be able to fill me in on all the details.

"Is everything all right, Officer? It was a terrible explosion, and with those boys screaming and everything, I didn't know what had happened."

"Do you know them, ma'am? Are you the landlady?"

"No, I live next door, and I know two young men live there because I see them coming and going. I've never really talked to them."

"Do you know if they were both inside when this thing went off?"

"Yes, I think so. At least nobody else was around when I came out. One of them was on the sidewalk. I don't know how he fell out of the window."

"There are some glass doors up there."

"Oh, yes, but those have been closed for a long time. You can't actually open them. When the owner built the second-floor addition, he was going to put a balcony there but never did."

My partner joined me, and while we waited for the bomb squad, we took down the woman's name, address, and statement. After the other units arrived, we continued our investigation.

"12-Adam-5 to Control One. What was the destination of the G-units [ambulances] from our call?"

"12-Adam-5, stand by . . . 12-Adam-5, both G-units are out to L.A. County [Hospital]."

When we arrived at L.A. County Hospital, sure enough, both of our guys were there. One had been taken upstairs and was being prepped for surgery; he was in critical condition with head injuries. The other man had suffered hand and face burns and was still being treated in the emergency room.

Regardless of a patient's injuries, everyone starts off in the emergency room at the county hospital. While the hospital didn't look like the cheeriest place, I always thought if you were critically injured, it was where you'd want to be taken for treatment. If you didn't survive there, you wouldn't make it anywhere. The emergency room staff honed their skills on literally hundreds of critically injured people daily.

We found our man in one of the curtained cubicles.

"What happened? Looks like you guys had some fun."

"Man, I don't know nothin'."

"Then let me fill you in. Somebody in that apartment, where I believe you live, was stupid enough to fire a fucking rocket. Now, I don't know, but you do have burns on your face and hands. Does that help you any?"

"I told that stupid motherfucker not to do that!"

"Not to do what?"

"It don't take too much to guess what happened. Even you fucking pigs could figure it out."

"Well, you know how pigs are. We're a little slow. Why don't you fill us in?"

"I didn't take 'em. I don't know where they came from, but the guy I live with got 'em from someone. He said he'd seen one before and knew how to fire it. I thought he was just going to look at it."

"Now wait a minute. Why don't you just be straight with me and quit fucking around? You're both a couple of Panthers, right?"

"Yeah."

"What were you going to do, put one into the side of a police car?"

He lay there with a sullen look on his face, saying nothing. We knew that rocket launchers had recently been stolen from a National Guard armory, but I had no idea if these were part of that theft. Rumor had it that the Panthers wanted to do a hit on a police car with one of them.

"Go ahead. Tell me what happened."

"Like I said, man. I didn't bring the motherfuckers home, and I told him, 'Don't fuck around with 'em,' but no, he don't listen to me! That stupid shit takes the fucking caps off and says, 'Look at this!' Man, the next thing I knew, the room was full of smoke. I don't know what the fuck happened, but I know what he did. He started running for the door, but he was fucked up in the smoke and ran out the window."

"So let me see if I understand this. Your roommate launches the rocket in the room and then launches himself? If that isn't poetic justice, I don't know what the fuck is."

They were placed under arrest for a U.S. Title 18 section dealing with possession of stolen government property, as well as a California state section having to do with possession of unlawful weapons. We never received a subpoena on the case. It was transferred to the United States attorney's office, which handled the prosecution. Some police officers, maybe my partner and I, were damn lucky that these rocket launchers fell into the hands of two idiots and not experienced Vietnam veterans who had become members of the Black Panther Party.

BY THE EARLY 1970S A NEW GANG had come on the scene. I was working Central Division day watch at the time, and I remember seeing a sixteen- or seventeen-year-old black kid on Broadway just north of Eighth Street walking with a cane and an exaggerated, self-imposed limp. I'd never seen anyone who acted like this before.

"Look at that dude over there."

"Don't you know what he is?" my partner replied.

"What do you mean? Just some fool with a cane and a pretend limp."

"No, man. He's bangin' [a gang member]."

"What gang?"

"The Cripples. Didn't you see any 'Crip-Dogs' on morning watch?"

"No. I would've remembered anyone like that. What's the cane for?"

"Just part of the uniform. Same way with the Brims."

"The who?"

"Mike, where've you been? The Brims are the rivals of the Cripples. They're south-end gangs, and the only time we see them is on the weekend."

"What do they do up here in Central?"

"I don't know. Go to the movies and cop a G-ride [steal a car] home."

That was my introduction to one of the two largest street gangs in America. Mexican gangs had used bandannas as a part of their identification for a long time; now black gangs also adopted "colors." The blue bandanna soon became identified with the Crips, but the cane and limp were quickly discarded.

THE FIRST CRIPS STREET SHOOTING I was involved with occurred when a group of them entered a gas station on Olympic. The gas station attendant kept a shotgun inside the office area for protection. The Crips were by the gas pumps, and the young Latin attendant left the office and confronted them.

"Go away! Get outta here! You don't belong here."

The group felt challenged, and they stood their ground. They weren't doing anything, but they weren't leaving either. The attendant returned to the office and retrieved a twelve-gauge shotgun.

"I told you! Go away! Get outta here! I'm not frightened of you." He leveled the shotgun directly at the group.

One young man stepped forward. "Well, you can

kill me, motha-fucker."

And the attendant did just that. The shotgun blast caught the defiant young man full in the chest, killing him instantly.

The Latin man was taken into custody for 187 of the Penal Code—murder. The district attorney declined to prosecute, because the attendant gave a plausible explanation for his fear. It seems that one of his friends operating a service station nearby had been shot in a recent robbery. The decedent also had a significant criminal history, including arrests for robbery.

THE BRIMS WERE A MUCH SMALLER and less powerful gang. They were easy prey for the Crips and in need of protection themselves. Their trademark was the "stingy brim" hat, which made them easy to identify.

Around the area of Adams and Central, graffiti began to appear identifying a new gang—BSV. Blood Stone Villains had arrived. It was the first time I saw the word *blood* in a gang name. Very soon the Brims were absorbed into the new gang, which became known simply as the Bloods. It was only natural that they too would select a color, and that color would be red.

In the early days there were just Crips and Bloods. By the mid-1980s in Newton Division the Crips could be known as Four Deuce (42nd Street), Four Trey (43rd Street), Five Trey, or Five Deuce Broadway Crips. The Bloods could also be identified as the 52 BSV, 56 BSV, or Mid-City Gangsters. Some Blood gangs still kept the old name Brim, such as Harvard Park Brims and Van Ness Gangster Brims, but they were Blood gangs.

Just because you were a member of the Bloods didn't mean that you were necessarily safe from other

Blood gangs, and the same went for Crips. The wrong color shirt, tennis shoes, or shoelaces could make the wearer a victim of a drive-by shooting. The words are called out from a darkened vehicle: "You Crippin'?" You better have the right answer, but at night it's hard to tell who's asking.

With the growth of the Bloods and the Crips, it seemed as though every week there was a new gang "set." A set is simply a subgroup of the larger gang, such as the Grape Street Crips, who are part of the Crips gang but operate autonomously. You might know that Five Deuce Crips were responsible for a particular crime, but you had no idea who the members of Five Deuce were. When I was a sergeant in Newton Division, two officers set out to change that.

CARLOS SANCHEZ AND RUSS SAWYER developed their own card file system to keep track of gang members. Every time they'd stop a group of gang-bangers, they'd ask about their gang alliance. Other officers before them had developed card files on gang members, but Sawyer and Sanchez added a unique twist to the technique. They developed a rapport with the gangs. Russ Sawyer could rap with gang-bangers like no one else I have ever met. He was simply amazing. It was almost like he was a performer, and Carlos Sanchez was the straight man.

They were a rare team, with Sanchez able to talk to the gang members Sawyer couldn't reach, and together the information they needed was obtained. They also began to photograph gang members and kept the pictures in their card file. However, the city attorney felt that maintaining files of photographs on persons who had not violated any specific law verged on an unconstitutional act, and the practice was stopped.

Before long, detectives began to call and ask Carlos and Russ about various gang members. There was no question, crimes were being solved through the knowledge Sanchez and Sawyer had about Crips and Bloods.

Their work was even more amazing when you consider that street gangs simply do not like the police. The two officers could alter their approach so markedly from one gang member to another that these kids would talk to them when they wouldn't talk to any other police officer. Complaints about their actions were exceedingly rare. These officers afforded gang-bangers a measure of respect but would still arrest them in a flash if they violated the law.

As gang violence increased steadily, the police department responded with a new unit—Community Resources Against Street Hoodlums (CRASH). It was originally named TRASH (Total Resources Against Street Hoodlums), but parents took umbrage with the implication that their children were refuse, and the name was changed. Initially uniformed officers assigned to CRASH were simply gathering information on gang members, much as Sanchez and Sawyer did.

The CRASH mission was ill defined, and its officers did not handle investigations at first. Then detectives were also assigned to the unit, allowing the investigation of crimes irrespective of the division of occurrence; the common denominator was simply gang involvement. Eventually CRASH units even handled the investigation of homicides committed by gang members. If there was a homicide, and the victim or suspects were thought to be gang members, CRASH was called in. Most south central division homicide detective units were handling about 125 to 150 homicides annually, not including gang murders. With the tremendous upswing in gang violence, divisional homicide detectives were drowning in case overload. By calling in CRASH units to handle gang murders, detectives were freed to work on other cases.

CRASH not only helped the detectives but also had a direct impact on patrol. You'd be at a gang-related homicide scene, and CRASH would arrive and agree to take over the investigation. The two or three patrol units tied up at the scene were immediately kicked loose by CRASH, which meant your men could return to patrol.

IF YOU READ THE NEWSPAPER, you thought that the only thing gangs were doing in south central Los Angeles was driving around shooting each other. Once it became fashionable, the *Los Angeles Times* newspaper would keep its readers abreast of the latest carnage in the inner city with the insinuation the police were powerless to stop it. It wasn't always so newsworthy.

"Hey, Sarge, press room on line one."

"Newton Division, watch commander's office, Sergeant Middleton. May I help you?"

"This is the press room. Got anything going tonight?"

"Yeah, one homicide, a drive-by shooting."

"Who's involved?"

"Right now, I don't know who the victim was. Some black guy on the street."

"How about the shooters? They in custody?"

"No, not yet."

"Who did the shooting? Do you know?"

"We think it was a gang thing. The suspects are black, but that's all we know right now."

"OK. What else you got?"

I don't remember how many calls of that nature I fielded, but they were many. In Parker Center, the police administration building, there was a press room to handle the contingent of reporters from various newspapers and news services. They came and went as they pleased and weren't responsible to anyone on the department. Usually on morning watch each division would regularly receive a call from the press room inquiring about any significant crimes that might warrant press coverage. As long as it was black-on-black crime, they didn't show too much interest. An event in West Los Angeles changed all that.

The Westwood area has several movie theaters that attract thousands of young people on the weekends. One particular night a teenage Asian girl and her friends were walking along the sidewalk. A group of gang members were driving slowly past them. Shots were fired from their car, and the young girl lay dead on the sidewalk. Gang violence had come to Westwood. The Crips had found new targets on the west side.

News of the drive-by shooting brought banner headlines. Talk of a wave of murders in West Los Angeles was detailed in stories. Suddenly black gangs were killing more than just each other or Latin gang members. Now it was news. That year West Los Angeles Division had fewer than 20 murders, Newton Division more than 125. From that time on, drive-by shootings were a hot topic, and no longer would they be blithely dismissed with "What else you got?"

THE REAL POWER OF THE CRIPS and the Bloods wasn't to be found in gunning down innocent teenage girls in West Los Angeles. They took a page from organized crime and began to realize the profit potential in the sales and distribution of narcotics. Initially their efforts were rather clumsy and based within the neighborhood. In the area around Sixty-Second and San Pedro streets, faint wafts of piperidine were in the air. The word on the street was that somebody was "cookin'" dust.

When PCP is being manufactured, the cooking process employs the use of piperidine, which produces a smell that always reminded me of some sort of spice. The clandestine lab operator would try to conceal the smell by completely closing off the lab area to the outside environment. The danger in this approach was that the lab operator could be asphyxiated, which did occur on more than one occasion. In addition, using the wrong mixture of chemicals while "cooking" PCP could result in a massive explosion.

I was taking a class at the academy, and the inherent dangers of PCP labs were under discussion. The two instructors were veteran narcotics investigators who had become experts in dealing with PCP labs. They related a story that made a lasting impression.

"We were following this guy who had just picked up a kit at a chemical supply house. When I say 'kit,' I mean just that—a package deal that included all the necessary chemicals to produce PCP. Of course, when we interview these people, they say, 'We don't know what you're talking about. We don't ask what anyone is going to do with these chemicals.' At present, there is no violation of the laws in the possession of these raw materials. . . ."

Laws would later be passed prohibiting chemical wholesalers from selling combinations of raw materials that in effect comprised a recipe for PCP, but at this point it was all perfectly legal.

". . . We followed this guy from his supplier to his home. He unloaded several thousand dollars' worth of chemicals from his car and took them into his house.

It had been raining that morning, but he came back outside, poured the water out of one of the trash cans, and took it into the house.

"After about twenty minutes there was an incredible explosion. It knocked all of the walls down, and the lab operator flew out of the building, across the street, and landed in a yard. He didn't have a stitch of clothes on when he landed. Now picture a cartoon that shows a house blowing up, the roof flies into the air, and comes back down. That's exactly what happened, but when the roof landed, the walls were gone. He turned the basic three-bedroom single-family home into a pile of rubble.

"As you gentlemen know, sodium shavings are a part of PCP manufacture. Sodium and water produce at the very least a fire, which in the presence of flammable gases inevitably results in an explosion. By the way, he lived, and we booked him for possession of and manufacturing of phenyl cyclohexyl piperidine.

"We were never able to exactly reconstruct what happened. He didn't remember anything leading up to the explosion, but we think he put sodium shavings into the wet trash can. Bingo!"

Everyone, probably even the drug manufacturers themselves, was aware of just how dangerous it was to make dust. When you found a PCP lab, the fire department's hazardous materials team had to respond to ensure no one was overcome by the chemical fumes and no explosion occurred.

A couple of blocks north of Sixty-Second Street, officers on the P.M. watch uncovered a lab in full operation and arrested the owner. By the time we cleared roll call and went to the scene, the fire department hazardous materials team was already there. Following an inspection, they determined the building was safe for us to enter. The smell of piperidine hung heavy in the air. It was the piperidine that had caused the neighbors to call the police, complaining about the strange smells.

While this was a small-time operation, he had mixed enough PCP crystals to make more than two gallons of pure liquid PCP ready for sale. On the street this batch would translate into thousands of dollars. A cigarette would be dipped into the liquid sufficient to cover one and a half to two inches. One dipped cigarette brought a dealer $5 to $10, and those two gallons would have treated thousands. There's no doubt that many of those cigarettes would have been sold at Sixty-Second and San Pedro.

THERE WASN'T ANYTHING PARTICULARLY remarkable about the intersection of Sixty-Second and San Pedro. It was essentially a lower-middle-class neighborhood composed of mostly single-family homes, but times were changing. A new gang had started to operate, calling themselves the Six Deuce Crips, and they were dealing dust.

It could be midnight, and yet traffic was always heavy—the perfect situation for dope dealing. The lighting was poor, and because of the layout of the street and the houses, you couldn't get very close to the gang-bangers dealing dust without being seen. There wasn't any way Narcotics Division or the gang units were going to solve this problem. If we wanted to return that neighborhood to its original state, we would have to make the arrests ourselves. It was amazing how fast the picture could change with the gangs. One week a street would be quiet with little crime, and the next week a couple of dope-dealing gang members had turned the place into a PCP supermarket. That's what Six Deuce had done to Sixty-Second and San Pedro.

The Crips and Bloods were financing their gang

operations through the sales and distribution of narcotics. It wasn't about black pride or protecting your neighborhood; it was about dealing drugs and making big money. There was a need to protect your neighborhood, but only as it related to your drug-dealing operation. There was no competition for the drug market in Six Deuce Crips territory, or so they thought. Newton morning watch set out to put Six Deuce out of the drug-dealing business and perhaps out of existence.

It seemed as though everyone on the watch became part of the operation. If you weren't assigned a radio call, the standing order was "Drive by Sixty-Two and Pedro." If things were quiet, park your car in an alley, get out on foot, and try to sneak up on Six Deuce as they were in the process of making hand-to-hand sales of PCP. The results came immediately with many arrests, but still we didn't seem to make a dent in the narcotics trafficking. When the lab was taken down a few blocks north, there was but a momentary lapse in the PCP supply. Within a few days it was business as usual again.

Friday nights were the best for drug dealing. "OK, guys, listen up. Roll call. L-20 is Durham. L-30 is Allen. Middleton is L-50. 13-A-9 is. . . ." The watch commander finished the rest of the nightly car plan. "Remember, guys, Friday night. Sixty-Two and Pedro. Let's make sure everybody has some log entries from there. If you're not busy, go by there. Everyone's doing a real good job, but we want to keep the pressure on. Mike, you had that woman last night—where was she at? Over on Avalon?"

"Yeah, we had a duck [abandoned stolen vehicle] over there, and she came out just as I was getting ready to leave. She loves what we're doing. She told me she's lived there for thirty-five years and hates those Crip bastards as much as we do. She's really on top of things and named off the houses where the Crips live on that block. She's pissed off at one of the owners renting to this family who have a couple of Crip-Dogs for sons. She hopes we won't give up on the dealers before we drive 'em away or put 'em in jail. So let's keep in mind we have the support of people like her, and remember that when we're dealing with these dope dealers. When somebody comes out of a house and wants to know what we're doing, it might be somebody like her who really supports us."

"To go along with what Sergeant Middleton just said, so far we have no 181s [personnel complaints], and I want to keep it that way. I want to put these assholes in jail, but I want the police work to be clean."

13-L-20 was Sergeant Peter B. Durham, a top-notch sergeant—Petie to me. We had worked together for a few years, and it was always a lot of fun. Skulking about to arrest bad guys was something Pete loved more than anything else. Our watch had very high productivity when it came to crime suppression, and to Pete crime suppression equaled arresting criminals. Maybe you couldn't stop the type of crime they were committing at that moment, but they sure wouldn't commit any more crimes while they were in jail. Pete described police work as dispensing "a kind word and a smile."

The other sergeant working that night was Steve Allen, who was assigned to 13-L-30. He had the same attitude toward police work that Pete and I had. The three of us got along better and enjoyed police work more than any other group I ever worked with. Steve is a very competitive person. His brother, Dave, a Los Angeles city fire fighter, is very laid back, the antithesis of Steve. Dave once told me a story where he and Steve were playing a round of golf and Steve lost. This was unthinkable for Steve, who promptly threw his golf bag and clubs into the water trap, believing them to be of no further use. Dave confided, "I retrieved those clubs and still play with them today." Steve always wanted to be the best.

"13-A-93 to 13-L-50."

"L-50, go."

"On Sixty-Two east of Pedro, they're dealing on both sides of the street."

"Where're you at?"

"We're on foot, just west of Ascot Walk between a couple of cars. We left our car on Sixty-First." The officer was speaking very quietly into his ROVER.

"What's the best way to approach?"

"I think north and south. Put one unit at Sixty-First and Pedro and one unit back at Avalon and Gage. Have the Gage car come west to San Pedro, up Pedro to Sixty-Two, then make a right turn. As soon as they hit Pedro, the Sixty-First Street unit can come out onto San Pedro, go south onto Sixty-Second, and make a left. We tried parking at Gage and Pedro by the liquor store, but as soon as we got out of the car, you could hear people whistling everywhere [a common method to advise others on the street that the police are nearby]."

"13-A-9 to L-50. We'll take Gage and Avalon."

"50 to 9, roger. A-93, how close are you to San Pedro?"

"We're just off of Ascot Walk. We've got to move down some. It's pretty dark here, so I don't think it'll be a problem. There's nobody else on foot down here."

"Let us know when you've moved down enough and then direct everything as soon as the Crip-Dogs see us and start running."

"20 to 50."

"50 go."

"Where you at, Mike?"

"I'm gonna move over to Sixty-First Street and go

south from there. Petie, why don't you go over to Gage?"

"20 roger."

"L-50 to any unit in the vicinity of 61 and San Pedro. Meet me on Sixty-First west of San Pedro."

"A-71, we'll meet you in about thirty seconds. We'll come east on Sixty-First from Wall."

"50, rog."

"L-30 to 20 and 50. I'll be southbound on Avalon, and I'm gonna come west on Sixty-First. As soon as you guys hit the corner of Sixty-One and Pedro, I'm gonna start down from Avalon in case somebody books out in a car."

"This is L-50. I've got A-71 here with me. 93, how's it lookin' over there now?"

"93. No cars on the street right now, but we've got what looks like hand-to-hand [sales] goin' down right now on the north side of the street. Looks like the guys on the south side of the street have got somebody comin' up from the liquor store. I'd say it looks good right now. Hold on. Here comes a car west on Sixty-One, and they're stoppin' to talk to the guys on the south side of the street. Yeah, come now! It's somebody from the Crip house in the middle of the block."

"OK. 50 to 9 and 20, let's go. Let us know just before you make the northbound turn on Pedro."

"OK. We're comin' up on it now!"

"Me and 71 are movin'. Ready, Steve?"

"Rog. When I see the lights, I'll come down."

The trap was perfectly sprung. A-9 and L-20 rounded the corner from San Pedro onto Sixty-First Street first while A-71 and I came in right behind. 93 had come out from its concealed position and ran toward the dope dealers on the south side of the street. Steve Allen roared in from Avalon to block off the carload of Crips should they decide to throw it into reverse to escape.

On the south side of the street the potential customers hadn't quite reached the two dust dealers, and as the units passed them, they bolted on foot across a vacant lot at high speed. We had nothing on them, so nobody chased them down. For a split second the two dealers left behind didn't know which way to turn. The two officers from 13-A-9 were out of their car and face-to-face with the dust dealers.

"Freeze! Get your hands out where we can see 'em! Both of you! Get 'em out there."

"We ain't done nothin'." Crack! A vanilla extract bottle shattered on the sidewalk. They had busted their dust and began to walk away from the officers.

"Freeze! Freeze, assholes!" The two men were now running south through the vacant lot with the officers from 13-A-9 right behind them. It was pitch black, and even though these two idiots knew the neighborhood well, somehow they ran directly into a low fence. They were arrested without any further struggle.

The four police cars converged so quickly that the carload of Crips, who'd stopped to talk to the dope dealers on the south side of the street, never moved. As officers poured out of their police cars, the three Crips inside couldn't get their hands up fast enough. They were surrounded.

"It's cool! It's cool! Hey, man. We don't have no drugs."

The officers from 13-A-93 ran up the street on the grassy strip between the sidewalk and the curb. When they were even with the Crip vehicle, they used a parked car for cover and lit up the occupants with their flashlights. With guns drawn, they ordered the people inside, "Get your hands up where we can see them, and keep them there! Driver, you first. Out of the car and on the ground. You! You, in the backseat. Keep your hands up. All right, front passenger. Out of the car. Facedown in the street. Face down. Come on. Spread your hands out. OK. Passenger. Push the seat forward and come out the same door. Prone out next to your partner."

The driver of the Crip car was covered by Pete and me. A-93 had the two passengers under control. The two drug dealers who had been standing on the sidewalk on the north side of the street started to run to the east. They came face-to-face with 13-A-93, stopped, turned around toward the two officers from 13-A-71, and surrendered, dope and all.

The neighborhood took on a strange silence. It was after midnight. No lights were on in the houses, but you could see silhouettes at the windows peering into the night. What we were doing would make a difference to these people. Maybe not forever, but for a little while. It seemed that it was all you ever bought in police work—a little while.

A-9 marched the formerly fleet-of-foot drug dealers who had run into the fence back to the patrol car. In spite of nearly knocking himself senseless on the fence, the Crip-Dog who'd broken the PCP bottle on the sidewalk was still feeling confident. "Man, you ain't got fuckin' shit on me. All you got is a bunch of motha-fuckin' glass on the sidewalk, and that ain't shit."

I looked at Pete and just smiled. "What do you think, Petie? Do we have shit or do we have shit?" What the Crip-Dog didn't know was that Pete and I had developed a system for arresting dust busters. We would take a field interview card and place it directly over the remaining liquid. The PCP liquid would then soak into the card. This was placed in a small, sealable plastic bag along with pieces of the broken bottle and then placed in a glass evidence jar, which we carried with us just for this purpose so it could be sent to the police laboratory for analysis. Pete and I had a perfect record for PCP arrests, whether they busted their dust or not. We never lost a case, and these two were no exception.

"ALL UNITS IN THE VICINITY. 13-Adam-43. 211 in progress at Chapel's Chicken, corner of Vernon and San Pedro. 13-Adam-43, handle the call code three."

"A-43, roger."

This call would be more than just a robbery; it was a Four Deuce Crips caper. Four Deuce was a new faction, not yet involved with narcotics sales. They fancied themselves gangsters, and a robbery of the chicken stand fit perfectly into their method of operation.

I was about a block and a half from the call and pulled into the chicken stand within thirty seconds of the broadcast. The manager was already outside the store when I arrived. Chapel's was a well-known franchise operation that specialized in fried chicken. From all outward appearances the store at San Pedro and Vernon was doing very well. It was always busy, and I purchased many meals there myself.

"Officer! They just left! One of 'em had a gun. Three black kids. I've seen 'em in here before. They're part of that Crip gang from Forty-Second Street."

"Anybody hurt?"

"No, but he sure scared one of my girls waiting on him."

"Which way did they go?"

"They ran down the alley over there. The guy with the gun had a dark jacket on, and the others. . . ." The manager was a wealth of information. He remembered height, weight, and more about each suspect.

"13-L-50 to 13-A-43. Suspects have just left southbound in the alley east of San Pedro. Suspects are three male blacks. One suspect is armed with a handgun, is approximately eighteen to twenty years of age, and . . . What is your position right now?"

"43 to 50. We're northbound on San Pedro approaching Forty-Eighth Street."

"43, stop at the corner of Forty-Six and Pedro. I'm going to come southbound in the alley and see if I can drive them out toward you."

"A-43. We're at 46 and Pedro."

"I'm gonna go southbound in the alley now." The alley that ran southbound from Vernon was unusually long. For whatever reason, there was no outlet at Forty-Fifth Street, which meant that if the suspects wanted to cut through the alley to escape they'd have to run two very long blocks. We were in luck, and the plan worked.

"A-43 to Control One. We have the three robbery suspects in custody at the corner of Forty-Sixth Street and Crocker."

When I started down the alley, the three gangbangers ran for a couple hundred yards before they got to Forty-Sixth Street. When they hit Forty-Sixth and saw A-43 waiting for them, they ran east on the sidewalk with A-43 driving behind them. Unfortunately the young man who had the gun was able to toss it because he didn't have it on him when he was arrested, and we searched the alley thoroughly without success. He may have gotten rid of the gun, but he still had all of the money taken in the robbery.

As I arrived at the scene, the three suspects were already handcuffed and sitting on the curb. "Guys, I'm gonna go up and get the victim and bring her back here to see if she can identify these guys."

I talked to the manager and explained we needed to take the young woman to the scene where the suspects had been arrested to see if she could identify them. Our case would have gone straight into the toilet if we'd taken the suspects back to the scene of the crime to be identified. The law allows a police officer to eliminate a person as a suspect by bringing the victim to the suspect, but generally the suspect may not be transported anywhere for identification unless a lineup is performed.

The young waitress was petrified. She came from Guadalajara, Mexico, and had been in the United States for less than a year. She had a young child, and her husband was a construction worker. She'd gotten this job at night to earn extra money so they could move away from the inner city to a place where this kind of thing wouldn't happen. She didn't speak a single word of English other than what was necessary to order fried chicken dinners. When the Four Deuce Crips came up to the window, they looked like any other customers until one of them pulled a gun and demanded money. The young Mexican woman ready to take their order was suddenly looking straight down the barrel of a gun.

For as long as I can remember I've spoken Spanish and was called on almost nightly to translate. "*Señora, tenemos tres sospechosos. . . .*" We sat in my patrol car as I spoke quietly to her in her native language. She was so terribly frightened because she realized how close she might have just come to having her life ended. "We need you to come and see if they are the same men that robbed the store."

"I will try."

"I want you to understand that just because we've stopped somebody doesn't mean it's the right person. It's just as important for you to tell me that you can't identify him as it is for you to tell me that it's the right person."

"I understand. Does this mean that my family will be sent back?"

"They'll come back. They're with the Crips."

"We don't have papers. We came here because the money is better and it would be a place to start. I thought that if I got involved with the police, I'd have to go back, and my family, too."

"Ma'am, you're the victim of a crime. I don't care if you're legal or not. What I care about is putting these guys in jail if they're the ones that did it."

"Thank you."

"You don't have to thank me. Maybe you'll help us catch some criminals. I should thank you. If you're worried about immigration, I told you, I don't care about that." And I didn't care. Maybe it was because I understood life in the barrio. I had dealt with thousands of illegal aliens and found them to be law-abiding citizens almost without exception. It is true they violated the law when they entered the country illegally, but I couldn't find fault with them for this transgression. All of us came here from someplace else, with the exception of the Indians. If my family and I were living on the other side of that wire fence, I'd find a way to cross in search of a better life, and I wouldn't care how illegal it was. All this waitress and her husband wanted was to find a better life for themselves and their baby.

I drove her over to where the suspects were in custody. Keeping the inside of our car dark made it impossible for anyone to see the young woman in the backseat well enough to identify her. "That's the one! That's the one who had the pistol! He pointed it at me, and I gave him the money."

"What about the others?"

"I didn't get as good a look at them, but I think they are the ones. Yes, they were with him. I know they were. I remember them. I can't go to court. I can't say that."

"What do you mean? You just said they're the ones."

"What do you mean?"

"You're afraid they'll hurt you?"

"Or my husband. Or my baby. Every night he picks me up after work. What if they're there, waiting?"

"I've never had a case where someone identified a suspect and something happened to the witness. Never. Not once. If anybody comes around, you call us. I'll talk to the manager and make sure he understands."

"You think I will be all right? And my husband? And my baby?"

"Yes, I do."

All three of the suspects were at least eighteen and booked as adults. The manager did an audit of the cash register, and the amount of money the one Crip had on him was within a couple of dollars of the missing amount. About two weeks later the preliminary hearing was held, and we were all in the courtroom together.

The young woman and her husband were seated in the first row. I walked over and sat down with them. "Are you ready to testify?"

"I can't identify anyone. I don't remember anything."

"Don't be worried. You'll remember when you see them here in the courtroom."

"I'm not saying anything about them."

"What do you mean? What did they do? Tell me, what did they do?"

"They came to the window and said I'd better not tell anyone."

"Do you know who these guys were?"

"I don't know their names, but I've seen them before with the same guys that robbed us."

"Did they speak Spanish?"

"No. They just pointed their finger at me and put

it up to their lips like I should be quiet. Then they pointed their finger at me again like it was a gun and laughed. One night a car came and stopped by the curb. At first I thought they were customers, but the guy in the front seat just stared at me, and then he raised his hand, his right hand. He had a gun."

"Did he point it at you?"

"No. He just pointed it up, and they drove away."

"Did you tell the manager?"

"No, I didn't tell anyone. Sergeant, I know you want to help, but you're not there all the time. They'll kill me if I talk, so I'm going to say they're not the ones."

"You have to tell the truth."

"I have my baby and my husband. I'm going to say they're not the ones."

I called the prosecutor aside and explained the problem. She had already told him through an interpreter that she would not identify the suspects. "Sergeant, if I put her up on the stand and she says that, our case is history, and these guys walk. Do you think you could find any other witness to identify these guys?"

"Well, the manager saw the tail end of it, but his testimony isn't going to be as strong as hers could be. I talked to her, and she's not identifying them because she's been threatened."

"By these three?"

"No. Other Four Deuce Crips came up to the stand and held their forefingers up to their lips, indicating she must be quiet. Then they pointed their fingers at her and pretended to pull the trigger on a gun. One carload stopped in front of the place, a guy looked right at her, and held a real gun up in the air."

"How does she know they're Four Deuce?"

"Shit, she works right there, man. She sees these

assholes every night. Forty-Second Street is three blocks from the chicken stand. You're the prosecutor. Got any ideas? Put me on the stand, and I'll tell what happened, including why she won't testify."

"I'm not going to put you on the stand. I don't think the judge'll buy it. I understand what you're trying to do, Sergeant, and I'm not saying you're wrong, but it's just too flimsy. I'm sorry. You're going to have to wait until next time for these guys."

The judge entered the courtroom, and the armed robbery case against the three Four Deuce Crips was dropped. As they were leaving, the one who had had the gun looked smugly at me and, with his arms crossed in front of him, held four fingers up on one hand and two on the other, the sign of the Four Deuce Crips.

After the courtroom emptied, I walked over to the court clerk and asked to speak with the judge.

"Is there something you wish me to tell the judge?"

"Yes, that I would like to speak with him."

The clerk looked very exasperated as he walked into the judge's chambers. When the door opened, I fully expected him to come out and tell me the judge was unavailable. "The judge will see you."

"Sergeant, what can I do for you?"

"Your honor, the reason this case was dropped is because the witness has been threatened by Four Deuce Crip gang members and is afraid to testify for fear that her husband and child will be killed."

"Are you telling me that the three men in court today threatened her?"

"No, sir. After we arrested these guys, other Crip gang members came to where she works and made hand gestures to let her know she better be quiet, and if she didn't, she'd be shot. Another time, somebody in a car pulled up and had a gun in his hand as he looked at her. She's seen those same people with the suspects in the past. Your honor, she works three blocks from where these gang members hang out."

"Did you tell this to the district attorney?"

"Yes, sir."

"Why did he drop the case?"

"He didn't think that the court would find the story believable, but your honor, I work in that neighborhood every night. I know these gang-bangers, and I know the way they terrorize people. I'd like a chance to get up on the stand and testify about what she told me. I don't blame her for what she did. We can't be there every minute, but it just seems like we owe it to her to stand up to these people."

"Well, Sergeant, I suggest you go back, talk to your detectives, and get this case refiled right away. Yes, that sounds like an excellent idea."

"Thank you, your honor."

I spoke with the robbery detectives later the same morning and explained what had happened. I was expecting an argument, but they liked the idea of trying one more time. The armed robbery charges against the Four Deuce Crips were refiled.

A couple of nights went by, and sure enough, our gunman was standing on a corner just south of the chicken stand. I couldn't wait to break the good news to him. He was with his girlfriend and a couple of other Four Deuce gang-bangers. I called for another unit, and when they arrived, all three of us approached the group. He remembered me right away.

"Hey, man. No hard feelin's, but you motherfuckers didn't have shit."

"I guess you Crip-Dogs just walk every time, don't you?"

He had an ear-to-ear grin as he said, "Hey, what

can I say? What can I say?"

"Try this. I'm gonna put your fuckin' ass in jail on that robbery charge if it's the last thing I do. As a matter of fact, you should have a subpoena in a couple of days because, 'homes,' your case has been refiled. You gonna be in YA so fast that your toothbrush will have to take the next bus. In fact, I think somebody's gonna make you a cell block spinner [forced participant in homosexual activities]." He was no longer smiling.

About three weeks later we were back in court for a preliminary hearing. The young woman got on the stand, was sworn in, and testified that these were not the robbers. I followed her and, after qualifying as a court expert in Spanish, testified about her initial identification of the suspects, the threats made against her, and my knowledge of gang activity and the systematic terror brought on the neighborhood by Four Deuce Crips and gangs like them.

"The defendants are held to answer for 211 of the Penal Code for the crime of robbery." A trial date was set, but the case was never tried as each of the defendants plea-bargained to a lesser offense and was sent to the California Youth Authority in Chino.

THE BEST WAY TO DESCRIBE the transition of gangs during my years on the streets would be a loss of innocence. Some people would say the gangs were never innocent and were only about crime and one group imposing its will on others through collective force. When you contrast the Businessmen of Newton Division with Six Deuce and Four Deuce Crips, the groups aren't even in the same league. The old Newton gangs were lightweights compared to the violence and terrible influence of their successors.

Eliot Ness and his men fought street gangs while

attempting to enforce liquor and tax laws. The same type of battle is going on today, only it's about narcotics. When the Four Deuces commit a robbery, it is very possible that the money goes to buy guns to protect their ability to sell drugs within a territory they've staked out for themselves.

The Panthers with their quasi-social movement were really nothing more than street hoodlums. They wanted to be urban guerrillas, a self-styled American Bader Meinhof. This German urban terrorist organization advocated the use of random terror against the state to create a feeling among the general population that no one could protect them except the terrorist organization itself, a model alive today with the Irish Republican Army (IRA). The problem with the Panthers was that they were basically criminals, not social zealots. Huey Newton started as a small-time drug dealer who took a few college classes, helped create an organization, and ended up back at his roots, killed in a drug deal. The Panthers might have elevated themselves above gang status if they had been more selective in recruitment, but with rare exception they were little more than street punks with guns.

By the end of my police career gangs were no longer about social movements or turf; they were about drugs. Grandmothers of little boys not much different from me could no longer chase the gangbangers away with an iron skillet. The gangs were too powerful, and life had become very cheap along the way.

Chapter Six

DEADLY FORCE
When Death Is Close Enough to Touch

"I WANT ALL OF YOU TO TAKE TIME and look carefully at the pictures being passed around. Every one of these officers started out in this classroom. All of them had this class, and they all heard the words I'm going to tell you. Every one of them is now dead. I want you to look at them. I want you to look at their faces. I want you to see the blood. Remember—none of these men thought it would ever happen to them.

"The first picture is Officer Thomas Scebbi. Notice what he's holding. He was trying to broadcast a help call, and he died with the mike in his hand. Look at him. I don't want you to ever forget the look on his face. He's dead. On June 20, 1958, he and his partner stopped a man they thought might have been involved in a burglary walking on the sidewalk. It was supposed to be a routine FI [field interview], and that's the problem. Routine. . . ."

To this day, I can remember seeing Officer Scebbi sprawled across the front seat of a 1958 Chevrolet police car with the mike in his hand. I don't recall seeing any blood, but I'll never forget the look on his face. It scared the hell out of me.

The central thrust of our police academy training regarding officer-involved shootings was not the "dead officer" class. It was made abundantly clear that most officers involved in shootings would not be injured and that most officers who were shot would not die. We were really taught survival skills.

Our training dealt with such things as recognizing when to use deadly force, what to do when confronting an armed suspect, what to do if you or another officer is shot, and being taken hostage by a suspect. On March 9, 1963, Officer Ian Campbell was murdered after he and his partner surrendered their weapons and were taken hostage. This event became pivotal in officer survival training. There was a never-ending debate on whether it was correct to give up your weapon or risk being shot by a suspect who had you at gunpoint. One training bulletin reminded us that all wounds were not fatal and that if you'd lost your weapon you still might be able to kill your attacker by thrusting a pencil or ballpoint pen into the jugular vein or carotid artery of the suspect. The bulletin concluded that religious conviction in such times of crisis may be beneficial, as it was for Carolyn Flemenco.

The philosophy of the Los Angeles Police Department during my entire career was to study officer-involved shootings at great length in an attempt to learn what went wrong and how the shooting could have been avoided. This knowledge was then incorporated into officer training so the same situation would not be repeated. Some shootings cannot be prevented. When a suspect pulls a gun on a police officer, the officer has two choices: use deadly force on the suspect or let the suspect use deadly force on him. At that point there's nothing particularly sociological about it. It's essentially kill or be killed. It isn't possible to argue with those who believe any killing in any situation is wrong, including in defense of one's life. People with convictions like that shouldn't be police officers. During the hiring process I was interviewed by an officer from Personnel Division who queried me on what I thought about using deadly force.

"OK, Mike. Here's the deal. Some guy pulls a gun on you or your partner. Are you going to blow him out of the tub or what?"

I was rather surprised at his frank and rather colorfully worded question. My response was simple. "I don't think I'd have a problem doing that. It doesn't seem like you'd have much choice."

AFTER I'D BEEN A LOS ANGELES police officer for about a year and a half, I fell in love with a young woman who lived in the Midwest. I decided it would be easier to convince her to marry me if I moved there, so I left the LAPD, taking a job with a small police force near her hometown.

One terrible night a help call was broadcast. When my partner and I arrived, we found a state police officer murdered by sniper fire from an extremist group. Ironically, we had just had coffee with the trooper and his partner only a few minutes before. Less than fifteen minutes after I had held his lifeless body in my arms and laid him on the ground next to his police car, I was involved in a shooting. Armed with a police-issue twelve-gauge shotgun, I killed one of the suspects wanted in connection with the officer's murder. No event was more pivotal in my entire police career. In one brief period I saw what those police officers who answered Officer Scebbi's help call saw and understood firsthand what the use of deadly force was like.

I remember having the suspect in my sights and thinking, This is it. A tremendous flame came from the shotgun barrel, but there was no sound, no feeling of the shotgun's recoil against my shoulder. It was as though the events were happening in slow motion. My conscious thought was not to kill the suspect but only to stop his flight as well as protect my own life. Officers congratulated me immediately after the shooting, but I didn't feel like a hero.

On my way home later, I drove by children playing outside and people on their way to work this bright summer morning. How could it all look so normal when everything had changed for me? I felt dirty. I don't really know if it was the murder of the police officer or the shooting of the suspect that made me feel this way.

Now the innocent question often asked by citizens—"Have you ever used your gun, Officer?"—became very intrusive. As often as not, my response would be, "No, I haven't."

MOST OFFICER-INVOLVED SHOOTINGS, usually shortened to *OIS*, weren't like mine and weren't like Scebbi's. By the time I made sergeant, I'd been to many OIS scenes. As a police officer you just follow the directions of your sergeant or the shooting team. The shooting team for most of my career was headed up by Lieutenant Charles Higbie. As a sergeant at the scene of an officer-involved shooting, you would deal directly with the investigators, and that meant dealing with Lieutenant Higbie. He commanded the scene with absolute power, regardless of anyone's rank. At an OIS, Higbie wasn't a lieutenant; he had the authority of the chief of police, and everyone knew it—or so you thought.

A CENTRAL DETECTIVE RECEIVED a call that a natural death had occurred. It was a little unusual because the call came to the homicide room. The friend of the victim telephoned in the news about an older man who had just passed away, probably because of a heart attack. The caller was understandably distraught over the loss of his best friend. No problem. Homicide detective Rodgers would go to the scene, take the appropriate report, have the coroner pick up the body, and that would be that.

When Rodgers arrived, he parked in front of the hotel on Eleventh Street and went in. "Someone call about a man who died?" he asked a man standing in the hall next to the front lobby.

"I did. He's down here. He was my friend." Without warning, the man produced a pistol and fired two shots, one striking the detective in the chest and the second in his arm. Such a scenario is called "suicide at the hands of the police." Someone wants to kill himself but doesn't have the guts to do it, so he pulls a gun on a police officer, maybe takes a few shots, and the desired result is achieved. Two more shots rang out as the wounded Rodgers managed to remove his gun from its shoulder holster and return fire, killing the man.

Lieutenant Higbie was at the scene before my partner, Frank Long, and I arrived. Higbie was a big man whose look never changed over the years. Short, flat-top haircut, white short-sleeved shirt with a tie, and no jacket. It didn't matter if it was raining or cold; he always dressed the same. Rodgers had already been transported to White Memorial Medical Center for treatment, and the scene secured. Frank and I rounded up witnesses to various portions of the incident so they could be interviewed by the OIS team. We were all standing out on the sidewalk when Commander Hoover arrived at the scene. He had no particular duty there, but in Central Division members of the command staff would frequently visit a shooting scene. Sometimes they had legitimate business, but most of the time they were just curious or playing at being police officers again.

The news media had also arrived, and Commander Hoover was talking with them on the sidewalk. Lieutenant Higbie looked over at Hoover and the newspeople, then back at me. "Excuse me, Officer Middleton. Does Commander Hoover appear to be giving a news conference?"

"Yes, sir, I believe he is."

"Excuse me just a moment."

The cameras were rolling for Hoover's impromptu news conference regarding the officer-involved shooting that Lieutenant Higbie was just beginning to investigate. Higbie walked up behind the commander and for a moment had an incredulous look on his face. He then placed one of his huge hands on the back of Hoover's collar, pulling him backward and out of camera range. "Excuse me, gentlemen. The commander and I have to speak for a moment."

I don't know what Higbie said to Hoover as he walked the commander over to his car, but at that point a furious discussion ensued. Well, not exactly a discussion. Higbie continually pressed his forefinger into Hoover's chest as he talked, making the slightly built commander recoil with each jab. When Higbie was finished, he turned and walked away from the commander, who simply got into his car and drove away. Higbie approached the newspeople and said, "I'll be about thirty more minutes, and then I'll be happy to give you a real news conference regarding this incident." That night on the evening news only Higbie appeared on camera.

WHILE ASSIGNED TO NEWTON DIVISION as a young patrol officer, I was to learn firsthand what it feels like when death really is close enough to touch.

"Mike, after roll call we're going down and hit the Pill Palace [so named because of the large volume of illicit sodium secobarbital pills sold there]. Couple of our guys got jumped yesterday when you were off, and one's still in the hospital."

"Sounds good to me, Ben. What're we going to do?"

"We're going to meet with a couple of other units, swoop in, FI everybody standing out in front, and run 'em for warrants. If anybody goes inside the restaurant, we'll bring 'em back out and FI them too."

I already had a bitter taste in my mouth about this location. It was the same place where my partner had told other officers I was a coward when I didn't get out of the police car first. I hadn't forgotten that incident.

After roll call Ben and I went code six at the Pill Palace along with two other units. There was usually a crowd in front, and this night was no exception. We parked our patrol car in a gas station lot immediately adjacent to the restaurant. As we walked down the sidewalk, several people were moving in our direction. Other officers had come in from the opposite side, and the crowd was drifting in a northerly direction toward us. I ended up talking to a man in front of the restaurant.

"Come here. I want to talk to you."

"What for? I ain't done nothin'. I'm goin' home."

"Yeah, maybe. Come here. I want to talk to you." Standing behind him, I started to pat him down for weapons.

When you search a suspect for weapons, you start by having him place his hands behind the back of his head, legs spread apart somewhat. First you check the wrist area, move to the armpits, then you check the chest area, moving the hands down to the waistband, around to the small of the back, then the crotch area, and finally down each leg to the shoes.

When I got to his waistband, the suspect's hand immediately came from the back of his head to his waist. He was armed with a .25 automatic pistol tucked into his belt, and he planned to use it.

"He's got a gun!" I yelled. I held both my hands on his weapon. I felt a pull on the right side of my Sam Browne as he moved his right hand back to my six-inch .38 service revolver, trying to yank it from the holster. Suddenly he jerked hard on my gun. The stitching on the holster's backside began to rip, but fortunately my weapon didn't come out. I moved my right hand to my weapon, feeling the suspect's hand on my pistol grip as I tried to pry his hand from my gun. Another officer came face-to-face with the suspect and hit him squarely in the jaw with a force that was so great it knocked both the suspect and me to the sidewalk.

"I'm gonna kill you, you motherfucker! I'm gonna kill you!" he hissed in my face. We were lying on the sidewalk, our faces no more than three inches apart. His hand had moved from my gun back to his own weapon. There were four hands on that .25 automatic, and at one point he had a slight edge. The gun was now pointed directly into my stomach, but I had my hand over the trigger guard, which kept him from shooting me. Then I turned it back into his stomach, but I couldn't get my finger on the trigger. If I'd been successful, I fully intended to shoot him with his own gun.

Ben came out of nowhere and dropped, knee first, onto the suspect's head. The blow only temporarily dazed the man, but it made him loosen one of his hands gripping the gun. Now I had a chance to use my right hand, and with a tremendous swing I took aim at his face. His head jerked back, my fist missed, and it went squarely into the sidewalk, but I felt no pain. Raising the same hand, I tried again and slammed the side of my fist into his mouth as though I were striking a desk in anger. His upper and lower front teeth caved in; his other hand returned to his weapon, which was now back into the pit of my stomach. Again Ben dropped, knees first, into the suspect's head. This time it had no effect at all.

"Ben, shoot this fucking guy!"

"I'm afraid I'll hit you!" Down came Ben again, with a thundering blow from both knees into the suspect's head. This did the trick. The suspect was momentarily unconscious. For the first time I took control of his gun. It was fully loaded with a round in the chamber. There was no safety on the weapon and could have been fired at any moment.

This was the first time I came really close to being killed or critically wounded. It was also the first time I knew what having a partner really meant. When I was in trouble, he was there. It would have been easier for him to reach down and pop this guy in the head with a round, but he didn't because he was afraid of injuring me. Ben was in danger, too. If I'd lost control of the weapon, I would have been the first one shot and Ben the second. I was Ben's partner and depended on him. He in turn relied on me. That night we came through for ourselves and each other.

No charges were ever filed against the suspect, who was arrested for the attempted murder of a police officer. The district attorney explained that filing charges would be a waste of time. In the struggle the suspect had sustained irreversible and significant brain damage and ended up little more than a vegetable, confined to a wheelchair.

It easily could have been me confined to a wheelchair, paralyzed for life from a bullet wound. My partner, the young man with a gun, or I could have been killed. I had learned a valuable lesson on that sidewalk on South Avalon. From that moment on I knew how serious police work could really be. If you weren't careful, it could be deadly serious.

ONE PARTICULAR MORNING WATCH shift in Newton Division, a thick fog was making its way north, settling over the whole area. On nights like this the air [radio transmissions] was very quiet. I'm not sure if the criminals didn't want to venture out or if it was just good sleeping weather.

Unit 13-A-11 was traveling northbound on Central Avenue, passing the Veterans Club in the 2100 block of the street. The Veterans Club was not for veterans and wasn't a club. It was more commonly known as the "shine parlor," but I never saw anyone getting shoes shined there. In reality it was little more than a gambling den. Vice made dozens of arrests over the years before the place was finally shut down using an old law called *red light abatement*. Originally this law allowed the police to get rid of houses of prostitution by literally having the court order the building leveled. However, you had to have a significant track record of criminal activity before this drastic step was taken.

Working A-11 was my longtime friend C. W. Carrington and Mike Dominguez, a young and very talented police officer. As they drove by the shine parlor, C.W. saw a man in the phone booth in front of the establishment and chuckled.

"Mike, look. There's a sore loser. I'll bet he's stiffin' in a phony 211 call so he can get his money back."

Carrington and Dominguez continued on their way to Newton Station, but as they pulled into the station parking lot, their plans were interrupted.

"All units, and 13-Adam-11. 211 in progress at the Veterans Club, 2135 South Central. 13-Adam-11, handle the call code three."

"13-A-11, roger." Carrington believed they were probably answering a phony call. Several other units also began to respond to the location. I was among them.

C.W. parked the police car about a hundred feet north of the club. The two officers walked cautiously down the sidewalk toward the front door of the shine parlor. C.W. spoke to three men standing together about fifty feet north of the club entrance.

"Anything going on in the shine parlor?"

One man responded. "No, man. Ain't nothin' happenin' in there." The trio then bolted past the two officers. Things were different now. Thoughts of a stiffed-in call evaporated.

Carrington moved out into the street, walking near the cars parked next to the curb so he could use them for cover if needed. Dominguez had armed himself with a shotgun as he left the police car and continued down the sidewalk, staying close to the buildings.

Suddenly the door of the club opened, and two men came out. They turned and walked directly toward Dominguez. One had a shotgun, the other a revolver. When they saw the officer, they turned and ran in the opposite direction. Quickly they rounded the southernmost corner of the club and disappeared into the fog.

Neither officer gave chase but proceeded cautiously toward the front door of the club. No cars were parked directly in front of it, and C.W. was now exposed should another suspect depart. The door swung open, and out stepped a third robbery suspect. He was armed with a sawed-off shotgun and, upon observing C.W., leveled the weapon, ready to shoot the officer. C.W.'s weapon had been directed toward the corner of the building where the suspects had fled. Now he whirled to the right, preparing to engage the armed suspect.

Mike Dominguez's shotgun discharged with a thunderous blast, shooting the suspect in that split second before the man was able to shoot C.W. Simultaneously C.W. had taken aim and fired one round that struck the suspect just after the shotgun pellets found their mark. Miraculously, the suspect did not return fire, but retreated back into the club and closed the door.

C.W. got out his ROVER and broadcast, "13-Adam-11. Officers need help. 2135 South Central. Shots fired."

"All units. Officers need help. Shots fired. 2135 South Central. . . ."

As quickly as the shooting had started it was over, and Carrington and Dominguez were again alone on the sidewalk, waiting for more officers to arrive before entering the shine parlor to search for the shootist. In the interim Carrington decided to pursue the two original suspects who had run around the corner. When he got to the corner of the building, C.W. could see no trace of them.

"13-A-11. Two additional suspects have fled westbound on the south side of the shine parlor. . . ." C.W. continued to broadcast a description of both men.

Additional units arrived and positioned themselves east of the shine parlor and began to search on foot. Almost immediately a second shooting erupted. Another officer saw one of the suspects and fired a round at him but missed.

There were still customers inside; the robbers had forced them to strip and then stolen their valuables. The officers outside ordered people to get dressed and come out one at a time through the front door. Extreme caution was called for since the wounded suspect was still inside. It was very probable that the exiting victims would not identify the robber for fear of being shot. All the males who came out were being viewed as potential suspects even though they were being treated as victims. We had only a very basic description of the suspect and what he was wearing, but clothing descriptions can be unreliable; it's easy for a suspect to change clothes.

Mike Dominguez, who had his shotgun at port arms position, was standing in front of the door as the victims exited. I parked my car and moved over by him along with several officers who were watching the people come out one by one. About a dozen people had exited when a woman yelled, "That's one of 'em! That's one of the men that robbed me!" She was pointing at a man just approaching Mike Dominguez.

The man she pointed to was acting very nonchalant and showed no signs of his multiple gunshot wounds. He was heading away from the group when the woman's voice rang out. The man quickened his pace, and instantly Dominguez butt-stroked him across the jaw with a shotgun. Down he went and was handcuffed before he knew what had happened. He had switched clothing with one of the victims thinking he'd get by the officers outside but hadn't counted on such a vocal witness.

A short time later the officer-involved shooting team arrived, headed by Lieutenant Higbie.

"Sergeant, are you in charge?"

"Yes, sir."

"And you are . . ."

"Sergeant Middleton."

"Names and serial numbers of the officers involved?"

The lieutenant delivered a rapid-fire series of

questions about the officers and the crime scene. I was beginning to feel pretty good about the whole thing. It was my first OIS as a sergeant, and I hoped Higbie thought I knew what I was doing. Then he asked me a question I was fairly sure I knew the answer to and responded.

"I think they were—"

"Sergeant, I don't care what you *think*. I don't want to know what you think. I want to know only what you *know*. Do you understand?"

"Just a moment, Lieutenant. I'll get the answer."

"Very good, Sergeant. That's what we need, the answer."

I would encounter Lieutenant Higbie many times over the ensuing years, and he never had to remind me again about knowing the answer. He was a total professional and earned my immense respect and admiration. Even if he chewed someone's ass, the next sentence always seemed to be encouraging. If you earned his praise, it meant something. He wanted you to do well, and he wanted to make you a better preliminary investigator at the shooting scene. He certainly did that for me.

"ALL UNITS. OFFICER NEEDS HELP. Shots fired. Officer down." There are no more horrendous words on the air than these.

It was early in the evening, and I was assigned to Newton mid-P.M. watch—strictly rock and roll all night long. You hit the streets at 6:30 P.M. and were out until 2:30 A.M, the busiest time period to answer calls for service. About 8:00 one night as I was southbound on Central at Slauson, those dreaded words came over the radio.

It took me about ninety seconds to respond to the call, and by the time I arrived, several units had already gone code six at the location. The fire truck and ambulance were parked a few doors down the block. The officers had taken up a position behind a police car positioned in front of a house next to where the call was. They had their guns drawn and pointed toward the house. I ran in a crouched position from my car to join them.

"What's up?"

"It's Puis. He's down, in there."

"Who's in there with him?"

"A couple of units are searching the house. We think the suspect fled, but we're not sure yet. Don't know if anyone else is with Puis yet."

The answer came over the radio from an officer inside. "All units. The location is secure, and we need an ambulance. We have one officer down."

The waiting paramedics heard that transmission and ran for the front door, carrying their emergency medical cases with them. The fire fighters immediately retrieved the gurney from the ambulance and followed them into the house. I wasn't far behind.

Officer John Puis was in the kitchen, lying on his back on the dirty linoleum floor. The room was bare, devoid of any furniture; the smell of rancid cooking oil hung heavy in the air. Scanning the room with my flashlight, I could see cockroaches hugging the wall along the floor. All of us were on our hands and knees, waiting for words of encouragement from the paramedics—words that would tell us John was going to be all right.

Puis and his partner, Donald Tinsdale, had gone to the house with another unit and Sergeant Joe Van Fleet for a "violent male mental." A young woman had called about her brother. He had ongoing mental problems and had assaulted their mother earlier in the day over the use of the family car. He had tried to strangle her when she refused to give him the keys.

The sister contacted the psychiatrist at Los Angeles County General Hospital who had been treating her brother and told him what happened. The doctor immediately said that her brother should be admitted. His sister hoped to transport him to the hospital herself but wanted the officers to be there to help out if problems arose.

"Where's your brother now?"

"I think Joe's sitting out on the screened porch."

"Does he have any guns? Are there any guns in the house?"

"Definitely not, officer. We don't have any."

The four officers walked down the driveway to the back of the house while Sergeant Van Fleet remained with the woman. When they reached the porch, the officers called to him.

"Hey, Joe, come on out. We want to talk to you."

"Fuck you! I'm not going anywhere."

One of the officers tried to open the screen door, but it was latched. As he looked onto the porch, he could see Joe standing in the shadows.

"He's naked and holding something. Looks like a broom or maybe a rifle."

Officer Puis heard only the reference to a broom and was unaware the man might be armed. The officers forced open the porch door as Joe retreated inside the darkened house. As Puis ran into the kitchen, he heard the slam of a door that led into an adjacent bedroom. Hot on the suspect's trail, John had his gun out and ready in his right hand. He decided to kick open the bedroom door.

Standing in the dark, Joe was waiting, a .22-caliber bolt-action rifle at his shoulder and pointing directly at Officer Puis. At the exact moment the door was forced open, Joe fired one round, hitting Puis in the right shoulder. It was as though he'd been struck with the full force of a baseball bat. His right arm became useless, and his weapon dropped to the kitchen floor. Wounded, he maneuvered himself against the wall for support while he tried to collect his thoughts and figure out what had just happened.

"I've been hit, but I'm OK," Puis yelled to the other officers. Puis didn't want any other officers running into the room. He thought the suspect was pinned down in the bedroom, because he couldn't see another exit. With great effort Puis picked up his gun from the floor with his left hand and decided to use the stove for cover.

The room was almost black, and John counted on the cover darkness would give him as he moved into position. He focused his attention totally on the door, not realizing that a nearby street lamp cast dim illumination through the kitchen window. Faint light, but enough to give Joe a clear outline of his target. Joe took aim and fired again.

The bullet entered Puis's neck and traversed through his body, ultimately slamming into his spine, producing instant and total paralysis from his chest down. Puis dropped to the floor.

"I'm hit again. Don't come in. He's in here. I'll try to come out myself." Puis was sure that if another officer entered the kitchen he would likely be shot by the suspect, not realizing Joe had fled into the night. The paralysis started to subside, so that by sliding backward Puis was able to retrieve his gun, put it on his chest, and start inching toward the door. His strength fading fast, Puis could move no farther and stopped near the kitchen door.

The first time I saw Puis, I thought he was dead. His eyes were partially open, and he wasn't moving. Very quietly I asked one of the officers in the kitchen how it looked. I didn't want John to hear me. He responded, "He doesn't look good, but just a second ago they asked him a question, and he didn't sound bad."

The paramedics were working rapidly but not frantically on Puis. The bullet in his shoulder was probably not too much to worry about since there was an exit wound. The bullet in the neck was another matter. It was still in there. The bullets probably hadn't traveled ten feet before striking Puis, so they hit with maximum power. The paramedics placed a pressure suit on him and inflated it. Developed during the Vietnam War, this device envelops both legs so that, when inflated, the pressure forces the blood from the legs up into the torso, giving an emergency blood supply.

"OK. Everybody move in close. We're going to put him on the backboard, then the stretcher. I want two guys on each leg. We have to be real careful lifting him. Don't know where one bullet is, and we don't want it to move." The paramedic in charge made sure each officer was properly positioned. The idea was to lift Puis yet keep him immobile. It was crucial his body didn't move, because the bullet could shift with catastrophic results. Everyone did a spectacular job. Puis never showed any sign of discomfort as he was moved to the board and then onto the stretcher. Even as he was taken out of the house, the officers handled the stretcher so gently it seemed to float to the ambulance.

"Who's going with us?" the paramedic asked.

"I will."

"OK, Sarge, you'll have to ride up front because we're going to be pretty busy back here."

I must have looked very worried, because the paramedic added, "Look, all his vital signs look real good. I don't think anything major has been hit. Why don't you tell him you're going with him?"

I looked into the back of the ambulance. Puis was staring directly at me, and I tried to sound reassuring. "You're gonna be OK. I'm going with you, but I've got to ride in the front. It's too crowded back here."

Los Angeles County General Hospital is huge and the emergency room constantly busy. It took us about fifteen minutes to pull up to the ER entrance at the rear of the hospital. As we left the shooting scene, the paramedic who was driving radioed the hospital, advising them they had a police officer who had been shot twice. The medical staff was ready.

A doctor and two nurses came running through the large double doors as soon as the ambulance came to a halt. This was the first time I had ever seen medical staff come out to meet the ambulance.

The gurney from the ambulance was out and Puis on his way to emergency almost the instant we stopped. I had to run to catch up with them. The doctor was assessing the wounds on the run. Puis still had his uniform shirt on, forcing the doctor to pull aside the clothing to look at the shoulder wound.

Inside the emergency room is a central area separated by curtains where the most seriously injured receive initial treatment. Once inside, the curtains close, and the real work begins.

"OK, everyone. You, too, Sergeant. Grab hold. We're going to leave the officer on the backboard and move him over to this gurney. Everyone ready? OK! Now!" Instantly Puis was transferred to the larger hospital gurney.

"Nurse, cut this shirt off. Don't move him. Cut the uniform belt, too."

"Doctor, just a moment. I think we can just undo the belt without any difficulty, and I'll pull the holster off and we can slide the belt off. It'll be easier, and we won't ruin his equipment."

"Sergeant, I don't care what you do! Get it off, now!"

Another man lying on a gurney nearby apparently had been receiving treatment prior to our arrival. He seemed to have some sort of cut that had already been sutured closed. "Hey, what about me? What's gonna happen to me? I been cut! Doc! Doctor—"

"You, shut your mouth!" The doctor barked. "Understand?" The doctor was all business, focusing on the police officer, who needed him more. Nothing more was heard.

Clearly the doctor's attention was on the neck wound. You could tell only where the bullet had entered, but it could have gone anywhere inside the body. Puis was having some difficulty breathing, which made the doctor believe that the bullet may have lodged in the lungs.

"Sergeant, you're going to have to step outside now." The nurse who appeared to be in charge spoke in a matter-of-fact tone.

"No, I'm not. I'm not going anywhere unless he goes somewhere, and if he does, I'm going with him. He's my officer, and I'm not leaving him. I won't be in your way."

The doctor spoke without looking up from his work on Puis. He was in another world. "Officer, when I press here, do you feel any pain?" Puis shook his head slightly. "Don't move your head. Can you talk? Sergeant, you can stay."

"Yes." Puis's response was soft. Even that short word seemed labored.

After about five minutes, Puis was taken to x-ray. "Sergeant, just a moment. I want to talk to you." The doctor stopped me from following Puis. "I know you're really worried about your man, but I don't think the bullet's in his neck. It's somewhere in the upper chest. He seems pretty stable, but until we know where that bullet's resting, we've got to be very, very careful. It could be resting against something, and if he moves, it could be bad."

The x-rays confirmed the doctor's suspicion but not his worst fear. The bullet had traveled from the neck down to the thoracic (chest) cavity, nicking the edge of one of Puis's lungs, and come to rest against his spine. As the doctor and x-ray technician peered at the white screen, the doctor exclaimed, "Do you believe it? I think that bullet had eyes! It missed all the important stuff."

From there we went upstairs to a ward devoted exclusively to gunshot and knife wounds. The emergency room staff had done its job well. The new team of doctors was concerned about the amount of blood inside Puis's upper chest revealed in the x-rays. Surgery to remove the bullet couldn't begin until his chest cavity was clear. The only way to alleviate this condition was to place a chest tube in him, suction off the blood, and monitor the subsequent flow.

I had seen several people who needed chest tubes, but I'd never seen one put into a conscious person. These doctors were experts at treating this type of injury and wasted no time in preparing for the procedure.

"Officer, what's your first name?"

I responded before Puis had a chance. "John."

"John, we're going to put a chest tube in you so we can pull off the fluid that's in there. It'll look like it's all blood, but it's not. There's not a tremendous amount, but it'll help you breathe easier. You're having a little difficulty breathing now, I can tell. I want you to understand we can't give you an anesthetic because it'll affect your breathing. I'm going to cut very quickly, and we're going to put the tube in. It's going to seem like you can't breathe, but you will be able to breathe throughout the procedure. You're going to be just fine. We've done a lot of these."

I bent down next to John and talked quietly to him. "John, don't worry. These guys really know what they're doing. I'll be right here. Grab hold of my arm. I'm not going to let them do anything I think will hurt you."

Two doctors then positioned themselves on Puis's right side. One had a scalpel and the other a forceps-type instrument clamped around a rubber tube that was so long it looked as though you could have inserted it about eight to ten inches into the chest.

"OK, John. We've got to do this now. It's going to hurt, but it'll be over very quickly. Hold on to the sergeant's hand." Before Puis could grasp my hand, the first cut was made, and he grabbed my right arm just above the wrist. The doctor made several rapid cuts through the wall of Puis's chest, about five inches below the armpit. Puis winced as each cut was made and let out a low groan. As soon as the chest cavity was pierced, a stream of blood an inch thick shot out over the doctor and onto the floor. Puis began to gasp.

"I can't breathe! Oh, God, I can't breathe! Mike!"

"Officer, you are breathing. You *can* breathe. If you couldn't breathe, you couldn't talk." The doctor's matter-of-fact tone was meant to reassure not only Puis but me. The forceps were inserted, and Puis was past groaning. He screamed. I was sure he'd pass out, but he didn't. His grasp on my wrist tightened so much I thought my bones would snap. The doctor with the forceps lifted the lungs to make sure the tube was on the bottom of the chest cavity so that all the fluid would be sucked out. Puis's eyes were staring straight up, his mouth open as though he wanted to speak but couldn't. Maybe he wanted to be able to take a deep breath but couldn't get any air. He looked so frightened.

The forceps were withdrawn, and immediately one of the nurses swabbed the area around the opening where the tube had been inserted with Betadine. Several layers of white adhesive tape were applied to hold the tube in place as well as seal the opening. The lungs function because of negative pressure inside the chest cavity, so when the machine was turned on and the suction took effect, Puis's lungs were instantly able to inflate fully, and very quickly he began to breathe normally. As fast as the painful procedure had begun, it ended, and his viselike grip on my wrist eased. At about the same time the chest tube was inserted into John Puis, the suspect was apprehended following a second shoot-out less than a block away from the original scene.

After about twenty minutes Puis started to drift off to sleep. I pulled a chair up next to the gurney and watched him for a long time. I don't know when the procedure started or stopped or what time he fell asleep, but I felt as though I had to stay and watch just in case.

I don't remember falling asleep in the chair, but I woke up at about 6:00 A.M. and discovered someone had covered me with a hospital blanket. Puis was still sleeping. I telephoned the station and told them everything was going well.

Following what seemed to be just a brief period of recuperation, John Puis returned to work, fully recovered. He was later awarded the Medal of Valor for his selfless actions that night.

WHEN A POLICE OFFICER IS SERIOUSLY wounded, the effect on officers at the scene is significant. As a supervisor, I had to train officers to be aware of this in an attempt to minimize its effect. One time a television news crew recorded an entire SWAT (Special Weapons Assault Team) operation during which an officer was critically wounded. That news footage was incorporated into the ongoing roll call training program at Newton Division.

The SWAT team was on the second-floor landing of a house, preparing to make entry, when suddenly the suspect burst through the door, butcher knife in hand, and attempted to sink it into one of the officers. Instantly a shooting ensued, and a SWAT officer was struck by a bullet that had already passed through the suspect. He slumped over and tumbled down a long wooden stairway in full view of many officers.

The news camera caught not only his fall but also the reactions of the other officers. For a brief moment officers were more concerned with the wounded officer than with the fact that additional suspects could still be inside. The traumatic impact of the officer's injury extended much beyond him. The whole group was affected, and that's usually what happens.

"PETE, YOU'VE GOT A RIDE-ALONG tonight. Some guy who's ready to go to the academy. Personnel Division sent him here."

The P.M. watch lieutenant seemed to enjoy giving Sergeant Pete Durham the news. Durham and I were both assigned to the A.M. watch and on our way to roll call. This lieutenant rarely left the station, but he knew how much Pete and I enjoyed being in the field. I sensed that the lieutenant felt he had put a damper on Pete's evening.

"Yeah, sure. Just have him wait down here. We'll be out of roll call in about fifteen or twenty minutes."

We had ride-alongs regularly on Newton morning

watch. It was popular because it was a busy division, and the sergeants were all active in the field. Usually a ride-along was a friend, a relation, or sometimes an officer's spouse who wanted to get a firsthand look. This, however, was the first time I'd ever seen a ride-along sent by Personnel Division.

After roll call Pete met the ride-along, filled out the necessary paperwork, then introduced him to me as Pete and I were riding together that shift. The ride-along seemed like a nice enough guy, anxious for a taste of patrol.

After we checked out our car and shotgun, the three of us left the station. I picked up the mike and advised communications of our status. "13-L-20 and 13-L-40 are clear. Control One be advised I will be with L-20." Even though we were in the same vehicle, as far as communications was concerned we were two separate units.

"13-L-40. Roger." The RTO continued to broadcast. "All units and any Newton unit available to handle in Hollenbeck [Division]. Officer needs help. Shots fired. Officers down."

"L-20 and L-40 responding."

"13-L-20 and 40 roger, and be advised. An ambulance is en route to the scene code three."

This was important information. The last thing you wanted to do was collide with the ambulance when you were driving the police car. You could never hear another emergency vehicle even if its siren was activated.

As we arrived at the scene, one officer was down in the roadway with the paramedics working on him. He seemed to be in a lot of pain. My immediate reaction was that this was good. It meant that he was still alive and conscious.

We parked adjacent to the ambulance. One look at the kid's eyes in the backseat, and I knew our ride-along was staying in the car. As I bailed out, I gave him his instructions. "Stay in here until we know what we've got."

Both officers were wounded but not seriously. They had been on patrol in a tough project apartment complex; in fact only a few blocks away Officer Jerry Maddox had been killed in a similar situation. These two officers had seen some juveniles acting suspiciously and decided to stop them to see what was going on.

The Pico-Aliso housing project was built in the early 1960s. The intent of this development and others like it was to make available low-cost housing that was different from the eastern slum scenario. Unintended by-products of the projects were a high crime rate and plentiful drugs. Hollenbeck officers weren't strangers here. Calls for service by the public were a regular occurrence; even calls from officers requesting assistance or help there weren't unusual.

As soon as the officers got out of their car, one of the juveniles opened fire with a handgun. Both officers were hit, and the shooter and his friends ran. Even though no Hollenbeck units were clear to be assigned the call, several heard the help call and interrupted their work to respond. Witnesses supplied the Hollenbeck units with a description of the suspects and the direction in which they had fled.

When Pete and I arrived, a Hollenbeck sergeant was already at the scene. I knew him from my early days in Newton Division, where he'd been a senior officer. He was pathetic. The sergeant was walking around from officer to officer as they arrived, writing down their names in his field officer's notebook. Two officers down at the scene, suspects outstanding, he's the only supervisor at the scene from his division, and the best he could do was write down the names of responding officers. His actions exemplified the very thing we constantly trained to avoid. He had lost control and was no longer a leader. It was embarrassing. At that moment I felt like putting him in the backseat with our ride-along. He was about that much use.

Pete and I had been to many officer-involved shooting calls and knew exactly what to do. Pete ensured that the transportation of the wounded officers to the hospital went smoothly and that a Hollenbeck officer went with them. Meanwhile, I went up the block and found some officers outside an apartment unit where one of the suspects had just been taken into custody.

An angry crowd had gathered, taunting the officers, who didn't seem to know how to handle the throng. As I was getting information about the arrested suspect, Pete approached, yelling, "OK, everybody, let's form a skirmish [straight] line and move these people back." Pete and I had dodged rocks and bottles before, and I'm sure he was concerned that if the crowd wasn't dispersed, sooner or later someone would find something to throw at us. "If anyone resists, place them under arrest, and I'll sign the booking approval."

An officer from Newton who had also responded to the help call approached me with some information. "Sergeant Middleton. Some Hollenbeck guys are upstairs searching, if you know what I mean." I knew just what he meant. If a warrantless search found the one piece of evidence linking this suspect to the shooting, it would be inadmissible in court, and the suspect would walk. An otherwise good case might be trashed by the actions of these officers. Immediately I went into the apartment. In the upstairs bedroom the officers had every drawer out and on the floor, mattresses flipped over, and clothes pulled from the closet. One officer was even removing the electrical switch plates from the wall.

"Wait, wait, wait. Guys, hold on—"

"What do you mean, hold on, Sarge? We've got one of the fuckin' shooters. This is where he lives. We're gonna find the gun."

"I couldn't agree with you more, but let's back out of here. Leave everything alone. Anyone found any evidence?"

"No, not yet."

"Good. Close up the apartment and let the shooting team and detectives conduct a proper investigation. I don't want that fuckin' asshole cut loose any more than you guys do, but let's do it right. Do we know for sure there aren't any other suspects in this apartment unit?"

"Yeah, every room's been checked."

"Come on, guys. Let's go." I knew they didn't like it, but it was the right thing to do, whether we found evidence or not. I'd seen this type of situation before; the fact that two of their fellow officers had just been shot had caused them to change the way they did police work.

IT'S VERY FRIGHTENING TO SEE AN OFFICER who's been shot. You know it could have been you. I saw many officers shot, and the impact never lessened over the years. It makes you realize how deadly serious police business can be.

My wife and I were watching the feature story on the late news—the funeral procession of Jack Evans, a motorcycle officer killed in the line of duty. I was working Central Division morning watch and preparing to leave for work.

"I hope I never have to do a death notification on

a police officer killed in the line of duty. That job always seems to go to the officer's sergeant."

Sometimes we don't get what we hope for.

About two and a half hours later I was having coffee with Sergeant Steve Allen, who was working the neighboring division, when a rather innocuous call came out. "Any Central supervisor available to responded to a CPI [city property-involved] traffic [accident] at College and North Broadway."

"See you later, Mike."

"OK. 1-L-50. I'll handle the call."

"L-50, roger. Respond code two."

When I said I'd handle the call, in my mind I visualized this traffic accident would be an off-duty detective involved in a collision after an evening of drinking in Chinatown. College and North Broadway was only a few blocks from a favorite police hangout.

I drove up Sunset Boulevard a few blocks and made a right turn onto North Broadway. As I did so, I could see a Los Angeles city fire department ambulance in the distance. A block away from the call, flares were laid out, blocking off traffic. The ambulance was parked facing south in the northbound lane, and its headlights blocked any view of the intersection. I parked the police car a short distance away from the ambulance and walked around it into the street. I caught a glimpse of two cars, one a black-and-white police car, and thought, Oh, a uniformed officer's involved in the accident. However, no broadcast had been made by anybody that one of our patrol cars was involved in an accident.

The far side of the police car appeared to be significantly damaged, but before I really started to inspect it, something caught my eye that didn't seem to fit. I was out of the glare of the ambulance lights, and there in the street was a white object only a few feet away from the open passenger door. I looked into the police car and saw a second white object. The driver of the police car was slumped over and partially covered by a sheet. Papers were scattered everywhere around the car. I couldn't bring myself to look at the face of either officer; not yet anyway.

There on the street was a three-ring binder. It was open, and I could tell it was a partially completed DFAR (daily field activity report). I reached down to pick it up and read the names. "Oh, Lord, no. It's Arthur." Officer Arthur Soo Hoo was the passenger; Officer William Wong had been the driver. I'd known Arthur since he graduated from the police academy. I was acquainted with his partner but didn't know him personally the way I did Arthur.

They had been assigned to Detective Headquarters Division, working a Chinese gang detail. Soo Hoo had ties to the neighborhood; his family ran a laundry barely a block from that intersection. Sitting on the curb next to the fallen officer was a young man. He spoke to me in Spanish.

"I was here when it happened. I ran over, picked him up, and held him close to me. Looking at me, he said, 'Help me! Help me! Oh, God, help me!' Then he didn't move anymore. I couldn't believe a police officer had just been killed. I wanted to help him, but it was too late."

The young man had blood all over the front of his shirt. As he finished telling me what happened, he shook his head and began to cry.

"I know you tried. Thank you. Please, sit down right here and wait for me. I'll be back."

"I just wanted to help him," he replied softly.

It was apparent that no one at the Central watch commander's office knew what had just happened. With information as sensitive as this you would always use a telephone instead of broadcasting it over the radio. There was a Gamewell [police telephone] box at the intersection, and as I headed across the street to use it, a paramedic walked up to me.

"Sergeant, we were the first ones here. Both officers were gone when we arrived, and we pronounced them [dead]. I've already called for more units, and my captain'll be here soon. I'm awfully sorry."

I thanked him with a wordless nod and dialed the station number.

"Watch commander's office."

"This is Middleton. I'm at College and North Broadway. Do you know what we have here?"

"No. An accident, right?"

"We have two dead police officers."

The desk officer didn't even set the phone down as he yelled to the watch commander, "Lieutenant! Lieutenant! Two officers have been killed at College and North Broadway!" I could hear the footsteps of the watch commander as he ran from the office to his car.

"Mike, the lieutenant's on his way." Within two minutes Central watch commander had arrived at the scene.

According to several witnesses, Officers Wong and Soo Hoo had been driving east on College and were turning left onto North Broadway. They entered the intersection on a green light and were broadsided by another car careening south on Broadway. An investigation would determine that the impact speed was more than eighty-five miles per hour.

This wasn't just an accident. These men were fleeing from a drug transaction gone wrong. Incredibly, the suspects were not seriously injured, and after the accident they had continued their flight on foot, leaving their disabled vehicle behind. One officer was dead and the other dying. Only one person had attempted to stop the felons: the young man seated on the curb with blood on his shirt and tears streaming down his cheeks. I returned to talk to him, our only known witness.

"Tell me what happened."

"When I saw the crash, I ran over to the police car, and I tried to help the officer. Then he died. I was so mad that I ran to the other car and grabbed the man who was driving. Other people were here by then and standing in the street, just staring. I was fighting with this man, and I called for someone to help me, but nobody came. The other men in the car pulled the driver away from me, and they ran away. I couldn't stop them all by myself; I tried."

It had been approximately an hour since the officers were scheduled to go end of watch, and family notifications would have to be made immediately. William Wong was divorced, but Arthur Soo Hoo's wife would doubtless be worried when her husband didn't arrive home on time and didn't telephone to say he was working over. As plans were being made for family notifications, I noticed a Chinese couple standing on the corner. The lady called me over.

"Excuse me, Sergeant, my nephew's a police officer, Arthur Soo Hoo. He works in Chinatown and always comes by to check on us at the end of his shift, but he didn't come by tonight. I'm worried about him. Who are the poor officers in the car? Are they all right? That car looks like Arthur's."

What a shock to have Soo Hoo family members at the scene. I knew the laundry was only a short distance away, but I really didn't think that a death notification would be made within fifty feet of the dead officer still lying in the roadway.

"Just a minute, ma'am. I'll have to see who this car was checked out to."

"Thank you, Sergeant. My husband and I will wait right here." The man and woman stood together, she stoically clutching her purse in front of her chest and he with his hands by his side. Looking at them, I somehow believed that they already knew the truth in their hearts and that I was stalling for time.

Walking away, I crossed the street and approached the lieutenant. "You're not going to believe this, but Soo Hoo's aunt and uncle are standing over there. They own a laundry just up the street. Soo Hoo always comes by to check on them before he goes end of watch, and that's probably where they were going when they got hit. I'm afraid if we don't tell them, they'll be on the phone to Arthur's wife before we have a chance to talk to her in person. They should be told, and maybe we can take them with us when we tell her."

"OK. Sounds good."

"I'll do it."

"Thanks, Mike."

As I walked back across the street, I knew that when I got to the far corner I was going to tell these people that their nephew had been killed. On many occasions I had notified family members of deaths, but never anything like this. I had no idea what words to choose.

"Ma'am, sir. Please come over here so we can talk. Let's sit here on the [bus] bench." The three of us sat down. I looked into the woman's eyes, and the words came to me. "Something very terrible has happened. Arthur is gone."

"Oh, no! He was just a baby!" she moaned. She began to sob, and her husband put his arms around her as both of them cried together. I got up quietly from the bench, leaving them to grieve privately. Soo Hoo's immediate supervisor arrived, and I advised him that family members were at the scene, they had already been notified of the officer's death, and why.

There were still many duties to perform. This was

a crime scene that had to be protected until photographs were taken and the traffic accident reconstruction team completed its preliminary investigation. Grieving would have to wait.

Chief Daryl Gates also arrived. He stood completely separate from everyone else, reminding me of a sentry guarding the scene, making sure everything was done properly. This wasn't just a fatal traffic accident; these were two Los Angeles police officers killed in the line of duty. That made it different—very different.

The fire captain at the scene approached me. "Sergeant, I'm going to have my men circle the car and hold sheets up while we remove the driver. The shotgun pierced one of his legs, and we may have to sever it to get him out. His head's basically exploded. It's just not something I think your officers should have to see."

"Thank you very much, Captain. That's very considerate of you." Then I made sure all the police officers still at the scene were away from the car as the fire fighters worked to remove the body of Officer Wong. The incredible force of the impact had killed him instantly. Wong took the full brunt of the accident as the suspects' left front fender and bumper went into his door. Earlier, when I had walked around the car looking for evidence and any personal effects of the officers, I could tell the impact had been tremendous. Pieces of brain matter and flesh were scattered around the point of impact.

Another sergeant and I ran the license plate of the suspects' car and went to the address we got from DMV. There a woman told us that her husband had come home about thirty minutes before and left in a hurry for Mexico. She knew he was in some sort of trouble but said she didn't know what he had done.

And Mexico is where the suspects remained. They

fled to the state of Guerrero, and the federal police refused to assist Los Angeles police investigators in apprehending them. The federal Mexican police knew why these men were wanted but had no desire to challenge the violent drug ring the felons were involved with; no surprise to anyone who knew the Mexican police system. It wasn't the first time they had refused assistance or outright hampered an investigation involving persons who had killed American police officers.

SOMETIMES THE DEATH OF AN officer reaches far beyond the original incident. A life has been lost, and families are changed forever. The news media effectively portray the grieving widow and her children as the flag is presented by the chief of police. Their sorrow is very real. In a different sense, sometimes others die as well.

The murder of Dewey Johnson resulted in more than one police casualty. Nothing could bring Dewey back, but part of Archie Nagao was lost as well. Dewey's partner had been critically wounded in the same firefight that killed Dewey. The visible wounds had healed, but others lingered below the surface.

Archie Nagao had returned to light duty. I was working the mid-P.M. shift in Central Division when Archie came back to work and was assigned to the desk. He had become increasingly quiet since the shooting.

A few months after the Medal of Valor ceremony honoring Nagao and his deceased partner, I was in the locker room following the completion of mid-P.M. watch, about 2:30 A.M. As I was changing out of my uniform, Nagao walked up and opened his locker, about ten feet away from mine.

"Hey, Arch. Everything OK?"

His locker was open, and he had just removed his uniform tie. He was still assigned to Central desk and had worked overtime on a lengthy crime report. Archie looked at me quickly, then straight ahead, and shook his head no. He stepped closer to his locker, almost as though he were seeking refuge.

"What's wrong, Arch?" I walked closer to him.

He said nothing, just stared down at the floor.

"Is it Dewey?"

He nodded, still mute.

"You blame yourself?"

For the first time he spoke, very softly. "Yes."

"You don't have your Medal of Valor pin on. How come? Where is it?"

There was a pause before he answered. "At home." Something in his answer made me believe that there was a deeper meaning beyond the pin being simply left at home. Archie continued, "In my closet."

"Have you ever worn it?"

"No."

"Did you ever take the plaque out of the box?"

"No. It's still in there. I put some things on top of it." During the entire conversation Archie stared at the locker room floor.

"Let's sit down and talk for a few minutes." The locker room was very quiet, and we sat on the stationary benches lining the rows between the lockers. I straddled the bench facing him, while Archie slumped down and faced his locker, staring into it. His hands were clasped, his elbows resting on his knees.

"How can you be a hero when the hero died? Is that it?"

He nodded again but still said nothing.

"You earned that medal. You know that, don't you?"

His gaze remained fixed on the locker. He shrugged, almost imperceptibly, and said nothing.

"Archie, initially you didn't even return fire at the guy who shot you. You directed your fire at the one who shot Dewey. Those were heroic actions. That's why you got the Medal. You didn't get it because Dewey was killed. You didn't get it to make you feel better. You got the Medal of Valor because you risked your life to defend someone else. It wasn't just your partner. It was all the people in the jewelry store, too. That's why you got it, Archie, because you were brave."

His eyes were glistening with tears, but he said nothing. Just continued to stare into his locker.

"Did you do something to cause Dewey's death?"

There was a minute pause, and he spoke almost inaudibly. "No."

"Then what?"

"It's just that I didn't . . ." His voice began to quiver, and he stopped speaking.

"Didn't keep him from dying. That's it, isn't it?"

"Yes." He then turned for the first time and faced me. He spoke slowly. "I should've done something for him. Something to prevent it. I don't know. Something. Something." His voice trailed off. He then stared back at his locker, nodded, and said, almost inaudibly, "Something." His head lowered, and he said no more.

Over the years I counseled several officers who had been involved in shootings. Each officer needed to know that his feelings were not unique. I remember my own situation. There was no one to talk to who could understand from personal experience what I was going through. Then I told Archie a story I'd related to other officers. I hoped the result would be the same.

"After my shooting I felt guilty for a long time.

Part of it was because I was the one who had survived. Why wasn't I the one who took that bullet? Then I felt anger at being the one who shot the suspect. It didn't seem fair. It was as though something in me had been lost which would never be given back. I could never be the person who existed before going to that call. Right after the shooting, people came up to me and slapped me on the back, like I was a hero. I just felt dirty; dirty about the whole thing. I wasn't a hero. Just a guy in a certain place who was called upon to act. Nothing more. I don't know how anyone else feels who's been in a shooting, but that's how I felt." I paused for a couple seconds and asked him, "Does this make any sense to you?"

He turned his head back to face me, nodding, and replied, "That's how I feel, too. I don't want to be a hero. I just want Dewey not to be dead. To be like it was before."

"Archie, it's never going to be like it was before—not ever."

I told him of my experience in Newton Division when the two children had been murdered. I explained to him what Dr. Gray had recommended to me. I didn't know if Archie had been to see a psychologist other than the visits required by the department after being involved in a shooting. He never offered to tell me, and I didn't ask. "I don't know if that will work for you, but it did for me."

It occurred to me that each time a police officer has a traumatic experience, that officer is changed. A new person has to emerge as a result.

Some months went by, and I happened to see Archie in uniform, wearing his Medal of Valor pin. I pointed to it and smiled. He smiled back and said, "Yeah, I took that box out of the closet."

"Is the plaque on the wall?"

He nodded. "Yes."

Chapter Seven

THE CRIMES

"All Units! Any Unit Available to Handle . . ."

POLICE WORK IS ABOUT MANY THINGS, but first, last, and almost always it's about crime. I would estimate that I was involved in the investigation of more than twenty thousand felony crimes and participated in at least three thousand felony arrests. Sometimes these arrests involved crimes where my partner and I did the preliminary investigation; sometimes the investigations were done by other officers, and my partner and I simply made the arrest.

You remember the first time you do anything. I remember my first felony investigation and arrest vividly. They occurred simultaneously, and it was really something.

My academy class was called the "Christmas Class." It lasted a few weeks longer, but it also meant you were put out on the streets in Central Division to direct traffic for three weeks during the holiday season. It was Saturday, Christmas Eve. At about noon my sergeant drove up to the intersection of Seventh and Broadway, where I was directing traffic. He told me I'd have to take over traffic control at Fourth and Hill because the officer working there had gone home ill. There were a lot more pedestrians and cars at that intersection, but since Fourth Street was one-way, it was actually an easier assignment. Everything was going along smoothly until 4:05 P.M., when a man came running up to me at the intersection.

"Officer! Come quick! There's a man robbing the Lewis."

My worst fears were realized. He wasn't able to tell I was a recruit from the academy. He thought he was talking to a real police officer. I might be in trouble.

"I'm sorry, sir, I didn't hear what you said. The Lewis?"

Impatiently he yelled, "The Lewis! The Lewis!" and pointed at a large sign that read Lewis Hotel. "He's downstairs now, trying to break in."

"You say he's trying to break into something?" The two of us began to run toward the hotel.

"Yes, he's robbing the basement storeroom."

"You mean he's burglarizing the storeroom."

"That's what I said!"

We had been told at the academy to be wary of the word *rob*. Robbery is the taking of property by the use of force or fear. It is a crime of violence, while burglary simply involves gaining entrance to a location with the intention of committing a theft. We had been warned always to question a witness or victim who used the word *robbery*. People never mistake robbery for burglary but often mistake burglary for robbery.

"Did you see any weapon, like a gun or a knife or anything?"

"No, he just had a big screwdriver."

As we entered the lobby, I told the desk clerk to telephone the police station and tell them an officer needed a backup with a burglary in progress. The wooden stairwell leading to the basement was pointed out to me. Standing at the top of the stairs, I could hear the burglar working one floor below. No matter how many times you enter a building or traverse a flight of stairs to apprehend a suspect, it's always a tense moment. If you're not nervous, you're stupid.

We had made lots of practice arrests at the academy. Tactics were explained, and officer safety issues emphasized, but this time it was different. This time it was for real. Taking my gun from its holster, I quietly walked down the stairwell, staying to the side in hopes of not alerting the burglar with a creaking stair tread.

Near the bottom I took my hat off and, holding it in my left hand, peered around the corner. A man in his twenties was busily prying at the storeroom door, oblivious to my presence. I quietly stepped out onto the basement floor; he still hadn't seen me.

"Police officer! Freeze! Put your hands out where I can see them and drop the screwdriver." My God, it was working. He did just what I said. Just about the time I was starting to feel very professional, I realized my hat was still in my left hand. Quickly I returned it to its proper resting place, hoping the suspect didn't realize that he knew more about his job than I did about mine.

"Turn around! Face the wall. Keep your hands up. No, interlace your fingers behind the back of your head."

If I screwed up one more command, he was going to think this was a calisthenics class. Fortunately, he was patient and went along with the program. It didn't dawn on me at the time, but I'm sure my gun had a lot more command presence than I did, and it was, after all, pointing right at him.

I reholstered my weapon and moved toward the suspect. Unsnapping my handcuff case, I removed my cuffs. It's a critical part of any arrest, and my training came through. Even though I would perform this procedure thousands of times in the next twenty-one years, this was the first time I'd ever done it on a real suspect. After finding no weapons in a cursory search, I snapped the cuff on his left hand and moved his hand to the small of his back.

"Leave your other hand where it is." He complied, and I reached up, took his right hand, moved it also to the small of his back, and secured the other handcuff to his wrist. In the distance I could hear voices. Two Central officers came running down the stairs. Holding my arrestee by the left biceps, I took a few steps toward the officers.

"There's only one suspect. He was prying the storeroom door open. His screwdriver's on the floor over there."

"OK. Are you from the academy?"

The suspect's head whipped around. He realized he'd been arrested by a rank amateur.

"Yes. I was directing traffic at Fourth and Hill when someone told me there was a break-in, so I came over and found him."

"We'll just need your name and serial number for the report. We'll take care of everything from here. Good job."

After giving them the necessary information, I started to leave.

"Hey, Middleton. Don't you want your cuffs back?" One of the officers had recuffed the suspect with his own and held out mine to return.

"Oh, yeah. Thanks!" Sheepishly I grabbed them, went up the stairs and out to my intersection. The traffic had taken care of itself during my absence, which proved I probably wasn't needed there anyway. However, standing on that corner and watching the traffic, for the first time I felt like a real police officer.

A CLASSIC CRIME SCENARIO INVOLVES the strong taking from the weak, and as a police officer you intercede to bring everything back to right. It was always an especially good feeling when the bully's hand was trumped.

"12-Adam-5. See the man regarding a grand theft. . . ."

The call was on 103rd Street. I was assigned to 77th Division morning watch, and it was about 1:30. My partner and I pulled up to a well-maintained single-family home in the heart of what is known to many as Watts. True enough, Watts is a high-crime and often poverty-stricken neighborhood, but there are also some nice homes there. Most of the citizens who live within the Watts confines are just everyday people who work hard, try to raise their families to obey the law, and instill good values. We were at the home of one such family.

A couple who appeared to be in their seventies invited us in. They asked us to follow them into the living room so we could see the empty space.

"It was right there. Yes, sir, that's where the television was. Those two boys from next door came in and just took it. Said they needed it. Actually, both boys don't live next door; his friend lives somewhere else—I don't know where. We've known this family over twenty years."

"Sir, excuse me. The next-door neighbor came in and took your television?"

"Like I said, Officer, just walked right in and picked it up. Said they needed it."

"Where are they now?"

"Well, the car's gone. Must've gone somewhere."

"When did this happen?"

"About three hours ago."

"Why didn't you call us right away?"

"I did! You're busy, I know."

"I'm sorry, sir, we just got the call. You're right, we've been very busy this evening."

The man's wife looked out the window and exclaimed, "They're back! They just parked on the street next door."

It was amazing. Our police car was parked in the driveway of the couple's home, plainly visible. In fact, when the two suspects returned home, they parked in front of their home and couldn't have been more than twenty-five feet from our black-and-white.

"Which one lives next door?" my partner asked.

"The taller one. You know, officers, it's a good family. That boy has just taken to running with some bad company."

"You folks stay in the house. We'll go over and try to straighten this out." We walked out to the sidewalk and approached the two young men.

"Hey, guys, I think we've got a little problem we need to talk about," I said, still believing we'd be able to resolve the problem and perhaps not make an arrest. At that moment the one who lived next door assumed a boxing stance and delivered two quick left jabs to my forehead.

I had made a serious mistake. I gave some weight to the fact that he lived next door, a stupid assumption on my part that could have resulted in serious injury. The victims neglected to tell me that the young man was also a professional boxer. Those two jabs felt like a couple of hammer blows. I fell backward and literally bounced on my ass.

Encouraged, his friend promptly took a roundhouse swing at my partner, who ducked and grabbed the suspect's right hand. My partner looked overweight, but he was as strong as a bull. He wrenched the young man's arm into a rear wrist lock in preparation for handcuffing. I was about ten feet away and could hear his humerus (upper arm) bone snap. This turned out to be a real benefit. When the suspect's arm broke, all his interest in fighting was lost.

As quickly as I hit the ground, I was back up. It was frightening to be knocked down so convincingly and be put at such a tremendous tactical disadvantage. When I got to my feet, the suspect was still standing in a fighting stance. Maybe his fight training had taken over, because any other person would have fled or been on top of me. Immediately I hit him in the side of the head with my baton. It was an unopposed shot and landed squarely. He recoiled, and I hit him again. This time he parried the blow with his left wrist.

He turned and ran into the street, where I tackled him. It worked out very well. We both landed, but he turned out to be my cushion. I grabbed his hair and scrubbed his face back and forth in the street. I knew if I had to fight this guy he'd probably win, and I needed to gain the upper hand right away. He screamed as his face went back and forth on the asphalt.

"Mama! Mama!" His cries did not go unheeded. Mama flew out of the house. I never saw her until she landed on my back.

"Leave my baby alone! He ain't done nothin'!" She was a large woman and had come to rescue her son. She meant business. The first thing she did was to bite my forearm with the force and tenacity of a pit bull, but I never turned loose of her son and continued to rub his face back and forth in the street.

"Lady, get the hell off me! We're arresting your son for grand theft."

This had a positive effect. She climbed off, releasing her dental grip on my arm.

"What do you mean, theft?"

"As soon as I get him cuffed, I'll tell you!"

"Mama, he's lyin'! We haven't done anythin'."

"What'd the two of you steal? What was it? I told you to stay away from him." The young man was clearly scared—not of me but of his mother. She appeared to be switching sides, which was fine with me.

"You stop fighting, and I'll stop rubbing your face in the street."

"OK! OK!" As fast as the fight had started, it was over. I honestly think he allowed himself to be handcuffed because of his mother. She was going to be around a lot longer in his life than we were. He might have a good left jab, but I'm sure she could hold her own with him.

"Officer, I want to know, and I want to know now, what do you mean about my son stealing? What do you think he stole?"

"A television from your neighbors."

"What do you mean? We already have a television."

The elderly gentleman spoke up. "You have two televisions now. They took it right into the house."

"That's a lie! That's a lie!"

"Ma'am, it would be very simple if we could just look. Maybe there's an explanation for everything."

She looked my partner in the eye, and she was mad. "Are you callin' me a liar?"

"No, ma'am, I'm not. Not at all. I'm sure you haven't done anything, but if we could just check, I'd really appreciate it."

"Well, all right, but I'm going with you."

"Of course, ma'am; it's your home. My partner and I really appreciate your help." The two of them walked into the house, and in about fifteen seconds I heard the woman wail.

"Sweet Jesus! My son's a thief!"

Her son heard it, too. His head dropped. He knew he was in big trouble, and it didn't involve the police or the courts.

When she came out, she apologized profusely to her neighbors, and they understood. It was my turn next. "Officer, I don't know what to say. Hope I didn't hurt you too bad, but I thought you were, well, you know, sometimes the police, they—"

"I understand. You thought your son was in trouble, and you came to help him, but you could've been arrested, too. Let me show you my arm." Removing my jacket, I rolled up my shirtsleeve, and displayed a set of teeth marks that had drawn blood. "I understand what you were doing and why, but you can't just jump on top of a police officer. Son or no son, you'll get arrested. Look, let's just forget it. Return the TV, and we'll call it even as far as you're concerned. Your son and his friend are going to be arrested for what they did. He'll be able to call you from jail." She was now in tears and ran into the house.

SOMETIMES CRIMES BECOME "SELF-SOLVERS," when the actions of the criminals involved settle the case with little or no help from police.

"12-Adam-5. Handle in Newton Division. Shots fired, Fifty-Fifth and Avalon. Be advised. The victim from your call may be at L.A. County General [Hospital]."

This was not an area that generated police calls. It was a long block taken up entirely by a factory that had no entrance onto Avalon. Just one big wall. We got the call at about five in the morning, and there was no one on the street. A car was parked about a hundred feet north of Fifty-Fifth on the west side of the street. It looked as if the driver was sleeping.

We pulled our police car up behind the vehicle, and I lit up the car with the hand-held spotlight. There were bullet holes in the back window and maybe some in the windshield as well. With our weapons drawn, we approached the car. On the driver's side there were bullet holes in the glass.

Using my flashlight, I carefully lit up the backseat to make sure no one was hiding. When I got even with the driver's door, you could see a man slumped over against the door. My partner could see the face of the man from the opposite side of the car.

"Mike, I don't think that guy's going anywhere. He's got a fuckin' bullet hole in his forehead."

I carefully opened the car door, but the man didn't move. I touched the back of his neck, and his skin felt cold. He'd obviously been dead for a few hours. In the front seat of the car was a bag of money. There were fives, tens, and twenties inside and more spilling onto the floor. Some of the money was covered with blood. In the dead man's right hand was a .32 semiautomatic pistol.

I moved around to the passenger side to get a better look. His eyes were about three-quarters open, and I carefully inspected the bullet hole in his forehead. A trickle of blood traced down his forehead and into the corner of one eye. The blood had congealed but still looked tacky to the touch. He'd also been shot in one hand and twice in the chest.

He hadn't been alone in that car. The passenger seat also had blood all over it. Blood was smeared down the passenger window, and there were bloody handprints on the armrest. On the floorboard was another semiautomatic pistol. On the seat, on the dash, on the floor, and in the backseat were spent cartridges. There was a slight smell of burned gunpowder still present inside the car.

"Hey, partner. Know what I put my money on? This is a 211 gone wrong. This guy and the other asshole had an argument over the money."

"You could be right, Mike."

I was right, at least about the robbery. As the

morning progressed, we found our second shooting victim dead in the emergency room of the county hospital. These two had canceled each other's tickets. They'd robbed a liquor store at about 3:00 A.M. in Hollywood and apparently fought over the dividends. The victim had gotten their license number as they drove away and given it to Hollywood Division. The car belonged to the dead man in the driver's seat. No robbery was more simply or cleanly solved.

NOT EVERY VICTIM IS HELPLESS. There are times when the intended victim can gain the upper hand on the suspect even if it's inadvertent.

"1-Adam-71. See the man about a possible burglar at the rear of the hotel on Hill between Third and Fourth."

When my partner and I arrived, the ambulance was already at the rear of the hotel. They were tending to what appeared to be simply a lump on the ground.

"Hi, guys," the paramedic greeted us. "I don't know what you've got here, except he took one hell of a fall. He's got some pretty good head injuries. We're going to [back]board him and take him to County General. He's pretty screwed up; look at his fingers."

On each finger of both hands, the fingernails were peeled back, and there were bloody abrasions on most of his fingertips.

"What do you make of that?"

"Hey, you guys are the cops." He smiled.

We helped load the injured man onto the backboard and then helped move him to the ambulance gurney. The man had been unconscious but was beginning to come out of it and moaned periodically. However, he wasn't responsive when we asked questions of him. After the ambulance left, we began our investigation. We really didn't know if we had a crime or simply an injury. You could smell alcohol on the man, and he could have been a drunk who simply fell.

We were inspecting the area for evidence when a voice called out, "Officers! Officers! Up here! I'm up here! I'm the one you want to see."

"Where are you at?"

"I'm on the fourth floor. I'll meet you out in the hallway. I can tell you what happened."

We went around to the front of the seedy hotel and climbed the stairs to the fourth floor. Probably at one time it had housed middle-class people who worked in the downtown area, but now it had a transient trade with only a few regulars who paid on a monthly basis. Saying it had seen better days was paying the old hotel a tremendous compliment.

By the time we got to the fourth floor, the man was waiting in the hall for us.

"Did you call?" my partner asked.

"Yes, sir, I'm the one. Come on into my room. I'll show you what happened."

This caller was obviously a permanent resident of the hotel. The room was furnished with old but still serviceable pieces.

"I was asleep when I heard some noises. So I got up and looked out my window. Always sleep with my window open. And I could see him, right over there." When you looked out the window, you could see a fire escape for another wing of the hotel. A person who stood on the fire escape would be about eight to ten feet away from the man's room. It was a big eight to ten feet because between that fire escape and the window was a four-story fall onto a walkway leading to the rear entrance of the hotel.

"Yup, watched him take off his shoes and climb onto the top of the railing. He was perched up there on top of it. His feet were on the railing and his hands, too. Don't know how he kept his balance. Then, just as he leaped, I screamed at him, 'Get away!' loud as I could."

"Did he make it?"

"Nope. Must've thrown his concentration off. He hit the wall just below the window."

"What happened next?"

"Couldn't see him. Heard him, though. Screamed all the way down. When he hit, didn't make any more noise. Like I said, I must've thrown his concentration off. If he would've made it, I'd have plowed him with my baseball bat." With a self-assured smile he reached over and tapped the top of his bat, leaning against the wall next to the window.

Looking at the outside brick wall, you could see marks for about ten feet straight down where the man had tried desperately to grab on to anything. This accounted for his ripped-back fingernails.

"OK, sir. Just need you to sign the report, and we'll be on our way."

When we arrived at County General, staff members at the emergency room nursing station directed us to one of the cubicles. As we approached, a doctor came out. "What exactly happened?"

My partner and I explained the circumstances surrounding the man's failed burglary attempt. "How's he doing? He didn't look too good at the scene."

"I know. His vitals looked bad when he came in, then all of a sudden he rebounded and woke up. I don't know how to explain it."

When we walked into the cubicle, the man looked at us, said nothing, and then stared straight ahead. He never said a word, and we booked him as a John Doe at the hospital. Although charged with attempted burglary, he was ultimately dealt with as a psychiatric patient.

When you worked Seventy-Seventh Division morning watch, most of the time you didn't have time to simply patrol. When I was first assigned, the captain said, "Mike, you'll hit the ground running here, and it won't ever stop." Most of the time his words could not have been truer.

One particular Saturday morning the air was unusually quiet. Fred Early and I had been working together for a few months. I benefited from Fred's patrol experience, and duty with him was never boring. Very sadly, a couple of years after this morning Fred was shot to death by a burglar.

"Mike, it's pretty quiet. Let's check the shine parlor at Seventy-Seventh and Main. Ever been in there?"

"No. I can't even place the building."

"It's a gambling joint, but they deal pills, too. Looks really small from the outside, but it opens into a lot of individual rooms. We took a couple of guys with guns out of there the other night; I think it was while you were on days off."

Fred drove by the shine parlor going south, made a left on Seventy-Eighth Street, then turned into an alley going north back to the rear of the shine parlor.

"12-A-45. Show us code six at Seventy-Seventh and Main on the southeast corner."

"12-Adam-45, roger."

"No, Mike, it's 7700 South Main. Give 'em the exact address in case we need help. I've been in here before, and it's confusing if you don't know which door to go into."

"12-A-45, the correct address of our code six location is 7700 South Main."

"12-Adam-45, roger on your code six location."

The place looked deserted. The first room we walked into had some pinball machines and a bowling machine that used miniature bowling balls.

There was no one in the room, but you could hear people talking. We walked through a curtained doorway into the next room, where four or five people were just standing around.

It was a very confusing place. There must have been five doors leading to other parts of the building from the room we were in. It reminded me of a maze. The smell of cigarette smoke and wine hung heavy in the air. Fred walked through one of the doorways and found two people shooting craps on the floor.

"OK, guys, break it up. Come out here; I want to talk to you."

Now we were getting down to business. "The rest of you, get your hands out of your pockets. Walk over here, face the wall, and put your hands behind the back of your head. Everyone leave your hands out where we can see them."

"Ahhh! You motherfuckers!" Without warning, a man came running into the room with a four-foot-long two-by-four board in his hands. He swung with all his might directly at my head. If I'd had my gun in my hand, I would have dropped him, but the only thing I could think of was to put my arm up to protect my face. He hit the back of my forearm with such force the board broke.

Fortunately, my jacket protected my arm from getting cut, and amazingly enough, my arm didn't break. The man whirled around and struck Fred full in the face with the remaining three-foot-long piece. Fred fell backward through the same door he had just come through. I took my baton from its ring and hit the man squarely in the face. He screamed and dropped the two-by-four but didn't go down. Instead he lunged at Fred, who in the interim had managed to get to his feet. They had a grip on each other's collar, and the man was groaning like an animal, spitting in Fred's face. Fred turned quickly to his right, flinging the man into the wall.

For the first time Fred was able to get his baton out and hit the man repeatedly in the face. Each time the suspect was hit, he retaliated by striking Fred with his fists.

"Fred, I'm getting help!" I started to run to the front door. One of the men I'd told to place his hands behind the back of his head had moved to a position directly in front of the curtained doorway. The others had scattered.

"Motherfucker, you ain't goin' nowhere." He reached out with one hand and pushed me in the chest.

As soon as the words were out of his mouth, my baton came crashing into his face. He was about six-four and must have outweighed me by thirty pounds, but my baton equalized our weight and size. Grabbing his face with both hands, he staggered out of my way. I ran past him, out the front door, and back to the alley where our police car was parked. The keys were in my hand as I approached the vehicle, but it seemed to take forever to open the locked door.

"12-A-45. Officer needs help. 7700 Main."

"12-Adam-45. Roger. All units. Officer needs help. Officer needs help at 7700 Main."

I ran back into the shine parlor. The man who tried to keep me from leaving was still holding his face, and as I came into the room I gave him another shot for good measure as hard as I could into the ribs. He had had enough and ran for the door. Fred was now fighting two suspects, the man who initially attacked with the two-by-four and another man who had appeared out of nowhere. Fred's face was a bloody mess. I pulled one suspect off and ran him across the room, driving his face into the wall. As the man bounced off the wall, he struck me full in the face with his fist. My baton was still in my right hand, and I tried to deliver a shot to the side of his head, but he successfully blocked it with his left arm, much as I had done earlier.

He ran for the curtained doorway, and I tackled him. As we fell through the doorway and into the game room, we ripped the curtain off its track. Both of us got to our feet at about the same time, and once again he tried for the front door.

I was able to get hold of the back of his shirt. He was only about five-seven, which gave me a significant advantage. I moved him counterclockwise, away from the door. Now I had a good grip on him and ran him as hard as I could into the bowling machine. His legs hit the front of it, and he tumbled forward. I pushed him as hard as I could, and he slid down the alley, forcing his head underneath the pinholder. His head was stuck, preventing him from escaping. His arms and legs were flailing as he tried to free himself. I climbed onto the machine and handcuffed him while his head was still stuck under the pins.

"Help me get out!"

"Fuck you, asshole!"

When help arrived, we took several people into custody for a variety of charges. Fred had finally gained the upper hand on the principal suspect, the man who attacked us with the two-by-four, and he was arrested for assault with intent to commit murder. Normally, if a suspect struck you with a two-by-four you would arrest him for assault with a deadly weapon, but based on his attempt to strike me in the head, the charge was elevated to attempted murder. A blow of that force with a piece of wood that size could easily have resulted in a fatal injury. Fred and I spent the rest of our shift at the emergency room being patched up. Fred received the worst of it, having been struck in the face several times.

A preliminary hearing for the attempted murder suspect was held within a few weeks of his arrest. Shortly after the proceedings began, he started talking to imaginary persons he thought were in the courtroom. It didn't take long for the judge to suspend the hearing and order a psychiatric examination. Ultimately the man was found incompetent to stand trial and committed to the Atascadero State Mental Hospital. Even though he had tried to kill us, Fred and I believed justice had been served because the man was insane.

WHEN YOU'RE ON PATROL, you're trying to find trouble—crimes in progress, suspects about to commit crimes, or suspects who have already committed a crime and are fleeing. Most of the things that catch your attention turn out to be nothing. A quick glimpse of a shadowy figure in an alley as you go past turns out to be a discarded water heater. A suspect with a coat hanger stuck into the window of a car turns out not to be a car thief but a car owner trying to unlock his car and retrieve his keys. Every shift is like that, but you keep looking, keep asking questions, keep going up that alley, because one of those times it won't be a water heater.

"Did you see the guys between those houses?"

"Yeah, one of 'em had a car battery."

"Let's go code six."

"12-Adam-5, show us code six Adam, 9100 block Hoover. Possible 459 [burglary] from vehicle suspects."

My partner was Phil Shattuck, and we were assigned to Seventy-Seventh Division morning watch. We had just handled a radio call for a burglary alarm a few blocks away and were returning to the station ready to go off duty for the night. Phil was my regular partner and a lot of fun to work with.

"12-Adam-5, roger. All Seventy-Seventh units, be advised. 12-Adam-5 is code six Adam with possible 459 from vehicle suspects, 9100 block Hoover."

The two men we'd seen were next to a car parked in a driveway serving a duplex. I decided to pull the police car directly into the driveway behind their car instead of parking on the street and walking up. This would put us closer to the suspects should a foot pursuit ensue, and pulling the police car in suddenly might disorient the suspects with the element of surprise. We didn't know that these two men lived in one of the duplexes, but we were partially right in our assumption—the battery was stolen.

As soon as I brought the police car to a stop, both Phil and I got out. Phil spoke first to the man carrying the battery.

"Come over here. We want to talk to you."

"What do you want? We haven't done anything. We live here. Hey, hey, come out! The police are here!" he yelled inside the duplex. Both men walked rapidly toward us. The man who had the battery set it on the hood of the car in the driveway. Three other people came out of the apartment and joined the two men. One was an obviously pregnant woman.

"Step over here; I want to talk to you," I said, motioning to one of the two original men. Simultaneously Phil called the other suspect toward him. At this time I was beginning to think that perhaps we didn't have a crime but just someone working on his car. The woman stepped in front of the man I'd just spoken to.

"You motherfuckers don't have any business here, and he hasn't done anything! He's my husband, and he isn't goin' to talk to you." She was now standing about eighteen inches away from me, yelling in my face.

"Ma'am, just step aside for a second." I placed my hand on her shoulder to guide her aside. "I just want to talk to your husband, and—"

"I'm pregnant, motherfucker!"

With this she delivered a crashing blow with her clenched fist right between my eyes. The force drove my glasses into my face, cutting the skin above both eyes. What was left of my glasses fell to the street. I'd been caught off-guard and was knocked back against the trunk of the police car. Her husband seized the moment and stepped forward to deliver a karate kick to my chest. I rolled off into the street, but he was right there and kicked me in the back. I got to my feet as quickly as I could and ran for the driver's door of the police car to put out a help call.

Simultaneously Phil's suspect took a roundhouse swing at him, which Phil ducked to avoid. Coming up with his baton, Phil literally put it down the man's throat, severing several teeth at the gum line. This suspect was neutralized. He staggered around in a circle, screaming with pain. That left Phil with my suspect to fight, and the fight was on.

The fourth suspect had originally been an onlooker, but when I got to the driver's door of the police car, he decided to enter the fray. As I reached in and grabbed the microphone, I received a punch to the left side of my face, knocking me into the police car. I landed on my back with the fifth suspect, who'd been joined by the woman's husband, on top of me.

Still clutching the microphone with my right hand, I broadcast, "Officer needs help. Ninety-First and Hoover." With my left hand I was throwing punches at both men while they were landing unopposed shots to my face one after another. After broadcasting the help call, I threw the mike on the floor. I didn't want them to seize the opportunity and pull it, cutting off our only means of communication.

I was in deep trouble. If they wanted my gun, it was theirs for the taking. I drew my knees back and began kicking in an effort to knock them off me. Several kicks landed, but I couldn't say who got hit or where. However, the desired effect was achieved; the men temporarily backed off, and I climbed out of the police car.

My baton was still in its ring. I drew it out and with two hands began to strike at the men who continued to land punches. The pregnant woman now joined the fracas again. No matter how fast I struck them with my baton, they were still landing blow after blow on me. The husband gave several karate kicks. I could hear sirens coming, but it seemed like an eternity before the first car arrived.

Just before the units pulled up, I got lucky. A two-handed baton shot struck the fifth suspect on his right wrist. It was a tremendous blow and broke it, ending his participation in the battle.

As the first police car arrived, the husband ran down the driveway with me in hot pursuit. When he got behind the residence in a small yard area, he started looking for a place to hide. When he realized I was right behind him, he ran for the side yard fence and started to climb over it. For the first time, I drew my weapon.

"When you get to the top of that fence, I'll blow your fuckin' brains out, asshole!"

He looked at me, looked at the fence, and jumped back, raising his hands in the air. "I give up!"

I reholstered my gun and drew my baton. "Not yet you don't, fuckhead!" I then delivered one more shot with my baton into his ribs. He collapsed onto the lawn.

"Get up, asshole, unless you want more." He literally jumped to his feet. I handcuffed him and marched him back to the front of the house.

As we came up the driveway, police officers were everywhere. They hadn't even missed me. No one knew I'd gone to the rear of the house. It was a mistake on my part not to advise someone; I had assumed the first unit saw me running down the driveway, but they hadn't. I was lucky it didn't cost me.

All five suspects were taken into custody. While I was chasing down the husband, Phil remained by the police car, subdued his suspect, and directed the initial units to take the other three people into custody. Although Phil and I had taken some lumps, we were lucky not to be seriously injured. I had two black eyes, my upper and lower lips split open, and bruises on my chest and back.

Later I was told by one of the officers that our sergeant had ordered the backup officers not to use their batons. That order was instantly remanded when the fifth suspect knocked our sergeant flat on his ass. After that, all restrictions were lifted. It was too bad I didn't get a chance to see it because this sergeant's father was a high-ranking member of the police department, and the sergeant believed he should receive extra credit because of it. Seeing Sarge take one on the chin was the high point of the event as far as the officers were concerned.

All five suspects were charged with battery on a police officer, a felony in California. They were held to answer to felony charges at the preliminary hearing, and a trial date was set. By the time the jury trial began, all were free on bail. The trial started on a Monday and ran through that week. Phil and I about lived at the courthouse.

On Friday night three of the suspects came into contact with Seventy-Seventh Division officers again.

This time the husband of the pregnant woman tried to shoot a police officer with a high-powered rifle. My decision to throw the mike on the floor had been a good one, because in the midst of this fight they ripped the microphone from the car, preventing the broadcast of a help call. Fortunately, a citizen placed a call to the station requesting help, but one officer was severely beaten before assistance arrived.

On Monday morning, when court resumed, three of the defendants were no longer on bail. Their attorney had seemed very confident of acquittal during the trial week, making several snide remarks to both Phil and me during those first five days. His confident air had vanished. The district attorney insisted that no plea bargain would be made. If they wanted to plead guilty, that was fine, but they would be cut no slack.

Late that morning a compromise was struck. All suspects would plead guilty to the initial charges, and the three who had been rearrested would plead guilty to battery on a police officer. They were sentenced as misdemeanants and received two consecutive one-year sentences in the county jail. This meant they would spend at least eighteen months in jail, probably the same amount of time they would have received if sentenced on felony charges. The pregnant woman also pleaded guilty but was given probation. The man who swallowed Phil's baton was allowed to plead guilty to simple battery and sentenced to six months in the county jail.

Criminals such as these receive little attention from the news. Other times the press seizes on the acts of felons to such an extent that they become instant personalities. Such is the case with serial killers. In a macabre sense these murderers become media darlings, grabbing headlines and conversations. Sometimes when the identity of the killer is known, that name becomes a household word. Jeffrey Dahmer and Ted Bundy are known to people who may have only sketchy knowledge of their crimes. Other times, when the names aren't known, newspapers and television give identities suggested by the crimes—the "Green River Killer," the "Night Stalker," the "Skid Row Slasher."

A Central Division unit had gotten a call to the L.A. City Library that indicated a body had been found. My partner and I were working P.M. watch and responded as well to see if we could assist. When we pulled up to the library to assist at the homicide scene, we didn't realize this was part of the work of a serial killer who became known as the Skid Row Slasher.

Around ten o'clock that evening, a woman had come to the library to return some books. She came up the south steps, a rather desolate place at night and not a place for a woman to be walking alone. However, it's only a few feet from the night book depository, and that's where she stumbled across the body. At that hour homeless men would find shelter there for the night. That evening, perhaps less than an hour before she tried to return her books, it had become a killing place.

Veteran homicide investigator Chuck Hughes from Central Division was dispatched to the scene along with other detectives. Detective Hughes would become an integral part of a task force assembled in response to the killings.

The victim was lying on his back, staring at the vaulted arcade ceiling. The cause of death seemed undeniable. His throat was shredded by dozens of slashes. The cuts were deep, some starting behind the ears and continuing across his throat. The larynx, esophagus, right and left carotid arteries, and right and left jugular veins were all severed. In looking at the victim's right hand, one could see characteristic cuts called *defense wounds*. He had tried without success to fend off his attacker. Curiously, the amount of blood one would normally expect at such a murder was noticeably absent. He would not be the only Slasher victim I would see.

Three weeks went by. It was now only a few days before Christmas. The downtown area was decorated for the holidays, but not everyone shared in the joy of the season. The despair experienced by the homeless at that time of year took on additional meaning. The Slasher continued to stalk his prey, claiming two more. He returned to familiar territory for his fourth victim.

Another call involving the discovery of a body at the library was dispatched, and Frank Long and I responded. This time the victim was lying on the ground at the southwest corner of the library in an area concealed from view by some bushes. He was a transient who frequented the library grounds and, like many of the homeless people, found the area suitable for sleeping.

Again the characteristic shredding of the throat was present. As before, the carotid artery and larynx had been severed. An autopsy would reveal that this man had choked to death on his own blood. With every gasp he had drawn more and more blood into his lungs until he lapsed into unconsciousness. This time there were no defense wounds.

The Slasher was a ritualistic killer, and his distinctive trademarks were clearly evident. The body appeared to have been arranged carefully. Fifteen feet away was a pool of blood with drag marks visible in the dirt. When he was found, the victim's face was covered with a jacket. His pants were unzipped and down around his hips, with the empty pockets pulled out. The most unusual idiosyncrasy had to do with the victim's shoes. They had been removed and carefully arranged so the toes were pointing at and nearly touching his bare feet.

Investigators Rick Jacques of Robbery-Homicide Division and Chuck Hughes were dispatched. The Slasher task force had been formed, and these two experienced detectives became the leading investigators on it. I watched them go carefully to work. There was strong evidence to connect this crime with the others, evidence the detectives would keep to themselves. Other homicide investigators came to the scene, and they spoke in hushed tones to each other. They knew something, but they weren't about to let anyone else know what it was.

This was the last time I was to see a Slasher victim. Frank would be at other Slasher murder scenes, but without me. The Slasher's rituals became darker and more bizarre as the killings continued, including glasses found at the scene that had once been filled with human blood. The glasses also bore smeared lip prints, indicating the killer drank the blood of his victim as some sort of macabre toast.

This investigation was different from anything I'd experienced before. Some police officers would act as decoys, lying in filthy alleys disguised as transients. Everyone was involved at some level, whether you were assigned directly to Slasher details or checking alleys for the elusive serial killer.

Ultimately the Slasher, Vaughn Greenwood, would claim thirteen victims before he was identified and apprehended. He was tried and convicted for nine of the murders and received a life sentence for each.

TO BE A SUCCESSFUL POLICE OFFICER, you've got to be a team player. This is particularly true in the inner-city environment, where there are no single-officer patrol units. Two officers who work together are partners. No matter what shift you worked or what division you worked it in, it was you and your partner. You were a team, and you found success or failure together.

You work with a lot of police officers over the years, but you have only a few real partners. In looking back, I would have to say that I had very few, but the best one was Frank Long. There were dozens of officers I really enjoyed working with and a few that I was teamed with for months at a time. Partnership involves much more of a bond than just working together. Next to my wife, my partner, Frank, is my best friend.

Not every partnership was that good. Sometimes you could be stuck with an officer you just didn't get along with. Usually when that happened it was only for a month, the length of a deployment period, and you went your separate ways. When I was a police officer working Central P.M. watch, I had the partner from hell. He gave me shingles, which made me break out in painful sores that itched yet hurt to touch. I went to see our family doctor, and he diagnosed the problem as being created by tension at work. He gave me medicine to control the shingles but told me it wouldn't be solved permanently until the stress was reduced.

You never knew what this guy would do. He was a constant embarrassment and driving me nuts. What made it worse was that he liked me, and I didn't want to hurt his feelings. I had never refused to work with someone, but I was approaching a point where I would have to talk to my sergeant and tell him I wanted to change partners.

Very quietly I devised a plan. There was an officer assigned to a foot beat on the same shift. When I first met Frank Long, I thought he was self-absorbed and totally obnoxious, but as I got to know him better I saw a different side and realized that my judgment had been hasty. I decided to ask him to give up his foot beat position and come work a radio car with me. This would not be an easy task. Regularly we would pick up him and his partner and take them to coffee, so I decided to approach him the next night.

"Now let me get this straight. I give up my foot beat, the job where I don't have any radio calls to answer, I get off on time every night, I'm not stuck in court the next morning after getting a few hours' sleep, where I get code seven [meal period] whenever I want, to work a radio car with you?" He wasn't nearly as excited as I'd hoped he would be.

"Yeah! We could have a blast working together."

"Let me think about it. This means one radio call after another, never getting code seven, and never getting off on time."

"It'd be fun!"

He paused for what seemed like forever, then said, "OK. I don't know how in the hell I get talked into these things." That was the beginning of not only a good partnership but a great friendship that has lasted more than twenty years.

Frank and I were working 1-A-71, a car that had geographic responsibility for the area around Metropolitan Hospital. The city of Los Angeles contracted with hospitals throughout the city to handle emergency medical treatment for suspects, arrestees, and injured police officers. Metropolitan Hospital was the contract facility for Central Division. Whenever someone came into the hospital for treatment and the injury appeared to be related to a crime in some way, the police were called. If it was known where the crime occurred, the division for that area was called to handle the case. If not, it was assigned to a Central Division radio car. Frank and I were regulars at Metropolitan Hospital's emergency room.

Over the years we developed good friendships with the doctors and nurses in the emergency room. On a nightly basis they treated some very tough customers. We were concerned for their safety and made sure we did everything we could do to help.

One night Frank and I were called to take a crime report at the hospital, nothing out of the ordinary. The victim had been raped. Again not terribly unusual, but what made it stand out was that the victim was a nurse, and the crime scene one of the upper floors of the hospital. A few nights later another nurse was attacked. It was now apparent the rapist was working within the hospital in the early hours of the morning.

We approached our sergeant, told him of the problem, and described our plan to capture the rapist. Frank and I decided the best course of action was to dress as doctors and work undercover. Since we were apparently working the same hours as the rapist, the plan had possibilities. Our sergeant agreed, and next we talked to our friend, Doctor Verdano, an emergency room physician. He in turn cleared everything through hospital administration. We were then outfitted with hospital greens and stethoscopes. The only shirts they could find that would fit belonged to the doctor and had *Verdano* stenciled across the pocket. The nurses immediately christened us the "Verdano brothers."

As "doctors" we had just come on duty and were standing behind the counter in the emergency room.

In came two Los Angeles city paramedics with the victim of a stabbing. The man had only a superficial leg wound requiring stitches. The paramedics wheeled him in on a stretcher from the ambulance, stopped in front of the counter, and looked at us.

"Where do you want this guy?"

Frank quickly moved around the counter, approached the victim, placed his stethoscope on his chest, and calmly stated, "Take this man directly to the morgue." Frank could always get away with saying the most bizarre things. I think it was his disarming manner. I nodded my head in sad agreement.

The paramedics had a look of total shock on their faces, as did the injured man, whose eyes had grown quite large at "Dr." Verdano's diagnosis. An emergency room nurse deftly moved in. "Don't mind them. Right this way, please." As the gurney began to move toward the emergency room, the patient's expression changed to one of utter relief.

The paramedic looked at the nurse and sarcastically asked, "Who are they? Frick and Frack?"

I turned to him and said, "No. Last time I checked, they were with the fire department."

Following Frank's failed diagnosis, we slipped quietly away from the emergency room, and the serious work began. The halls were dimly lit and very quiet in comparison to the hustle and bustle of the ER. You knew the rapist was lurking somewhere; you just didn't know where.

We spent four nights on that detail. Two things didn't happen. We didn't catch the suspect, and no nurses were attacked. I don't believe the rapist knew we were in the hospital; it was probably just chance that he didn't strike.

On the fifth night our sergeant called us into the watch commander's office. "Mike, Frank, I'm as committed to catching this rapist as you are, but we're just too shorthanded tonight. You have to work your regular car."

Back into uniform we went, putting the Verdano brothers temporarily out of practice. We stopped by the hospital to advise the emergency room staff we wouldn't be working the detail that night. At about 1:30 that morning we received a radio call and returned.

"1-Adam-71, see the emergency room personnel regarding a suspicious person at 1414 South Hope." When we arrived at the hospital, we were met by a security officer at the entrance to the emergency room.

"I think we have our rapist, officers. A nurse on one of the upper floors confronted him inside an x-ray room. He'd been hiding in there. I guess he was going to attack another nurse, but she surprised him. She was lucky and got away. Then she called us. He ran down to the next floor; that's where we caught him. He didn't even put up a struggle. If he had, he'd be in the emergency room receiving treatment! He's such an asshole; his mouth just won't stop running."

"Where's the nurse?" I asked.

"She's on the fourth floor."

"I'll go up and take a report from her, Mike."

"OK. I'll take care of the suspect."

The man was in a hallway just off the ER with a hospital security officer standing next to him. The suspect definitely fit the description of the rapist. He greeted me with "Well, here comes another fuckin' pig."

"Why don't you just relax? What's your name?"

"The rent-a-pig has my ID. You try to fuckin' relax with fuckin' handcuffs on. What am I bein' arrested for?"

"Well, you fit the description of someone who's wanted."

"Yeah, yeah, yeah. They told me all about it. I ain't the guy, but I hope whoever it was fucked her good!"

"You know, asshole, I really don't want to hear any of your shit. Now tell me, what the fuck were you doing upstairs?"

"I came in and wanted to look around. I wasn't doin' nothin'. Next thing I knows, some bitch was screamin' at me, these fuckin' pigs came, and slapped the cuffs on me. Maybe she thought I was gonna fuck her. She didn't look too bad, though. Probably could use a good fuck."

"You better cool it, guy."

A few minutes later, Frank returned with a crime report. In talking with the nurse, he found out that the man had done more than just surprise her; he had lunged toward her, his hands closed in a viselike grip on her neck. She turned quickly, and he loosened his grip. She screamed and pushed him back. He lost his balance and fell against a cabinet. The nurse was about two feet from the door and pulled it open. He tried to cut off her escape, but he was a fraction of a second slow. There was little doubt she had nearly become a rape victim.

"Frank, before we go, we've got to switch cuffs. He's still got the hospital security's cuffs on. OK, guy, put your right hand on top of your head when I take the handcuff off."

"Must be your partner. What took you so long? You fuck her, too? She looks like she needs it. Fuck all these bitches!"

Frank normally was pretty unflappable, but not with this guy. "Listen, asshole, shut your fucking mouth. Just shut the fuck up."

"You can't fuckin' tell me what to do! I'll say whatever the fuck I want!" And with that he pulled partially out of my grasp and was now facing Frank. Instantly Frank spun him around and, using a bar-arm control, choked him out cold.

So much of police work is chance. You can do everything right and come up empty night after night. Police officers can work very hard, and crime continues to go up. We worked hard to catch this rapist, but it wasn't police work that really resulted in his arrest. It was a chance set of circumstances—a victim freed herself; security officers were close by; he ran right to them. I felt those nights on patrol with Frank in that hospital in some way played a part in the arrest. Even though we didn't catch him, our presence increased the awareness of the hospital staff to the suspect, as well as the police department's response to their problem. He was in custody, and that's what mattered.

OVER THE YEARS FRANK AND I made many felony arrests together. Some were armed suspects; some wanted for incredibly violent crimes. We knew each other very well. I could count on him, and he could count on me. The most outstanding example occurred in a multilevel parking structure in Central Division.

Frank and I were assigned to 1-FB-97. The FB stands for a foot beat, and it was a very desirable job. Frank had finally made it back "to the beat." We made some good arrests in the garment district and convinced our sergeants to allow us to work a plainclothes foot beat. We further adapted the assignment to searching for suspects who had committed violent street crimes in our patrol area. After a few days we had made our first arrest. The detective in charge of investigations on the police team Frank and I were assigned to was Santo Guerrero. At the beginning of each shift we would usually meet with Santo or one of the other detectives if we had any questions regarding wanted suspects.

"Santo, I'm telling you, we need more suspects to look for. You've got to make them harder. The last guy was too easy."

Frank chimed in, "Maybe one with not so good a description."

"Good idea. Got any like that, Santo?"

"Middleton and Long, you guys are so full of shit, but now that you mention it, I do have a guy. In fact he's committed about a dozen armed robberies and stabbed several of the victims with a knife. Here's the package with all the reports. It's 8:30 now; you guys ought to be back by noon with him."

He handed me the manila folder with several crime reports in it. I looked at Frank. "Do you think it'll take until noon?"

"Nope. I'd say we'll be back by ten with your boy in tow."

Santo just shook his head as he walked back to his desk. We went into an interview room and spread the reports out on a table. Frank and I had actually taken one of the robbery reports. The best approach to apprehending this type of suspect is to look for habits or anything left behind that could be a clue to his whereabouts. There were no evidence reports to go with the ten or so robberies, which meant that he was careful.

"Frank, look at the days he's committing the 211s. Is there any pattern?"

"Yeah, he's hit four times on a Tuesday and a couple times on Thursday, but that's it. No, wait. That's not it. Two of those Tuesdays he's hit the same place—that parking garage right across from April's

Department Store on Hill. Where's the calendar?" Holding the handful of robbery reports, Frank walked over to the calendar mounted on the wall. "Mike, look at this! He's hit that garage on this Tuesday, and then, look: he hit again two weeks on this Tuesday." Frank was jabbing his finger at the dates on the calendar. "And the last time he hit was two Tuesdays ago."

"What time is he hitting?"

"Always in the morning."

We looked at each other without saying a word, gathered up the reports, went to the subterranean parking lot, and got into our unmarked police car. We went directly to the eight hundred block of Hill Street, parking our car on Olive, the next street over. We walked back to Hill Street, where there was an entrance to a stairwell that gave access to all levels of the parking garage. We went to each level and looked around to see if anyone was there. When we got to the fourth level, we stood looking out over a concrete railing down onto the intersection of Eighth and Hill, watching the people hurrying by.

"Look at that guy on the far corner. He fits the description," Frank said. When the light changed to green, the man walked west across Hill Street and began to move north. He went about twenty-five feet and reversed his direction, returning to stand on the northwest corner of Eighth and Hill.

"Frank, look what he's done. He walked north a little bit, then turned around to come back and stand on the corner again. All the people he crossed the light with are gone. He's with a brand-new group. He doesn't want anyone to see him for any length of time. Wouldn't it be wild if that was our guy?"

He now crossed the intersection when the light changed and was approaching the parking structure. When he got to the door that led to the stairwell, he stopped. He walked north again for about ten feet and stopped. He turned, went back to the door, and entered.

I walked over and opened the door to listen. The stairway was made of steel, and when anyone walked on the treads, it echoed all the way up to our position. I spoke very quietly to Frank: "Let's listen for this guy until he gets to whatever level he wants, and then we'll move."

I could hear the door opening to the first level, then "boom." The sound of the door closing resonated up the well, immediately followed by the footfalls of the suspect as he climbed to the second level. Again the door was opened and quickly shut. He then moved to the level just below us.

"Frank, if this guy comes up to our level, I'm going to try and get him to rob me. I'm going to walk like I'm going down the stairwell when he opens the door, turn around, and show him my back. Let's see if he does anything. You can cover me." Up to this point all his victims had been women who were robbed just after parking their cars and walking to the elevator.

As he climbed to the fourth floor, the sound of his footfalls thundered in my ears. Carefully I closed the steel door and walked toward a parked car about twenty feet away. I pretended to lock the vehicle and fumbled with my keys.

The design of the stairwell was rectangular in the corner of the parking level. This allowed Frank to position himself around the corner from the door. If the suspect were to come out the door, Frank would be within three feet of him.

Reflected in the window of the car, I could see the door opening. I couldn't see him, but I knew he was there. Looking down at my keys, I began to walk directly toward the stairwell. My heart was pounding. About five feet away from me was an armed suspect, and I was asking him to rob me. I decided to give him what I thought would be an irresistible opportunity. I hesitated, as though remembering the elevators at my back about fifty feet away. Still staring at my keys, I turned around and began to walk away from the door.

I heard the door open and footsteps behind me. As I turned, Frank flew from his position, tackling the suspect with his left arm while holding his gun in his right hand. He yelled, "Drop the knife, or your fuckin' brains are in the lot!" Above the man's head, arm extended, was a knife he was preparing to sink into my back—the same knife he had used to stab so many women.

They went to the pavement, hard. Frank was on top and screamed into his ear, "Drop the fucking knife!" The man released his grip, and it clattered to the pavement.

Frank had done everything. It happened so quickly, all I'd done was get out of the way. As the young man of seventeen lay facedown, spread-eagle on the pavement, he spoke. "I'm glad you got me." He was handcuffed without further incident and taken to the station.

We walked into Santo's office with the suspect in tow.

"Santo! I was wrong. I said 10 o'clock. It's only 9:45."

Frank added, "He's always too conservative with his estimates. I knew it wouldn't take that long." Santo's jaw literally dropped.

"Don't tell me. It's the guy."

Frank and I looked at each other and smiled.

The teenager spoke freely about the crimes he had committed. He was a heroin addict, and his robberies were done to get money to pay for his habit. He didn't really have any explanation as to why he stabbed the women.

It was a great arrest, an incredibly lucky arrest, but not really blind luck. The suspect gave us a break, and we took advantage of it. What stands out more than the arrest was what Frank did. His quick action saved me from being seriously injured—or worse. While protecting me, he could easily have been stabbed. I'm not surprised at what he did or the way he did it. He was always there for me, and I hope I was always there for him. That's what being a partner is about.

"1-ADAM-95. SEE THE VICTIM of an ambulance attack on Flower south of Seventh Street at the multilevel garage." An "ambulance attack" meant only one thing—a woman had been raped.

"1-A-95, roger on the call. Is there a report unit available?"

"1-Adam-95. No U-cars [report-taking units] show clear."

"A-95, roger."

"1-Adam-95. Day watch 1-U-1 advises he will respond and meet you at the location of your call."

"95, rog." This was good news. We would investigate the crime, and the U-car would handle the paperwork.

The parking lot structure was a five-story concrete prefab. At seven o'clock in the morning it's not a place where one would expect a crime like this to occur. The garage would be filling with people who work in the downtown business area, and it isn't even a place you would think to patrol for crime prevention. In fact this was the only call I ever handled there. Frank pulled the patrol car into the parking structure. The ambulance had already arrived, and the paramedics were ministering to a young woman.

She was so severely beaten we couldn't tell how old she was. Her eyes were swollen shut, her mouth had blood caked around the outside, and you could see where her teeth had cut through her lips. Blood had run down the front of her business suit, intermingling with dirt from the floor. Her nylons were torn, and she'd lost both her shoes in the attack. Her right knee had a large laceration. We waited for a moment to let the paramedics finish checking her out before I broke in to inquire about the crime.

"Ma'am, could you tell us what happened?"

"What do you think happened? He beat me and raped me! He even made me suck him. I did everything he wanted, and he still beat the shit out of me!" She began to cry as her pent-up anger flowed out. "Where the fuck *were* you guys?"

"Ma'am, I know you're upset. I wish we'd been here, but we weren't. If you can just explain to me what this guy looks like, we'll put out a description and see if we can catch him. I have to ask you some very personal questions because we have to know what happened. If you'd like, we can have a female police officer come and take the report, but we need to have at least a general idea of what crimes have been committed."

"Officers, I saw him as he ran out the back! I got a good look at him and what he's wearing." The young parking lot attendant had been watching and spoke up.

"Mike, talk to her, and I'll get a description from this guy and put it over the air."

"Thanks, Frank. Can you tell me, ma'am, what happened?"

"I park here every day. I'm a legal secretary in the Broadway building. When I drove in this morning, I went to the third level. I saw the guy standing by the elevator. I hadn't seen him before, but I didn't think anything about it. I thought he was just waiting for the elevator. Most everyone that parks here pays by the month, and I recognize the regulars. I just didn't think anything about him. I parked my car and walked over to the elevator.

"That's when he grabbed me. He pulled me to the door and out onto the fire escape. No, it's not really a fire escape; it's the stairs if you don't use the elevator. He held his hand over my mouth, and I couldn't breathe. He took it away and told me if I screamed he'd kill me. Then he punched me in the mouth and said, 'I'm gonna fuck you, bitch. Get your panties off.' I pulled my dress up and tried to get my panties off when he slapped me and knocked me down. He got really mad, and said, 'I told you, get them fuckin' panties off!' Then he got on top of me and forced his way inside me. He was holding my mouth, and I couldn't get my breath. I started whipping my head from side to side. I thought I was going to pass out. When he got off me, he took his hand off my mouth, then grabbed me by the front of my dress with one hand and slapped me with the other. He said, 'You ain't no good to fuck, so you can suck my cock.'

"He stood up, and I put him in my mouth. I started sucking him, and after I don't know how long he pushed my head back and hit me in the face again really hard. I think I passed out. Next thing I remember, he was going through my purse."

"What did he take?"

"He took some money from my wallet. Not much; payday's tomorrow. I think I had a five and a few ones."

"Was there anything else? A watch or a ring—something identifiable?"

"No, no there wasn't anything. Wait, yes there

was. He took two guitar picks."

"What did they look like?"

"They're custom-made for me. One's white plastic, and the other tortoiseshell. They come from a store in Hollywood, and the store name's stamped on them."

"What'd he do next?"

"He told me that if I called for help he'd come back and kill me. Then he ran down the stairs."

"Did you see which way he went when he got to the bottom?"

"No. When he got down to the next floor, I ran into the garage trying to find help. Somebody was just getting onto the elevator when I came out. I yelled for her to stop, but she just let the door close. I ran down the ramp until somebody came and helped me . . . I don't know who."

"Mike, this guy might still be in the area. The parking attendant saw him go up to the Seventh Street bridge over the freeway. Let's take him with us and see if we can find that asshole."

"Ma'am, the paramedics are going to take you to the hospital. We're going to catch this asshole." Turning to the attendant, I asked, "Is it OK for you to leave and go with us? Can somebody else watch the lot?"

"Yeah. There's two of us."

The three of us got into the police car, and Frank drove north on Flower Street to Seventh. The attendant had followed the rapist up the alley until he got to Seventh Street and watched him walk west on Seventh until he crossed the next street. By the time the attendant ran back to the garage, we were already there.

"Where was he the last time you saw him?" I asked.

"He was just crossing Figueroa."

"Did you see him when he got to the far side?"

"No. When he started to cross, I ran back. I would've tried to stop him, but this guy was huge, must've been six-four. Looked like a dude from prison who's all buffed from pushin' iron. Wasn't anybody I'd take on!"

Frank drove over the Seventh Street bridge and went a block or two on the other side. No sign of the suspect.

"Frank, maybe this guy went down onto the freeway. There's that bus stop, remember?"

Frank made a U-turn and returned to the bridge. We got out and looked down. Between the Seventh and Eighth Street bridges, there's a bus stop on the freeway with a path worn in the ivy leading to the pickup area. Frank and I looked at each other with the same thought. Frank said, "Eighth Street," and I knew he was right. The suspect had probably used a set of steps going to the bus stop, then walked south along the edge of the freeway, and down the Eighth Street on ramp. We ran back to the police car, and Frank drove south on Figueroa to Eighth Street.

"You know where he is? He's at that gas station, the one on the far side of the freeway."

"I'll bet you're right, Mike."

"How do you guys know? How do you know he's there?"

I looked at the attendant and said, "We just do. Are you gonna recognize this guy if he's there?"

"I'll know. I won't forget him!"

Frank pulled over to the curb just before the intersection of Eighth and Garland, where there was a gas station on the northwest corner. It had gasoline pumps and a building that housed two service bays and an office area. Parked in front of each service bay was a car. No customers were at the pumps. A soft drink machine was set against the wall between a service bay and the office entrance. Standing in front of the machine was the rapist, one hand resting against it as he gulped the soda.

I thought the attendant was going to jump into the front seat with us. "That's him! That's him! That's the fuckin' guy! How did you know he'd be here? All right!"

He was as excited as we were, but I wanted to make sure he didn't think he was part of the arrest team. "When we pull in, you stay in the car. If anything happens, duck. Got it?"

"Hey, I'm not goin' anywhere!"

The suspect's back was to us as Frank idled the police car into the gas station. The morning rush-hour traffic concealed the noise of our approach. Frank got out and went to the left of one of the cars parked in front of the service bay closest to the suspect. I positioned myself behind the passenger door of the police car, about fifteen feet away from the rapist. Although no one had seen a gun on the suspect, neither Frank nor I was taking any chances. The door of the police car would act as a shield if he fired at me.

It was amazing, but he still didn't know we were there. I then spoke. "I'll bet at this distance I couldn't possibly miss."

"If he does, I won't." Frank spoke calmly, his weapon pointed, as was mine, directly at the suspect. I intended to deliver a head shot if possible because this guy was far too big to fight. There's no doubt he could have beaten us both senseless. He was that big. The attendant's description was, if anything, an understatement. The suspect looked to his left and down the barrel of Frank's gun. Soft drink still in hand, he raised his arms above his head and turned to face us. He was probably sizing us up to see if there was any hope in taking us both on. I'm sure he realized very quickly that either Frank or I would have dropped him in a heartbeat.

"Put the bottle down and turn back around. Put your hands behind the back of your head. If you move, I swear I'll blow your fuckin' brains out." After giving the suspect his directions, I waited until he turned back around and then holstered my weapon. I walked toward him. Because of the size of this man, I decided to handcuff him before searching him.

"I want you to bring your right hand down and put it in the small of your back." He complied without saying a word. He knew the routine. The handcuff barely fit around his wrist. "Bring the other hand back."

"I can't get my hands that close together." He was so muscular there was no hope of cuffing him with a single pair of cuffs. Without a word Frank removed his handcuffs and threw them to me. Frank's handcuffs were snapped onto his left wrist, and our two sets hooked together. Never before or since had I handcuffed a suspect in this manner.

Now that he was neutralized, I searched the man for weapons and checked his pockets for evidence. In his left front pocket was a single five-dollar bill and in his right rear pocket a five-dollar bill and four one-dollar bills all folded together. The real prize was in his right front pants pocket. Two guitar picks, one white plastic and the other tortoiseshell with the name of a certain Hollywood music store imprinted on each.

I held the guitar picks up in my right hand so he could see them. "Why'd you do it? How come? She's a fuckin' mess, man. I'm gonna tell you something, asshole. When we finish with you, you'll be on your way to state prison, where you fuckin' belong."

"I got nothin' to say."

It was just as well. I was furious, and we had

what we wanted—the right suspect in handcuffs. As I walked him over to the police car, Frank had the witness move up to the front. The suspect never offered any struggle and sat quietly in the back seat. I filled out an FI card on him. He had no identification, so I wasn't really sure if the data he gave were correct. Using that information, I did an NCIC [National Crime Information Computer] check on him to see if he was wanted.

"1-Adam-95. Your suspect shows a felony want for escape from Ohio State Penitentiary."

"1-A-95. Show code four at Eighth and Garland. Suspect is in custody."

"1-Adam-95, roger. All units, code four on the felony want. Suspect in custody at Eighth and Garland."

Looking at him, I smiled and said, "Escape, huh? What were you in for?"

"Rape."

"Figures. You're not going back there for a while. First you'll do your California time for, let's see, rape, assault, robbery, and then, when you're done with that, you'll go back to Ohio, where they'll undoubtedly tack time on for your escape. You'll be right where you belong—in the joint." He stared straight ahead and didn't speak again.

We went through the preliminary hearing without any problems. When I saw the victim in court, I didn't recognize her. She was a very attractive young woman. Most of the damage done by the suspect had healed, at least on the outside. However, she told me of being constantly frightened of strangers. He had taken away from her something that may never come back again—a feeling of being safe.

At the rapist's trial the American Civil Liberties Union showed up because of a new court ruling that prohibited a woman's sexual life from being brought up. The ACLU was monitoring the case to ensure that the rights of the victim were protected. The trial resulted in the conviction of this man for rape with aggravated circumstances (rape with significant injuries to the victim) and robbery.

It was interesting working with the ACLU instead of in our normal adversarial relationship. They had sent a young female attorney who was very positive and helpful to our victim. She thought the police had done a great job. That in itself had to be a first.

This was an excellent illustration of what rape really is—a crime of power, a crime of violence, a crime that finds its root in one person exerting his will over another. Anyone who thinks provocative clothing or seductive mannerisms play a part in these actions is woefully ignorant. This wasn't a sex act. It was an act of savage brutality.

CRIME IS THEFT OF ONE SORT or another. Whether it's a television set, the life of a homeless person, or the self-respect of a rape victim, something's been stolen. Police work is about crime; it's about standing in the way of those who want something and don't care how they get it or whom they hurt. Sometimes you really felt that you made a difference, and it was good. I never felt better than that morning when I pulled those two guitar picks from that guy's pocket. We couldn't prevent the rape of that young woman, but I'm sure we helped another young woman somewhere, one we never saw.

In a span of twenty-one years I was at the scene of so many crimes and made so many arrests it's difficult to pick one that was the most outstanding. So much time is spent taking reports in situations where you're aware no suspect will ever be apprehended. Sometimes you're just going through the motions. Most of the arrests are just routine. There's nothing particularly spectacular about the events. On rare occasions it all comes together and you have the opportunity to conduct a preliminary investigation on a particularly heinous crime and follow it up with the arrest of the suspect almost immediately after. In my mind the arrest of that rapist was the best one I ever made. It was fitting Frank and I did it together.

Chapter Eight

IN RETROSPECT

MOST OF THE TIME POLICE WORK is serious business. That's part of the problem. It's too grim, sometimes unrelentingly. So many lives that touch yours will never be the same again. I suppose if you were to compare inner-city police officers to merchants, their stock in trade would be broken human beings. Sometimes it seems as though you never get out of the gutter, and you're rolling in garbage day after day.

There's a whole other side of police work that's positive. It's about all the good people and the good things they do. It's about remembering that you have negative contacts with only a small part of society. If you can remember and focus on only the bad parts of the job, it will consume you, and you'll never appreciate all the positive things you see and the good that you can do. You have to be able to keep a balance.

Humor is one way to achieve that balance. I used to tell young police officers that police work is much too serious to take seriously. If you can't laugh at yourself and see the light side of things, you'll be in deep trouble. Police officers can be great practical jokers. To some perhaps it seems more like "frat-house high jinks," but there's a reason behind it. There has to be an escape valve for all the things that build up inside an officer, and a good laugh can do wonders. Sometimes you pick the target; sometimes you're it.

WHEN YOU WERE A SERGEANT, you became a potential object of practical jokes, especially in the roll call room. You were a natural target, sitting up front with between fifteen and thirty-five officers in attendance. Almost nightly somebody would think of something to do to you. Some sergeants insisted on the roll call period being very quiet. In good conscience, I couldn't go along with this. I'd been too vocal as a police officer ever to insist that others be silent.

Newton Division morning watch had two guys who were classic practical jokers. C. A. May and Archie Cruse were as good at dreaming up things to do to you as they were at catching criminals. Their specialty was the paper airplane. They could fold a paper plane that would float in the air, but that wasn't enough. They gave the aircraft an added twist. Fire. They could fly a paper plane, fully engulfed in flames, above the heads of the roll call and put it right on target—the watch commander. I have personally dodged these flaming projectiles while still calmly continuing my roll call activities. How could you get mad? The whole roll call would be in stitches, and it kept you on your toes.

May and Cruse didn't limit themselves to paper airplanes. They could do a mean trick with paper dots. Before roll call they'd collect all the dots from the three-hole punches around the station. These would then be placed in a paper cup and precisely situated on top of a light fixture above the watch commander's desk in the roll call room. A thread was carefully tied around the cup and strung across the top of the other light fixtures all the way to the back of the roll call room. At what was deemed to be an appropriate moment, the thread was pulled, and down the dots came, showering the watch commander with paper snow.

The most successful application of the dots was played on a particularly fastidious Newton Division detective. The detectives were end of watch by midafternoon and wouldn't return until the following morning, so mid-P.M. and morning watch police officers would use the detective room to write reports. There were times when officers didn't clean up after themselves after using someone's desk, an ongoing complaint of the detectives, often with justification.

One of the detectives complained loudly and at length that he did not want anyone using his desk to write reports. Big mistake. Archie Cruse and his crafty band from morning watch decided to show this detective what the word *mess* really meant. The first night they simply poured dots from the teletype machine onto his desk. It wasn't a great amount; perhaps two cupfuls and easily removed. Instead of laughing with everyone else, the detective put on a real performance when he saw his desk. Demanding to know who had done the deed, he wanted disciplinary action taken by morning watch supervisors. The other morning watch sergeants and I were enjoying the scenario immensely, probably matched only by the detectives this guy worked with. It certainly didn't warrant disciplinary action.

Part Two, a day later. A cup filled with paper dots was left on the detective's desk. When he arrived as was customary at about 6:30 in the morning, Cruse and his merry band of men were peering through the windows from the outside. No small task in itself since the windows were quite high, but they gave a perfect view of the room and what was to come. The detective walked up to his desk and observed the cupful of dots. He had a bit of a sneer on his face as he swooped the cup off his desk, intending to move it and its contents into the trash in one movement. Too bad. The cup had no bottom, and dots went everywhere. He was furious. Off he stomped to the watch commander's office, again demanding something be done.

"We'd really like to help you, but we really don't know any more than you do. Sure it's not P.M.s? Maybe day watch did it."

"You guys don't care! You just don't care!" Off he stormed, back to the squad room.

Part Three, following day. This time the cupful of dots was placed on top of the ever-convenient light fixture. This tried-and-true method had already been field-tested on the morning watch commander, but a bit of a twist had been added for the detective. Instead of the merry band from morning watch pulling the thread, they fixed it so the detective would pull the thread, releasing the dots. The detective arrived at his desk right on schedule. He gave a slight nod of approval when he noticed nary a cup nor dots to be seen anywhere. Carefully removing his jacket, he put it over the back of his chair. Pulling the chair out, he prepared to sit down. That did it. The thread was tied to the chair, and down came the dots. He didn't bother to make another trip to the watch commander's office. He kicked his chair in anger.

"Archie, I think you better cool the dots. You've got him close to the edge."

"I know, Sarge! That's where we want him."

"Yeah, I know, but you better leave him alone for a while."

"But he's so easy to set off!"

"That's a fact, which makes it great, but I don't want him to go to the captain."

"Just one more time, Sarge! Then we swear we'll leave him alone."

"OK, one more time, but that's it!"

Part Four—the finish with a flourish. The cup was again carefully placed on the light fixture, the thread barely visible as it dropped from the light fixture and went under the desk, prudently attached to the detective's chair. He approached his desk as though the slightest untoward movement might produce some sort of deadly dot deluge. This time would be different. He had spotted the thread. Down on all fours, he followed its path under the desk and found its destination on the leg of his chair. Carefully he removed the thread and stood up, a triumphant smile on his face. He followed the thread upward with his eyes and stepped back a few paces and saw the cup resting on top of the light fixture.

Using his chair to stand on, he climbed up to remove the cupful of dots. Darn! The bottomless cup trick again! This cup was the biggest of all, a giant-size soft drink cup filled to the brim with dots. He let out a scream that could be heard all the way to the watch commander's office. "I'm gonna kill those fuckers!"

Ever the gentlemen, the morning watch crew went in to help him clean up the mess with careful allusions to the P.M. watch as the probable culprits. That detective never came back to the watch commander's office to insist officers refrain from using his desk to write reports. In turn we politely asked the officers not to leave a mess at his desk.

THERE WERE TIMES WHEN THE opportunity to "do" someone came along, and you just couldn't pass it up. Such was the case with the marijuana detection kits. The department had purchased them to familiarize officers with the smell of burning marijuana. Included in each box were several tablets and plastic marijuana leaves. The salesman who talked the city into this must have been incredible. What other boondoggles must he have peddled to other unsuspecting government agencies.

As one might suspect, the kits were not pressed into service as part of roll call training. I was a police officer III+1 assigned to Central Division, a quasi-supervisory position that brought me more in contact with the watch commanders and sergeants. I was still assigned to regular patrol duties but had additional responsibilities as well.

Team policing was an experimental approach to police work being tested in Central Division, and I was filling in as the watch commander for Team Thirteen. In the bottom drawer of the watch commander's desk sat one of the kits. It was a very quiet evening, and I started reading the instruction booklet. I could see why we hadn't used the kits. They were better suited for people unfamiliar with marijuana, those who never had any previous contact with the drug. As police officers, we saw the real thing on a nightly basis.

The pills in the kits looked like compressed alfalfa with no discernible smell until they were burned, sort of like synthetic marijuana incense. I couldn't resist. Taking one out and putting it in an ashtray, I lit it. You had to admit—it did smell like grass.

There had to be a practical application for this, and it certainly wasn't teaching police officers about smelling marijuana when they already knew very well what it smelled like. That was it! Someone who knew what it smelled like and smelled this would think someone was smoking grass right here in the police station. Smoking marijuana was a firing offense.

How could I use this? Wait a minute. Sergeant John Fitzgerald was the divisional watch commander. Perfect! John had been a sergeant for a number of years and a good guy, although a touch on the gullible side. If I knew John, he'd swallow this hook, line, and sinker.

The watch commander's office was surrounded by a series of rooms. One of the doors leading into the office had no glass above it and a flat ledge, perfect for placement of a smoldering "marijuana" pill. The doors leading into the office were open, and it was possible to see John from quite a distance. I went by the report counter, where several reports were waiting for signature by the divisional watch commander.

Next I headed for John's office. "John, the guys at the report counter say there's a bunch of them for you to sign."

"Thanks, Mike." John was up and away. With nary a witness in sight, I stood on a chair, placed a tablet on the ledge above the door, and lit it. I returned to my vantage point and waited for John to come back.

He returned and sat down, busily reading reports. The first whiff crossed his nose. His head snapped to the right. The detective in John was coming out. He was going to find the culprit. One of the rooms next to the watch commander's was a report-writing room. He charged in an effort to surprise the officers who were not only simply violating department policy but also the law. Alas, the report room was empty. John returned to his desk.

By now the pill was really smoking, but he apparently didn't see it, maybe because the smoke was the same color as the ceiling tiles, a break I hadn't counted on. It was amazing. John's head kept swiveling from side to side. Two possibilities were left. The Analytical [crime statistics] Office was in a line between John and me. With due stealth John crept up to the edge of the door and then, as if to pounce on the violators, quickly entered the room. Damn, it was empty, too. Only one possibility left—the captain's office.

I couldn't see the door to the captain's office from where I was sitting pretending to write a report, but as John moved out of my view I got up and positioned myself to watch him as he moved in for the kill. The pill had burned out, but John was still hot on the trail.

He grasped the doorknob to the captain's office and flung it inward, barging into another empty office. It was nighttime, and the captain had long since gone home. John returned to the watch commander's office, a look of real consternation on his face. Looking again in all directions, he tried to piece it together. Apparently receiving no answers, he shrugged his shoulders and started reading reports again.

I waited about twenty minutes before walking into the watch commander's office and sitting at the adjoining desk. I had the kit in hand, but John was still absorbed in report approvals.

"Hey, John, what's up?"

"Just finishing these reports. Wish those guys at the counter wouldn't save them up for so long before they give them to me."

"Yeah, I know what you mean." Holding the open box up, I pulled out some of the remaining cellophane-wrapped pills. "By the way, have you ever smelled any of these fake marijuana pills? I hear they smell just like the real thing."

John looked at me, smiled, and began to laugh.

"Mike, you are such an asshole!" John could always laugh at himself and enjoy a good joke.

There were times when a touch of humor had a practical application to police work. The central area of the city always had quite a few people on the verge of institutionalization. If they were delusional, they might seek the aid of the police in warding off what to them were very real demons. One such woman was an elderly pensioner who believed she was the victim of x-rays being beamed through the windows of her run-down apartment by aliens.

She called so many times that communications stopped sending units to the Grand Avenue hotel when she would complain about the x-rays. She caught on quickly and changed her approach, describing the aliens as "prowlers." This did get a unit dispatched, Frank and me.

We walked up to the third floor and knocked on her door. "Ma'am, police officers."

"Mike, I've been here before. This is some nut who keeps calling about x-rays or something. I thought they weren't sending any cars here."

An elderly lady opened the door. "Officers, I'm so glad you're here. I've had such trouble, frankly, I don't know what I'm going to do."

"Mike, it's her."

"What's the problem, ma'am?"

"It's the beams."

"Beams?"

"X-rays."

The solution was simple. Everybody told her she was nuts and not to call the police, but that didn't work because she didn't believe anyone was actually helping her with her problem. The x-rays were the problem.

"Yes, ma'am, we know. There's been a big outbreak. They've been beaming everyone." I looked at Frank, and he nodded seriously in agreement.

"Yes, ma'am, a real problem."

"That's why they sent us to fill you in. You see, this isn't a problem for the police. This is a problem for the X-Squad."

"Who are they? They never told me about this! I've been calling for months. They think I'm crazy! That's why I've got these drapes up. Got to keep every window covered to keep the rays out, and now they've started shooting them through the walls. The pains in my chest are incredible, but nobody wants to listen! Who did you say? The X-Squad?"

"Yes, ma'am. The X-Squad. Most of the officers aren't familiar with it. We're actually a liaison between them and the police. Before we go any further, can we trust you with this information?"

Frank looked at her, again very seriously, and spoke in a hushed tone. "It's very confidential."

"Yes, Officers. You can absolutely trust me. I'm so thankful they finally sent someone who understands!"

I walked over to the window and pulled the faded, threadbare drapes back a few inches as if to peer into the street below. Immediately I winced and recoiled as though the rays had struck me, too. I moaned in pain. "My God, those are strong! They're out there, all right. I could see a couple of them. You're obviously a very strong woman. May I use your telephone?" She nodded her head yes.

Picking up the telephone, I pretended to dial. "Hello, Middleton here. Yeah, we're over on Grand Avenue. Right. The rays are very strong. Are you sure? How soon? This evening? Just a moment. Ma'am, is it all right if they start the counterbeaming efforts tonight?"

"Praise the Lord! Yes!" She was listening intently as I spoke on the phone.

"Yeah, she said it was OK. You gonna send anyone to her apartment first? Didn't think so, but I wanted to make sure. So it's going to be a regular counterbeam operation? Very good. I'll let her know. Any reason for us to come back here? No? OK, then it's all taken care of, and we'll be moving on to the next location."

"What are they going to do? Is my problem going to end?"

"Here's the program. We'll begin counterbeam operations immediately. You won't see our men, but they'll be outside. I would say that by tomorrow morning you should be able to remove your drapes with no further need for the X-Squad. We also leave monitors on the rooftop to pick up any future beam attacks. I want you to understand, ma'am, even when the police aren't around, the X-Squad will be."

"Thank you! I knew that if the right officers came, everything would be OK."

Frank again nodded knowingly, and we left. As it turned out, the X-Squad did its job well. She never called again.

A MAJOR PART OF POLICE WORK is simply interacting with other people in moments of crisis. Many times that interaction weighs very heavily on you. It can be easy to forget the X-Squad and the dots and remember only children lying on bloody floors. It's too easy to remember Dewey Johnson instead of those officers who ran under the whirling helicopter blades.

Mostly I knew officers who day after day did the best job they could do with the tools they had. They tried to uphold the motto "To protect and to serve." They made mistakes along the way; they were at times influenced by personal prejudices; they were at best imperfect. I was that way, too.

One incident that happened to me was a microcosm of what police work was really about. It reveals the serious side as well as the positive nature of the job. On a February night several other officers and I were involved in a narcotics interdiction task force. Our job was to arrest drug dealers as they plied their trade in the Pueblo del Rio projects of Newton Division. I was a sergeant then and helping to supervise the operation. The detail was going smoothly, and several arrests had been made. Then it happened. A garbled message was broadcast.

"All units. Officers requesting an ambulance and a supervisor. Shots fired. Forty-three hundred block Long Beach Avenue."

Sergeant Charles Bridgeman and I were in the same car at the time of the call, and when we got to the scene Officer Jay Hernando met us. The smell of gunpowder was still in the air, and a man lay facedown near the railroad tracks. Jay approached me and began to explain what had happened.

"Sarge, we were headed back down to the projects when some people came running out into the street and flagged us down. They said this guy was threatening people with a machete, and we saw the guy walk from the liquor store parking lot out to the railroad tracks. You could see he was carrying some sort of knife; we didn't know what. I walked over and called out for him to drop the weapon so we could talk."

There was usually a crowd at the liquor store, and tonight was no exception. Several people were standing on the sidewalk just opposite us. Some of them were yelling words of support to Jay.

"He did what he could, but the guy just kept comin' at him! He tried not to shoot him."

Jay continued as though no one else had spoken. "The guy just held his knife up like he was going to stab me and started walking toward me. I was backing up, telling him to drop the knife. I told him to drop it several times, but he just kept coming at me. I backed onto the railroad tracks, and I stumbled, but I caught myself before I fell. When I tripped, he came at me a little faster so I stood up and fired one round at him. He fell. Turned out he had a butcher knife; looks like an eleven-inch blade at least."

"Where'd you hit him?"

"In the neck."

"Was anyone else out here?"

Pointing to the crowd, he said, "Probably most of those guys, Sarge."

I walked over to the suspect to see if I recognized him. He didn't seem to be moving, and I thought he was dead. When I rolled him over, you could see he'd been shot on the left side of the neck. Blood was shooting out about six to eight inches, and the stream was at least the size of my little finger. His eyes were open and staring.

This guy was on his way out and would be dead in a very short time. It was apparent his jugular vein had been severed. Maybe if I was able to stop the flow of blood, he could be prevented from bleeding to death. Looking at Charles Bridgeman standing next to me, I said, "I just can't let this guy die."

I'd never been confronted with a severed vein in the neck, but I decided to try to stop the flow of blood. Twice before, I'd encountered people bleeding to death and successfully intervened. One time I used my hands in a makeshift tourniquet to squeeze the bloody stump of a man's severed leg. Another time a robbery victim had been shot in the femoral artery, and I was able to apply pressure and stem the flow of blood. Both men lived.

"Here, take my gun, Chuck. I'm gonna sit down with this guy and see if I can stop the bleeding." Jay Hernando helped me pull the man over to a spot next to the railroad tracks. I sat down and leaned against the tracks, using them as a brace because I didn't know how long we'd be there. My legs were spread apart and I pulled the man, Richard Hinton, close to my body. His back was against my chest while his head rested against my right shoulder.

"I want you to listen to me and listen real good. I'm gonna try and save your life. I don't know if I can, but I'm gonna try. If you fight me or fuck with me, I'll roll your ass over and watch you die. Got it?" By laying it on the line to him, I figured he'd be less likely to put up a hassle.

He shook his head and said, "Yes, sir. Yes, sir."

By now, blood was shooting all over my shirt and pants. Some of it splashed into my face and got on the lens of my glasses. Placing my right hand in front of his neck, I felt around for the wound and, finding it, inserted my middle finger deep into the bullet hole. Interlacing my hands together, I pulled tightly against his neck. Never having done this before, I didn't know how much pressure to apply. Hinton began to choke. Too much pressure. When my grip was relaxed, he gasped, "I can't breathe!"

"OK. I won't press so hard."

We sat like this for what seemed to be the longest ten minutes until the ambulance arrived. Hinton didn't lose consciousness and never offered the slightest resistance.

The fire department paramedics took over, and Hinton was transported to the hospital. When the ambulance left, I walked across the street to the liquor store to wash up. I didn't realize what a mess I was until I looked into the bathroom mirror. It was a macabre sight. My face was splattered with blood.

After finishing up at the shooting scene, Bridgeman and I went back to the police station so I could change into a clean uniform. Then we went to Metropolitan Hospital to check on Hinton. Chuck spoke with the nurses, who told him the suspect was being operated on and would survive. A nurse looked at me and said, "Who stopped the bleeding? Whoever it was saved this guy's life."

I really didn't want any attention over the incident and simply responded, "Some officer at the scene."

Chuck Bridgeman was having none of this. "Don't listen to him. He's the one who did it!"

"Well, I'll tell you, Sergeant, you saved that man's life. Good work."

The next day a telephone call came to my house from the chief of police's office. The chief's liaison to the news media, Lieutenant Dan Cooke, was on the line. "Sergeant Middleton, the phone's been ringing off the hook up here. I understand you're the one that stopped the bleeding on the man one of your officers shot last night."

"Yes, it was me."

"I'd like for you to call back these people from the news media, and please cooperate with them. You did a fine job."

Ultimately stories ran in the *Los Angeles Times* and the *Los Angeles Herald Examiner*. KABC radio ran a weeklong editorial praising me and all Los Angeles police officers for their "selfless acts." Police officers save lives every day. What I'd done had been done before by countless officers. The difference was that Hinton was a suspect, not a victim. He tried to murder a police officer yet was in turn saved by a police officer. The fact that he had come at Officer Jay Hernando with a butcher knife played no part whatsoever in my decision to try and save his life. When I looked down at him that night and realized he was bleeding to death while I watched, it simply seemed wrong not to do something.

Only two police officers approached me and made negative comments about my actions. Myron Weddel, whom I'd known for some years, saw me in the locker room at the police academy and sarcastically noted, "It figures *you'd* save a guy who tried to kill a police officer."

"Thank you." Weddel's opinion had never meant anything before, and this stupid remark didn't improve my opinion of him.

The other comment came from a probationer whose name I didn't even know. "Hey, Sarge, how you gonna feel when that guy you saved goes out and kills a cop?"

My first instinct was to simply slap his face, but I refrained. "Kid, if that man were to kill an officer, I would grieve for that dead officer but not because I had saved the killer's life. Someday if you're confronted with the same situation, all you have to do is roll the guy back over, and only you and God will know what you've done. I'm not selling the program, kid; I did what I did because it was the right thing to do." I turned and walked away.

Ultimately I was nominated for and received the Police Star for my actions that night. With my wife and three daughters looking on, Chief Gates awarded the medal to me at a ceremony held one afternoon at the police academy. It was one of the proudest moments in my career.

Most of the time in police work you never knew exactly what difference you made. That night was different. Jay made a difference for those people being threatened by a man armed with a knife. Ironically, I made a difference for the man who threatened them. Without hesitation Jay had risked his life in service of people he didn't know.

For a brief moment in time I was cast in the light of a hero, but I wasn't a hero. I was just an officer confronted with a situation where I was able to make a difference. My actions were typical of the overwhelming majority of officers who act not out of desire for accolades but simply responding to a sense of duty.

BEFORE THAT WEEK IN APRIL OF 1992 when I watched the city of Los Angeles engulfed in a conflagration born of frustration and criminal actions, I had never seriously questioned whether or not our actions as police officers made a difference. South central Los Angeles seemed to have improved since those early days when I looked on the charred skeletons of buildings left over from the Watts riots. Things must have changed; I had changed so much.

Watching the fires grow and seeing the actions of the rioters, it struck me that this generation sensed no real progress or change. Many of the people looting and burning were unable to see their way out of the endless cycle of poverty and racial injustice. The old solutions of looting and burning became viable again.

It seemed as though my years on the department had become the years between the fires. I began to wonder how much of a difference we really had made. Maybe these weren't new fires but simply the old ones rekindled. Maybe they came from embers never extinguished. Perhaps we had only tended them all those years.

That was the problem with police work. You were confronted with situations you could never adequately be trained to cope with, and each time things were a little different from before. You were a little different from before. You always seemed to be behind the times, only reacting to what was occurring, never getting ahead of the game. There was never time. There were always calls to handle, victims to care for, children to try to save, arrests to make. Night after night you were plunged into this swirling mass. In a way it never changed, but in other ways it was always changing. When you put all the years together, it made you a police officer.